TRANSITIONS:
Schooling and Employment in Canada

TRANSITIONS:
Schooling and Employment in Canada

Edited by Paul Anisef and Paul Axelrod
York University

THOMPSON EDUCATIONAL PUBLISHING, INC.
Toronto, Ontario / Lewiston, New York

Copyright © 1993 Paul Anisef and Paul Axelrod

All rights reserved. No part of this publication may be reproduced or transmitted in any form or by any means, electronic or mechanical, including photocopy, recording, or any information storage and retrieval system, without permission in writing from the publisher.

Requests for permission to make copies of any part of the work should be directed to the publisher. Additional copies of this book may be obtained from the publisher.

Orders may be sent to:

United States	or	*Canada*
240 Portage Road		11 Briarcroft Road
Lewiston, New York		Toronto, Ontario
14092		M6S 1H3

For faster delivery, please send your order by telephone or fax to:
Tel (416) 766–2763 / fax (416) 766–0398

Cataloguing in Publication Data

Main entry under title:

Transitions : schooling and employment in Canada

Includes bibliographical references and index.

ISBN 1-55077-042-X

1. Youth - Employment - Canada. 2. Labor supply - Canada - Effect of education on. I. Anisef, Paul, 1942-   . II. Axelrod, Paul Douglas. III. Title.

HD6276.C32T73 1993   331.3'4'0971   C93-093209-9

Cover design by Mariana Grezova.

Printed in Canada.
1 2 3 4   96 95 94 93

Table of Contents

Preface viii
Contributors x

Introduction xiii
Jane Gaskell

PART I:
COMMUNITIES AND CONSTITUENCIES

1. **Getting There and Staying There: Blacks' Employment Experience** 3
   Carl E. James

2. **Gender Tracks: Male-Female Perceptions of Home-School-Work Transitions** 21
   Nancy Mandell and Stewart Crysdale

3. **Interconnected Transitions and Their Costs; Gender and Urban/Rural Differences in the Transitions to Work** 43
   E. Dianne Looker

4. **Transition of Adolescents into Science Career Pathways** 65
   John H. Lewko, Carol Hein, Rashmi Garg and Geoffrey Tesson

5. **Lifelong Education and Chronic Underemployment: Exploring the Contradiction** 89
   D.W. Livingstone

6. **Universities, Graduates, and the Marketplace: Canadian Patterns and Prospects** 103
   Paul Anisef and Paul Axelrod

PART II:
PERSPECTIVES AND RESEARCH METHODOLOGIES

7. Transitions: From School to Work and Back: A New Paradigm   117
   Alan M. Thomas

8. Education and Employment in Quebec: A Review of the Literature   129
   Pierre Dandurand and Roland Ouellet

9. Life Trajectories, Action, and Negotiating the Transition from High School   137
   Lesley Andres Bellamy

10. First Nations Empowerment in Community Based Research   159
    Schuyler Webster and Herbert Nabigon

11. Panel Studies of the Transition from School to Work: Some Methodological Considerations   169
    Harvey Krahn, Clay Mosher and Laura C. Johnson

Index   189

Preface

This volume presents new research by scholars from across Canada engaged in the study of youth, schooling, employment and social change. The aim of the book is to describe the multiple transitions that young adults encounter in their journey from school to the world of paid employment. Different contexts and conditions affect these transitions and the authors employ historical, qualitative and quantitative methodologies in identifying them. Particular attention is paid to the themes of gender, socio-economic status, ethnocultural origin, and region.

The qualitative accounts that inform much of the new research data are intended to provide the reader with more than a glimpse of the personal biographies of young adults. In analyzing their findings, the authors apply a wide range of theories, including developmental, sociological, and social/psychological. In addition, a number of the essays have implications for policy-making in the areas of education and employment.

This project was inspired by the "Strategic Research Network" program inaugurated in 1990 by the Social Sciences and Humanities Research Council for the purpose of encouraging collaborative work in targeted or "strategic" areas of study, in this case, "Education and Work in a Changing Society." Following an organizational meeting in December 1990, which included academics from York University, the University of Western Ontario, and the University of British Columbia, the Network members resolved to convene a series of conferences, the first of which was held in Toronto in October 1991. This book arises from that conference.

We would like to acknowledge the important roles played by a number of individuals and organizations that have facilitated the Network's activities, meetings and publications. Susan Houston, past Director of the Robarts Centre for Canadian Studies at York University, was instrumental in initiating the project and securing for it the sponsorship of the Robarts Centre. The Policy Research Centre on Children, Youth and Families hosted the Toronto conference in October 1991, and we are especially grateful to Laura Johnson and Lee Marks for their assistance.

Renée Cloutier of Université Laval served as a conference commentator and facilitated the inclusion of the chapter in this volume by Professors Ouellet and Dandurand. Etta Baichman-Anisef prepared a bibliography on schooling and employment, and has furnished valuable editorial assistance. Sara Costantini of York University's Division of Social Science has provided excellent secretarial service both to the Network and in the preparation of this book. Finally, we are grateful for the financial support received from the Social Sciences and Humanities Research Council, without which this project and publication would not have been possible.

Paul Anisef, Paul Axelrod
The Editors

Contributors

PAUL ANISEF is an associate professor in the Department of Sociology at York University.

PAUL AXELROD is an associate professor in the Division of Social Science at York University.

LESLEY ANDRES BELLAMY is a post-doctoral fellow in the Centre for Policy Studies in Education at the University of British Columbia.

STEWART CRYSDALE is an Emeritus professor in the Department of Sociology, Atkinson College, York University.

PIERRE DANDURAND is a professor of sociology at the University of Montreal.

RAGHMI GARG is an associate professor in the Department of Psychology at Laurentian University.

JANE GASKELL is a professor in the Department of Social and Educational Studies at the University of British Columbia.

CAROL HEIN is Research Associate at the Centre for Research in Human Development at Laurentian University.

HARVEY KRAHN is a professor of sociology and Director of the Population Research Laboratory at the University of Alberta.

CARL JAMES is a professor in the Department of Applied Arts at Sheridan College in Brampton, Ontario.

LAURA C. JOHNSON is a Toronto research sociologist and consultant on social policy issues.

JOHN H. LEWKO is Director of the Centre for Research in Human Development at Laurentian University.

D.W. LIVINGSTONE is a professor of sociology at the Ontario Institute for Studies in Education.

E. DIANNE LOOKER is a professor in the Department of Sociology and Director of Graduate Studies and Research at Acadia University.

NANCY MANDELL is an associate professor of sociology and coordinator of the Women's Studies Programme in the Faculty of Arts at York University.

CLAY MOSHER teaches in the Department of Social and Environmental Studies at the University College of the Cariboo, Kamloops, B.C.

HERBERT NABIGON is a professor in the Native Human Services Programme, School of Social Work, Laurentian University.

ROLLAND OUELLET is a professor in the Department d'administration et politique scolaires et directeur du Centre de recherche et d'intervention sur la reussité scolaire (CRIRES) de l'Université Laval.

GEOFFREY TESSON is an associate professor in the Department of Sociology and Anthropology at Laurentian University.

ALAN M. THOMAS is a professor in the Department of Adult Education, Ontario Institute for Studies in Education.

SCHULYER WEBSTER is an assistant professor, and Coordinator of Native Human Services, the School of Social Work, Laurentian University.

Introduction

Jane Gaskell

Interest in the transition from school to work fluctuates with changes in the economy. In good times, when young people seem to be moving smoothly from school to work, the linkages can remain unexamined. With unemployment or labour shortages, attention is refocused, usually on the school. We ask how the process works, what might be changed, and, the underlying political question: who is to be blamed for the problems?

At present, school to work transitions are again a concern. The context for this discussion in the 1990s is deindustrialization, recession and restructuring the economy, along with considerable criticism of the educational system. Recent reports such as the Economic Council of Canada's "A Lot to Learn" and the Conference Board of Canada's report on "drop-outs" stress how education is failing. Government policies including the "Stay in School Initiative" and the "Prosperity Initiative" are premised on the same assumption. As the federal government's introduction to the "Prosperity Initiative" states, "new approaches are needed to meet the challenges that confront us — challenges that threaten our ability to generate new jobs, our standard of living, and our social programs...Canadians must have the skills and access to the lifelong learning opportunities necessary to improve their job prospects and ensure their own prosperity. But Canadians are questioning whether our approach to learning, despite the efforts of so many talented educators and administrators, is adequate for the times" (Government of Canada, 1991: 1–4). In other words, the economy is in crisis and Canadians are looking to the educational system for some solutions.

The idea that education should fit people more smoothly into the workplace is not a new one. Two fundamental economic concerns have persisted through fifty years of Canadian debate about education and work: that education should contribute to economic growth, and that education should contribute to economic equality. But the balance between these two concerns shifts, and the way each is defined has changed over time and varies among researchers and policy advocates at any given moment. In our federal system, provinces retain jurisdiction over education, and there is considerable provincial variation. Even a brief look at educational research and policy over the past fifty years provides examples of both continuity and change.

After World War II, educators became concerned with economic readjustment and students' economic prospects. In 1947, the Canadian Education Association set up the Canadian Research Committee on Practical Education to "investigate the secondary school curriculum as it affects those students who enter employment from the various grades of the secondary school." The Committee questioned whether the current curriculum provided "the type of training which will enable these young people to assume the full responsibilities of citizenship" (McColl, 1950: 30). The issues were the high level of dropouts (59% of boys and 51% of girls, according to committee calculations); the provision of practical training; and the question of whether young people were "adjusting satisfactorily in their post-school careers." The Committee produced four reports before its demise, *Secondary School Education in Agricultural Communities*, in 1948, *Practical Education in Canadian Schools*, in 1949, *Your Child Leaves School*, in 1950, and *Two Years after School*, in 1951.

In its report the committee expressed concern about students' prospects for employment and argued for a more equal distribution of opportunity in society, at least in relation to social class. It noted that students from families below average in economic status were more likely to leave high school early. There was no analysis of ethnicity, race or language in the report, but it did address the issue of gender. All the analyses were done separately for boys and girls, on the assumption that young men and women moved in different worlds of employment. The committee recommended "courses for boys in business topics, shop work, agricultural science, farm mechanics and practical agriculture besides the academic subjects." (Canadian Research Committee on Practical Education, 1951: 27). It also urged "that the high school should provide courses for girls in business training, home economics, home nursing, child care and so on, besides a basic core of academic subjects" (CRCPE, 1951: 27). It further reported that girls were less likely to drop out, and better adjusted to school.

As the economy expanded in the 50s and 60s, enrolment increased and the system was differentiated. In the secondary schools, the Robarts plan in Ontario, the Parent Report in Quebec, and the Chant Report in BC all led to a streamed and expanded conception of secondary education. At the post secondary level, the college system was born, and universities multiplied and grew.

The 1950s' focus on practical education was transformed in the 1960s and 70s into a more general concern about Canada's supply of "human capital." The critique now came from economists, rather than educators. "Education is a crucially important factor contributing to economic growth and to rising living standards. This has been the conclusion of a growing body of economic analysis in a number of countries. This is the conclusion also reached in our exploratory analysis of the contribution of education to the growth of the Canadian economy and to the welfare of the its people," the Economic Council wrote (Economic Council of Canada, 1965: 71). The Council was concerned about secondary school facilities, drop-outs, the quality and methods of education, retraining and continuing education, and particularly about "the tremendous expansion required especially at the university and post secondary technical school level"(p.120). It recommended an expansion in educational investment that materialized to an unprecedented extent with the opening of new universities and community colleges, and the extension of secondary schooling and "manpower training."

Equity was seen to be served by the same policies. Individuals benefited from education by increasing their incomes, and society as a whole benefited from increasing productivity. The concern for equity was more apparent in academic work such as *The Vertical Mosaic*, written by John Porter in 1965, and in a variety of sociological studies that followed it (the Atkinson surveys; Belanger and Rocher, 1976; Breton,1972; Porter,1982), than it was in the work of the Economic Council. In his work, Porter stressed the inequality of non-Anglo cultural groups in the Canadian mosaic, and differences between males and females continued to be reported in most surveys. The 1970 report from the Royal Commission on the Status of Women reframed the discourse on sexual equity in education and at work, stressing the importance of stereotypes in school curriculum, and the dramatically different enrolment patterns of males and female students starting in the secondary schools.

By 1981, with unemployment up again, an aging and no longer expanding labour force, and a low rate of economic growth, the federal government became more concerned about the fit between the educational system and the labour market and the efficiency of both systems and their linkages, than about expansion. The so-called Dodge report (EIC, 1981) recommended more carefully tailoring of education to labour market needs, and more fully informing workers and employers about economic opportunities. Counselling students, planning more carefully, matching jobs and skills and monitoring labour market needs were among the recommendations and the concerns of the era. More emphasis was put on adult education as a way to prepare people for work, and to adapt them to changes at work.

In this scenario, there was no longer an easy fit between equity and educational provision. Investing in education only for those areas of the economy where there were "skill shortages" meant less investment in education for those who seem destined for low paying, and therefore "low skill" jobs. There was, the commission observed, a "trade off between equity and efficiency" (p.16). "Where equity and efficiency goals conflict, there are no hard and fast criteria on the basis of which decisions can be made as to the appropriate mix of equity and efficiency considerations." However, it argued, "there are situations in which the goals of equity and efficiency are mutually supportive. This is most clearly the case with respect to measures designed to better integrate women and native people into the labour force. To the extent that these groups acquire a greater diversity of skills and experience, equity will be increased, labour market adjustment processes will occur more smoothly and the economy will be able to adapt more easily to changes in the industrial and geographic structure of economic activity" (p.16).

The commission then recommended special measures for women and native people "to ensure the full productive potential of these groups is realized" (p.207). It also called for less investment in short term, low level skill development, the programs most often used by disadvantaged workers and the unemployed. Employment equity with its four target groups was introduced into the policy debate in the 1980s. Women, visible minorities, native people and the disabled were targeted for special consideration.

In the 1990s, education is again being examined in light of its contribution to the economy. There is a lot of emphasis on the importance of education for economic recovery in documents such as the 1990 Ontario Premier's Council report, *People and Skills in the New Global Economy*, and the most recent (and final) Economic Council of Canada report, *A Lot to Learn: Education and Training in Canada* (1992). Equity concerns are secondary in most policy discussion but they are articulated. They surface in attempts to get women into science and technology, improve learning opportunities for First Nations People, and implement employment equity programs.

But funding is not increasing. Testing and monitoring, efficiency and effectiveness, standards and targets remain the primary themes of educational reform. The papers in this book were written in this context and they reflect its pull. Should universities pay more attention to employers' demands? How can we recognize the economic value of learning that is not credentialed? What are the employment outcomes for young people graduating from different kinds of programs? How can we get more girls into science?

As a group these papers become a plea for more attention to the less often articulated problems of equity. Again and again, the authors point out, achieving in school and finding a job are organized and related differently in different communities. Youth are not a single category, for the diversities by region, sex, ethnicity, race and class remain huge. The economic consequences of schooling, and more broadly of learning, are dissimilar in different labour markets. Some groups fare much better than others. We need ways to study the processes that create differentiation and ways to sort out how the social, economic, historical and political context matters.

While the existing policy discourse shapes the research in many ways, the research also challenges received wisdom and provides analysis that allows new ways of seeing the problem. The research works in conversation with current policy and current public opinion. It will stimulate the thinking of researchers and policy makers, but provide no simple solutions. There is no consensus on modes of analysis, assumptions or conclusions, but one will find in this book information and analysis for debate and reflection.

Themes in This Volume

These papers employ diverse techniques, languages and conceptual frameworks in examining the process of school to work transitions. Setting out some of the most important ways in which these papers differ from each other may help to guide the reader.

Method and Data

The papers draw from different sources and kinds of data, all of which can contribute something to our understanding of school and work. The authors in this book most often use surveys of students and ex-students, employers, parents and university officials. The surveys are frequently combined with interviews and sometimes with the analysis of documents and observations.

Large surveys, especially longitudinal ones, which follow young people over time, are expensive and time consuming. Although Canada does not have the large national data sets that are available in other countries (especially in the U.S. with its "High School and Beyond" surveys), several large Canadian surveys have been carried out by the federal government, provincial governments and university based researchers. Krahn, Mosher and Johnson's reflections on their longitudinal survey of high school seniors and fourth year university students in three cities represents by far the largest data collection exercise in this book. The "relance" surveys on the transition from school to work referred to by Dandurand and Ouellet provide some large scale data for Quebec. The discussion by Krahn illuminates many of the difficulties of gathering and interpreting the data from very large surveys. The practical difficulties of finding funding, locating and keeping the sample as well as more theoretical difficulties of choosing the sample and interpreting the results are important to keep in mind.

Many researchers have chosen instead to work with smaller surveys, which allow different kinds of analysis. The studies reported by Looker, James, Lewko et al., Anisef and Axelrod, Livingstone, Mandell and Bellamy are targeted at fewer questions and/or smaller samples. They frequently combine interviews with quantitative data. By illuminating different pieces of the puzzle, they encourage us to rethink how larger surveys might be framed, and they provide questions for policy makers to consider in their own local communities. By studying employers (Livingstone), university officials (Anisef and Axelrod), high school seniors (Bellamy, Mandell), students in enriched science programs (Lewko et al.), 17 year olds in different communities (Looker), and a small sample of black youth over time (James), the authors provide a good picture of the experience of and pressures on Canadian youth.

Interview data generated in lengthy conversations with a researcher illuminate something different from written answers to open-ended questions, even when the research report from each includes examples of what people "thought" or "said." Quantitative survey data, where the possible responses are predetermined by the researcher, will have different uses again. Both researcher and reader must be sensitive to the context in which data are gathered and the way in which they are analyzed in order to find their meaning.

Theory and Assumptions

Most of these analyses provide descriptive accounts of what happens to young people or to institutions. Some rely on numbers, some make arguments about other people's data, and some rely on the words of participants. The role of the writer is not foregrounded, but as one moves from one paper to another, it becomes increasingly clear how the background assumptions of the researcher shape the project.

Different theoretical traditions underlie these papers. Developmental, psychological and sociological/status attainment theory are discussed by Lewko et al. Segmented labour markets, capital accumulation crisis and economic restructuring are the keys for Livingstone. Bellamy discusses Bourdieu's theory of practice and rational choice theory. James prefers the term "coping strategies." The sources of data are diverse for these researchers, but the different ways they analyze their data are even more marked.

Dandurand and Ouellet provide an overview of the shifts in theoretical framework among Quebec scholars, opening up to the English reader a wealth of scholarship on Canadian youth that is too often ignored. In the process they point to the links between the changing political situation in Quebec and its changing scholarly traditions. Their observations are also useful for looking at the assumptions and questions in English Canadian scholarship.

Each author in this volume wants to know something different about transitions to work, and each makes assumptions about what is really important for policy. For example, Lewko accepts the importance of science for competitiveness and asks why girls do not succeed. Looker has observed regional differences and asks how they shape transitions. Anisef and Axelrod focus on universities and the marketplace, while Livingstone is concerned with the nature of the capitalist economy. Thomas calls for greater attention to the learning of adults and to learning that is not credentialed.

Thomas also invites a reconsideration of the whole notion of the "transition" from school to work. As Krahn et al., Livingstone and Thomas point out, people make many transitions from school to work and back again, often learning and earning money at the same time. The traditional lock-step move out of public schooling into a paying job, which was examined by the Committee on Practical Research in the 1950s, is less common than it used to be, and using it as the norm against which other patterns are measured may well blind us to the advantages of more flexible patterns.

The scholarship on black youth, First Nations communities and women, again reflects the experience and political concerns of the authors and brings to scholarship and policy a set of questions that are too often marginalized. James wants to know how racism is part of the process for black youth. Webster and Nabigon argue for the insertion of First Nations values and culture into research. Mandell stresses the way gender tracks young people into the workforce. All hold up a critical mirror to research and policy that ignore the social inequities of Canadian society.

Despite the differences, there are themes to which all the papers return. Perhaps the most important is the necessity of understanding the social context of transitions. It is perhaps unremarkable to note that people take their desires, assumptions, and understandings from the communities in which they live, but this has too often been forgotten. There is no quintessential "youth." While some patterns are more common than others in Canada today, local labour markets, cultures, families and educational systems come together to create varied experiences for young people.

Some factors are particularly important. To point to class, gender, race and ethnicity may be relatively commonplace in sociology, but these factors are rarely evident in the official reports that politicians and economists generate. In this book, they are front and centre. Looker points out that gender has an impact on boys that is just as important as its effect on girls. Lewko shows that girls are academically equal to or more able than boys, but still plan to avoid the physical sciences. Gender continues to matter. While demonstrating how important racial issues are for young black people, James points to the assumption of privilege built into analyses that do not pay attention to racial issues. He argues that employment equity has worked mainly for white women. First Nations people similarly cannot ignore the importance of cultural traditions; their experience places it front and centre in any analysis.

Many gaps remain to be filled in the research and the policy debate. In this book, there is little analysis from the point of view of employers or educators, although these groups are central to bringing about change. There is no examination of the impact of social welfare policies, although the papers point to the role of the state in shaping the forms of social provision that surround the transitions from school to work. Historical analysis is limited, although all of the existing dilemmas have a history that needs to be understood. There is little examination of the partial perspectives and situated nature of university scholarship, although the differences among the papers, as well as the silences, point to its importance. While there is much to be done, this volume displays the diversity and some of the commonality, the information and some of the gaps, the agreement and some of the debate that infuses Canadian scholarship on the transitions from school to work today. If it stimulates discussion about what kinds of research are useful and for whom, then it will be serving an important purpose.

PART I
COMMUNITIES AND CONSTITUENCIES

1
Getting There and Staying There: Blacks' Employment Experience

Carl E. James

In 1984 and 1985, sixty young Black men and women living in Toronto and between the ages of 17 and 22, participated in a study which, among other things, explored the relationship between social conditions and Black youth experiences, their career aspirations and their perceptions of their chances to realize them. The participants included high school *"dropouts," "stop outs,"* grades 12 and 13 graduates, as well as students who were attending high school, college and university. The findings reported in *Making It: Black Youth, Racism and Career Aspirations in a Big City* indicated that despite the educational and social diversity of the group, their views and perceptions reflected similar patterns. They perceived being Black or a *"visible minority"* as particularly significant in terms of society's expectations of them, and consequently of their life chances and opportunities.

They held high career aspirations and were optimistic that they would achieve their goals despite social and economic conditions. It was found that:

> Their high self-concept and positive attitudes (coping mechanisms) seem to fuel high career aspirations and positive perceptions of their chances to succeed. Racism, therefore, has not led them to develop negative, low self-concepts; rather it has invigorated them to strive with particular intensity for career success (James, 1990: 114).

Seven years after those initial interviews, we revisited the respondents to find out about their plans, aspirations and experiences in the workforce. A number of questions guided this follow-up: were respondents still optimistic that with self-confidence, determination and education, they would achieve their goals? Did they still believe that their coping strategies could, and would help them survive? And now that they had been in the workforce for some years, how would they characterize their experiences? What was their perception of the extent to which being Black would influence their chances of success? Did they see racism as affecting their occupational opportunities and workforce participation?

Literature Review

Closely related to individuals' perceptions of their opportunities is the degree to which they feel that events are under their control rather than the control of others or of impersonal forces. This attitude, this sense of confidence and power to determine their own destiny, in preference to resigning themselves to social and economic forces, is of particular significance during the transition period from school to work. For as Burnstein et al., (1975) document, the point of entry into the labour force has profound consequences on one's work history and participation in society, as well as on one's perception of the future and the role and opportunities that will be afforded.

In going to work, individuals move into social spaces which may not be familiar to them in relation to other experiences such as school and community. For some minority youth this movement from school to work is perhaps the most significant transition into racially and culturally diverse environments they will have faced at that point in their lives. It is possible for this to be a *"rude awakening"* — an introduction to the subtle yet painful realities of racism in Canada.

The examination of the transition from school to work provides insights into how early work experiences and social issues such as racism and discrimination affect today's young Black people. Though initiatives have been undertaken to address the problem of race inequities in job opportunities for racial minorities, improvements are not evident in workforce participation today (Weinfeld, 1990). Therefore, in regard to this research, we might hypothesize that *if little has changed over the last seven years in terms of social conditions and racism, it follows that little will have altered for most respondents with regard to their internalized notions of race and their perceptions of its effect on their occupational opportunities and achievements.*

Research shows that because of inherent inequalities in the social stratification system, accessibility to, and participation in certain occupations are very strongly influenced by characteristics such as social class (Anisef et al., 1982; Gaskell and Lazerson, 1980/81) and race (Abella, 1984; Billingsley and Muszynski, 1985; Henry and Ginzberg, 1985; Zureik and Hiscott, 1982). In addition, attitudes of racism manifested in discriminatory acts influence the extent to which racial minority groups are able to participate fully in Canadian society and achieve success. In their 1985 study of discrimination at the early stages of entry level of the employment process of young people, Henry and Ginzberg (1990) concluded that:

> ...there is a very substantial racial discrimination affecting the ability of members of racial minorities to find employment even when they are well qualified and eager to find work... Once an applicant is employed, discrimination can still affect opportunities for advancement, job retention, and level of earnings, to say nothing of the question of the quality of work and the relationship with co-workers (p.20).

Studies show that young people believe that despite tough economic times, they can achieve their career goals through high educational attainment and hard work (Bibby and Posterski, 1985). Young Canadians have career aspirations, value work, and want to work. And despite the labour market situation, barriers to employment, and in some cases, dissatisfaction with their jobs, they continue to be optimistic.

In general, Black youth also have high career aspirations. They believe that achieving their goals requires adopting various strategies. For the majority of youth, education is seen as the most important strategy (Fuller, 1983; Head, 1975; James, 1990). But as Fuller notes about experience of Afro-Caribbean girls in Britain:

> Schooling and education provided an alternative and less undermining possibility in their search for greater freedom and control...Being aware of both sexual and racial discrimination, the girls did not assume that good educational performance was the sufficient requirement for obtaining such jobs, but they did believe it was a necessary one (Fuller, 1983: 172).

It is worth emphasizing that Fuller's respondents saw that education was not a *"sufficient requirement for obtaining"* jobs. Indeed, Head and James identified other strategies: "being on guard," "being aware of racism," "working harder," "proving self," "having a plan," and "being determined, self-confident and strong."

In Head's study, the youth tended to believe that individual effort, qualifications and ability were the important determinants of success. Two-thirds of the respondents stated that they did not feel their colour would influence the attainment of their personal goals, or as one respondent indicated, it "isn't colour which is important. Nothing can stop you if you're willing to try" (Head: 98). This optimism was also evident ten years later (James, 1990). However, as Fordham (1988) points out, race does have an impact on Blacks "persona" and aspirations for employment.

> Out of their desire to secure jobs and positions that are above the employment ceiling typically placed on Blacks, they have adopted personae that indicate a lack of identification with, or a strong relationship to, the Black community in response to an implicit institutional mandate: Become "unblack" (Fordham, 1988: 58).

In this chapter, we examine the experiences, perceptions and ideas of young Blacks in their initial years of full-time employment. This is done by briefly reviewing the 1984–85 results and then by discussing the 1991 data with regard to the respondents present social construction of race; of their beliefs and experiences and their perceptions of the current situation. Particular attention is paid to the challenges the young people face, both in accessing jobs and while on the job, as well as to the coping mechanisms they develop.

For this 1991 follow-up of the study, a selective sample of twenty-two young people (eleven males and eleven females) were interviewed.[1] They ranged in age from 24 to 29 years. Fourteen were employed full-time in permanent jobs, five had returned to university or college pursuing new career options, two were working at temporary full-time jobs, and one was unemployed. Attempts were made to select respondents who represented different types of experiences and points of view (Selltiz et al., 1965; Kirby and McKenna, 1989).

---

[1] Since the aim of this qualitative study is to look for "provocative ideas and useful insights," respondents were chosen because of the likelihood that they would offer the information sought. Selltiz et al. (1965) note that in experience surveys, a random sample is not necessary since the study does not intend to generalize to the population being sampled. The open-ended interview method which was used allows for a deep and thorough examination of the issue under investigation but must necessarily be limited to a small sample in order to be manageable (Dexter, 1970).

Discussion

The Social Construction of Race: Factors that Contribute to Black Self Image and Its Significance

In 1984–85, the participants contended that racial consciousness was one of the realities of living in Canada. They suggested that "having Black skin" seemed more important than "being a person," whereas having "White skin" did not require mention when referring to "Whites." For most participants, being Black in Canadian society also meant having to experience, and expecting to continue to experience racism that would lead to differential treatment and opportunity based on race. Participants expressed a need to be prepared for racism in employment.

> **Brenda:** ...More than likely the employer is going to be White and he is going to notice that you are Black and that is going to more than likely influence him ('85).

Many of the respondents felt that *being Black and female was a double setback*. Most females and a few males stated that although women were disadvantaged, Black women were doubly so due to their placement as double minorities. Many of the females admitted that gender and race were closely related and would determine what they would be likely to experience in the future. Sharon's comment was typical of many of the statements of females respondents.

> **Sharon:** Being Black and a woman means that I have two strikes against me to start with, but that makes things challenging ('85).

While recognizing that women have to struggle to compete in a "man's world," some of the respondents stated that race is more of an obstacle than gender. Most of the males in the study felt that they would have better chances than females but a few suggested that with current employment equity programs addressing equal opportunities for women, Black women might actually have an easier time than men. None of the female respondents believed that they had better chances than their male counterparts.

In 1991, the interviewees continued to claim that race was significant in terms of how they were perceived and treated:

> **Frank:** I think when you walk into a room, people don't see Frank, the first thing they see is that I am a Black male. I think that triggers off certain behaviours from other people, certain attitudes ('91).

The respondents also indicated how stereotyped the images held of Blacks were, particularly in job situations. These images helped to influence their construction of race.

> **Tracy:** Because people have preconceived notions of you, I feel that I always have to *dispel the myth*; I feel that I have to come into an office and say well, I don't understand patois, I've never been exposed to it. Not everyone has that background... There are a lot of Black Canadians.

Some respondents added that in certain situations, they would willingly take on the task of making up for the "ignorant" behaviour of some Blacks. Bryan, and others, admitted that this was a "responsibility," a "burden" that they have willingly undertaken in the hope that their behaviour would prompt employers to think "that the next Black they hire might be like me." Such respondents also felt a responsibility to educate employers and co-workers by dispelling Black stereotypes.

Given that many of today's Black young people are breaking into new areas of work, they expect to be scrutinized by employers and co-workers who might be influenced by stereotypes and are uncertain of their ability and skills. Tracy noted:

> You always feel that they are watching you to see if you could fit in... And it becomes quite stressful because you know that you are being watched; you know that you are the only Black person there. And you feel that you don't want to be this frontier woman and having to put up with all that.

Essentially, respondents' construction of their racial identities was in relation to their social position as racial minorities. Most felt that they had a responsibility to exemplify qualities outside of the negative images. Their construction of Blackness was done *in response to* dominant social preconceptions, prejudices and stereotypes, and not out of a sense of understanding of self, heritage, and community affiliation. Fordham (1988) points out that the construction of race by Blacks in White dominant society does not have its genesis in the accomplishments of a people who have chosen to *define themselves* racially, but out of the definition of race by the dominant culture.

Preparing for the World of Work: Beliefs, Perceptions and Aspirations in 1984/85

> **Roger:** I know that discrimination is something I'll go through, but I'm not worried about it. People that should be worried are people that are less knowledgeable than I. I have been to school. I basically understand a bit about the way the system works... ('85).
>
> **Christine:** Do you think I would be going to school doing everything if I didn't think that I would? I think the possibilities are endless. If you work you can get anything you want, no matter what, if you work at it ('85)!

The 1985 investigation indicated that the respondents believed that they could succeed (assuming they possessed the ability and skill), provided they were willing to *apply* themselves. Most claimed that: *"if you want something bad enough you will get it." "If you work hard, you can get anything you want no matter what."* They operated on the assumption that individuals control their own destiny, undetermined by any external or structural factors.

Generally, many of the Black youth held values that transcended colour and that were reflective of the White majority culture in Canada. They seemed to believe that they could not succeed if they operated with values outside the cultural norms of Canadian society. It is not that these youth wished to be *White*. They reasoned that by living in Canada, they must operate as full members of this society. Consequently, holding and internalizing the values of this society were necessary for success.

The extent to which the youth believed that they could overcome racism was a reflection of their perception of racism. They saw racism as a *hurdle* and not a *barrier*. Therefore, they felt that their coping mechanisms would enable them to overcome its negative effects. Some tended to believe that they could cope with racism by *ignoring it* or by considering it as *just part of life*. They seemed to conceive of racism more on the level of individual attitudes towards Blacks. The racial incidents that they and other Blacks experienced were perceived merely as the result of one particular individual's racism. They believed that if they avoided people who were racist, they could achieve success. Some youth believed that they could *get around* racism and achieve their career goals if they *made the right contacts*, obtained the appropriate educational qualifications, *worked harder* and *proved themselves*.

Seven Years Later: Does the Optimism Remain?

The young men and women who participated in this follow-up investigation appeared still optimistic but "*a little more realistic.*" The following comments by Jenny were typical of what many of the respondents said when they were asked if they still believed that *self-confidence, determination, education*, and *the right attitude* would help them to overcome the *hurdle* of racism and therefore achieve their career aspirations.

> Yes it will, but I guess because I am older and I've been out there I am now a little bit more realistic. I guess when I said that a few years ago I was a lot younger, ...sort of naive, not having to deal with what I've had to deal with. Education can get you where you want to go but still you have to have someone on the other side willing to give you that chance to get to that level of success. I don't think those things totally get you there...

What do you mean by someone on the other side?

> ...[T]he person who is going to hire. Say it is a job that you want — I mean you can have all the education, you can have all the confidence in the world..., but if that person doesn't want you or doesn't want to give you the chance whether it be because you are Black or female... — you need someone that's totally non-biased, totally neutral...

While the respondents admitted that the *hurdles* were not as easy to overcome as they anticipated seven years ago, they seemed not to be deterred from pursuing their career goals. Their movements[2] between school and work reflected the complexity of a process in which self-concept was related to race, education, experience in the workforce, aspirations, achievements, and perceptions of opportunities.

---

[2] The 22 respondents were at different stages of their occupational and career process. The following represents their movement over the 6–7 year period:
School to Work (completed grade 12), 3
School to Work (dropout high school), 1 (currently unemployed)
Dropped Post-Sec. (now working), 3
To Work now in Post-Sec., 3
To Post-Sec. Work now Post-Sec., 5
To Post-Sec. complete, now Work, 7

Race and Work Experience

In this section, the ideas and perceptions of the respondents in terms of their assessment of the role of race and racism in their experiences at work will be discussed. For the most part, they talked of the challenges they encountered around these issues.

The Challenges in "Getting In"

Getting hired for a job could be considered the most important step in one's life, in terms of establishing one's self-worth and beginning the process of achieving one's career goals. Some of the respondents talked of their interview experiences. Most noticeable were cases in which the applicants were the first racial minorities to be hired by the company. Some recalled being stared at by employees.

The "Look"

>Jenny remembered her discomfort when she was interviewed.
>
>The Director walked me through the office and everyone stopped and stared at me... They weren't just looking; I know the look. I have seen it before... They have never had to mix with minorities because I was the first full-time minority with the company.

The *look*, caused Jenny's concerns about how she would be perceived by others — a sensation she had experienced on other occasions. She cited her encounters both the first day on the job, and subsequently, as evidence that her fears were justified. She said that the Director asked if she had been introduced to the staff, and followed his question with, "*Oh well, we won't have any problems knowing who you are Jenny.*" Jenny contended that since everyone in the department was White, "*obviously he was referring to the fact that I am Black.*" She continued:

>This particular Director is not very comfortable dealing with minorities. It's obvious in his actions, his words — he's made some other blunders along the way...

Oh, Are You Brenda?

A number of respondents talked of the surprise reactions they received when they went for job interviews. For example, Brenda related how she was greeted by the interviewer with "*Oh, are you Brenda?*" Since she was the only person in the lobby that Sunday morning waiting to be interviewed, Brenda believed the question to be inappropriate. The way the interviewer said "*you*" gave her the impression that he was surprised to discover that she was Black. It sounded as if "*you are not what I was expecting...*" While at her current job, Brenda also learned from her supervisor that he too "*was surprised that [I] was Black for it didn't occur to him.*" It should be noted that Brenda has an MBA and in both cases had applied for senior positions — administrative assistant to the Hospital Administrator, and Senior Consultant in a consulting firm. It was possible, according to Brenda, that because she has no "accent," and because the organizations had little experience with Black applicants, the telephone callers merely assumed that she was White.

It's Who You Know

Harcourt: It's not so much what you know and what degrees you have, it's who you know. If a Black man has a degree, say in accounting, and he goes for a job, and there is a White guy who is good at accounting, but does not have a degree, but because he knows somebody there, he is most favoured to get the job. People today are more confident with who they know... When you talk to most of these people out there who do have the jobs that those people should have, ...you will find that they know somebody.

As in 1984–85, the respondents, like Harcourt, believed that: *"It is getting the right contacts, and who you know"* that will eventually help them in obtaining jobs and reaching their career goals. During both studies they cited education as important, but *"who you know"* is even more important particularly in competition against a White person for a job. As one respondent stated, while education can help, *"I have seen that who you know gets you further."*

Be Politically Aware and Conscious About Networking

But getting a job through contacts is only part of the process. As Brenda points out:

Education definitely gets your foot in the door. You need some kind of qualification and credibility... Other types of skills are important — like being able to talk...In Canadian society, talking goes a long way, [and] you have to be politically aware and conscious about networking... [i.e.] Just realizing that it is not only what you know but who you know and recognizing that every organization has politics. Every organization has an organizational culture and you have to be aware of that and know how to use it.

For many of the respondents, the process of getting a job involved using their skills and confronting the challenges, one of which was understanding how to use the organization's culture.

I Wasn't Aware of the Extent to Which It Existed

In 1984–85, respondents said that racism was a *hurdle, not a barrier*, and one that could be overcome. At that time, they expressed confidence that their ability and determination would enable them to achieve their career goals. They said that they knew that racism would not end, but they could side-step it. However, in 1991, they sounded less confident; racism now seemed more insurmountable.

Frank: ...Probably at that point in time, I wasn't aware of the extent to which it existed. I wasn't aware of the degree to which it is entrenched in large systems. I wasn't aware of the degree of how difficult it is to change somebody's mind with regards to their perceptions of other people, in terms of race, colour, sex... So I think the big difference between me now and then is that I am very aware of how deep a part of this society it is.

Frank pointed out how racism had affected his life in accessing jobs. For example:

> When I was first hired, the person who hired me took me aside and confided that he wasn't sure that the community was ready for a Black School Community Education Advisor because it wasn't a Black community...

Most respondents, like Frank, said that experiencing racism was a major challenge. Nevertheless, they remained confident that they could deal with this challenge. As Vanessa, a high school teacher, pointed out: *"You can't make that a reason to stop trying. Racism is something you will have to deal with... I don't think that racism should be used as a reason to curb your goals."* This confidence might be a reflection of the fact that to date, most of these young people had been able to obtain jobs.

The Challenges on the Job

Once on the job, there were other challenges, including the need to confront and deal with stereotypes that employers and co-workers might have of Blacks. Mention has already been made of respondents such as Bryan and Tracy, who felt that they had a responsibility *to make up for* negative behaviour of other Blacks. And there were other challenges dealing with clients and co-workers being caught between the expectation of members of their community and the job, loss of identity, loneliness, employment equity and the *glass ceiling*.[3]

You Don't Know What You Are Doing

Anthony, an immigration officer, reported that when in the course of his work he has had to take action which sometimes displeased clients, they asked *"to see his supervisor."* He and other interviewees who work in service occupations such as teaching and community work said that because they were more likely to be challenged by clients, they felt a particular responsibility to carry out their duties correctly and fairly so that when complaints were made, they could be confident that they had carried out their tasks correctly. Many of these respondents felt that because they were Black and in authority positions, their judgment was sometimes questioned.

You People

A number of respondents also talked of how they were expected to account for the actions of other Blacks and to deal with co-workers' attitudes. Anthony, for example, related an incident in which a co-worker, referring to a Jamaican client,

---

[3] The *glass ceiling* concept refers to limitations in achievement. Referring to racial minorities, Fleras and Elliot (1992) point out: "If not openly barred from certain occupations, many find themselves shunted into menial and unskilled occupations with little in the way of remuneration, security, or prospects for promotion (p. 100). And as Weinfeld (1990) notes: "equal opportunity exists for Canada's White immigrant groups. Visible minorities still have far to go ... ."

"*remarked that, that's all you people do is come here...*" Tracy, an ex-sales representative for a major hotel chain in Toronto, also talked of the comments and attitudes of her bosses and co-workers. "The sarcastic jokes at meetings, ...like, *'Well, we don't want any of the Caribana people to stay at our hotel. They'll just run it down and ruin it'*."

When asked how one dealt with such challenges, Tracy, commented:

> Well, I wondered how they could be so ignorant to think that I wouldn't be affected or hurt or offended at some of the comments. Most often, they would say: *'We don't mean you Tracy'* or *'We don't mean your friends or anything but you know how they can be'*... It became a personal thing after a while; I was offended personally.

Make Extra Effort to Help Blacks

In addition to representing the "*Black viewpoint*" to their co-workers, respondents also talked of having to respond to the expectations and pressures of Blacks. In particular, respondents who worked in service areas recalled cases of Blacks expecting favours from them, and their sense of obligation to respond positively.

> **Anthony:** I make a little extra effort to help those who happen to be Black in the office. Other officers show favouritism, so I do feel a little responsibility to try to help out any Black person as much I can without going overboard.

Anthony also said that Blacks' expectation of him was "probably one of the hardest things for me." Vanessa, a high school teacher, also said that she paid

> special attention to my non-White students, in particular, Black students... I tend to put a lot of energy into them because they are the ones that are going to get burnt the most...

Frank, a school community worker, talked of being caught between speaking out about issues related to Blacks, or initiating programs for Blacks, and being expected to address the issues of the "entire community." Frank said that for the first two years of his job, he felt burdened by the pressure and expectation of his community and that of his employer. He concluded, in retrospect, that he has managed to be fair to all parties.

I Represented the Conservative White Viewpoint

That many of the respondents were expected to speak on behalf of, and represent the viewpoints of other Blacks, was often a consequence of the fact that they were the "*only Blacks*" working with staff who had little experience with Blacks. As Tracy explains, being "*a pioneer*" made her think of why she was hired. Referring to the hotel industry, where the executives, as in her hotel, were exclusively White, she said:

> They are very concerned about looks and I kind of felt that I was certainly hired because I represented the conservative White viewpoint so I fitted in well with their scheme of things. I didn't rock the boat; I wasn't radical. I looked almost White...so they felt safe with me.

I Get Lonely Sometimes

In 1985, the respondents said that being female meant that they had "two strikes against them." But while they felt that being Black was more of a disadvantage, the 1991 sample of respondents, particularly the females seemed less able to articulate which of these factors was the greater disadvantage. However, most noticeable among the female participants was their feeling of loneliness, particularly in role settings in which they were "pioneers;" that is, the only Black employee or one of few.

> **Tracy:** You still feel like the odd one out even though you can go so far. It is nice to know you can reach the top and be alone is kind of different and I felt that's what I was experiencing...

> **Brenda:** ...You don't feel like you are part of the group. You feel like an outsider and sometimes you wonder, what should you do. Should you take up golf or should you, if you prefer a different type of sport, just stay with that... Everyone comes in on Monday and talks about how they went to the cottage, etc., all these things that are foreign to me. I guess I used to feel that people wouldn't be interested in what I was doing.

> I think it was a lack of confidence. Maybe because...everyone would be talking about things that they did and it never seemed to be the same sort of thing that I did. Or should I say that I went to the Congress of Black Women...

Is it lack of confidence or cultural difference?

> But how come they are not thinking that I might not relate to what they are saying?... So is it lack of confidence — that I would be even concerned about whether or not they can relate to it? Some people are so arrogant that they just talk — whatever they did it is important and it better be important to you.

None of the males in the sample talked of being lonely in the way the females did. This is probably a reflection of the fact that females have fewer same-sex colleagues, with whom they could interact, particularly in senior organizational positions. These colleagues might be busy trying to "fit in" as well. As Vanessa pointed out: "Men have a mentor system" which has benefitted them over the years.

Very Disappointed in Employment Equity:

> **Brenda:** I am very disappointed in employment equity. I think it is garbage... It seems to be working mainly for White women right now.

The above comment was typical of how many respondents felt about employment equity. They claimed that *"White women are benefitting from it more than Blacks."* But most agreed that if applied fairly, the legislation could benefit Blacks.

> **Frank:** Employment equity is correcting historical wrongs... I don't see people out of the goodness of their hearts doing that themselves. Unfortunately, we live in a place...where in order for good things to happen, it has to be legislated.

Most of the respondents had not used any employment equity programs, and when asked if they would, everyone said "yes." However, they hastened to add, as Frank did:

...employment equity doesn't mean people that are less qualified are getting in. It is giving people who have always been qualified a chance, but because of racism, they just didn't get the opportunity. So it is giving opportunity to qualified people.

A few interviewees said that they had made applications without using "the minority angle...'cause I felt that I really shouldn't use that advantage."

Sonia: ...I still feel kind of funny [using this advantage], although I have always been arguing that special measures have to be taken to encourage those groups that are not represented...

Black People in Entry Level Positions Are Not a Threat:

Brenda: I don't think that Black people in entry level positions are as much of a threat to the power structure as they are once you get more experienced and start moving up into more influential positions. So yes, it may look as though I have had things easy. I got an entry level job at Y.F., got a job at P., so what. The real trouble is going to start when I want to be a partner at P. or want to be the CEO instead of being the assistant at Y.F. So I don't think I can sit back now and say things have been easy and I don't really have to try hard...

Brenda was referring to the "glass ceiling" phenomenon (Weinfeld, 1990) that women and other minorities face in employment. Brenda, like others, perceived it as a challenge that would grow as they pursued more senior positions.

Ways of Coping with the Challenges

In response to the challenges they encountered during their early years in the workforce, the respondents developed various strategies which they contended would enable them to overcome their barriers to achievement. The strategies they constructed and employed to cope with race-related dilemmas grew out of, and were dependent upon, their understanding of the consequences of being Black, as well as on their work experiences, their perception of their opportunities and their occupational goals. Thus, their reliance on strategies enabled them to respond to, manage and control their situations in the workforce. Confidence in their strategies seemed to help them maintain their optimism.

Brenda: I am as optimistic... Maybe now I am more realistic and I think it is possible but with a big **BUT**, but you have to take certain strategies to get there. It is not going to be easy...but I can do it because I understand the hurdles and what you have to do to get over them.

In 1985, it was found that whatever the circumstances or situation, the respondents were determined to rely on their own abilities, skills and strengths as a way of coping. There seemed to be a preference for working within the existing social system despite the inherent disadvantages. All of the youth's strategies or coping mechanisms confirms their belief that ultimately they would be judged on their own merit.

Self-Confidence, Determination and Hard Work

In 1991, the respondents seemed to be employing the same coping mechanisms or strategies to ensure their survival in the world of work. Brenda's comment was typical of what many of the respondents said:

> I am definitely the first Black person in the Health and Social Service practice and I may be the first Black consultant in the Toronto office, I am not sure. But there aren't any others right now. I guess I feel an obligation to do well so that other Blacks will have an opportunity to join: 'cause I guess I still feel that maybe if I screwed up I would be an example of what Black people represent. It's like, *"Oh we had a Black person before and she didn't work out so we are not going to hire another one."* I don't know if that happens but I am not taking a chance with it so I am trying to give Black people a good reputation while I am here. The other reason too is that I think some people have a lower expectations of Black people and expect less than excellence from us so I like to prove them wrong in that area and surprise them. So when people say *"Oh, that's really good,"* I try to act as if that's the standard, that's the norm.

So the determination to *work hard* and *prove one-self* was not only a personal goal but also an obligation to be an *example* and to *make space* for other Blacks.

Some respondents seemed to suggest that *working harder* was not an indication of their lack of self-confidence or succumbing to racial stereotyping. Neither was it an indication that they were *working against a White person*. Rather, it was a way of *helping all of us*.

> **Sonia:** ...I don't subscribe to those kinds of competitive kind of ways of looking at work 'cause I realize that ...I am not opposed to White people. I am opposed to those who are in power, who happen to be White people who are misusing their power. But I think that it is in all of our interest, regardless of our race, that we tap into the talents of all of us because it's getting us all further.

The respondents, like Sonia, preferred to see the strategy of hard work in a positive light. They were not against White people, but the people in power who misused that power. This could also be interpreted as their attempt to maintain a positive attitude because they would have to work with Whites. Further, they argue that their talents and contributions were important to building our society.

But not all the respondents agreed that they had to *work harder* and *prove themselves*. These respondents felt that their work would be judged on its own merit. For example:

> **Vanessa:** ...I am not out to prove anything to anyone. Maybe I thought so at first but now I am just doing my best... You just have to do your work and your work will speak for you... If you are good and capable in your field, you really shouldn't have to do that.

However, this belief in meritocracy was not in fact evident in some of their actions. For example, Vanessa, a teacher, said that she tells her Black students that they have to be *"confident and self-disciplined because...there are individuals in society who are racist...and those individuals are in hiring positions...so they have to do well and try their best."* So, while Vanessa and others wanted to think that they were not succumbing to the pressures that racism exerts on them, unconsciously they operated with the knowledge that they had to work hard and prove themselves.

Place Blame on the System

In 1985, respondents suggested that they were likely *placing blame* on themselves and not *the system*. They reported that while they were *still somewhat optimistic*, that *self-confidence, hard work*, etc. *"are absolutely necessary to overcome racism, we can't do it alone."* Now they focus on the system.

Sonia: It has to be in concert with other people organizing other like-minds because you can't take on the system by yourself even if you prove to be the brightest, best...I don't think, no matter how optimistic and brilliant I may be, I am not getting anywhere unless it's with other people.

Frank: Back then the focus was on us as individuals and we weren't placing blame really on the system... We were in our own naive way sort of putting the onus on us to achieve according to whatever standards that are out there that we did not set for ourselves and we, I guess, internalized those standards. Right now I feel that any change that needs to take place needs to be...so you can change the very structure of these systems and until then I feel that as an individual, or as Black individuals, we need to look at ourselves as a people and the strengths that we have...

Seven years later, the participants seemed more informed of the extent to which *the system*, compared to *the individual's* effort, could influence their achievement. Thus, as Frank pointed out, rather than living up to the standards of the system that might not serve their interests, they must work to change the *structure of the system* in order to meet their needs. In doing so, the respondents were shifting their focus from themselves as incapable if they fail, to themselves as *strong people who have always had a lot to offer the world*.

The System Is Not Perfect

One question asked of the interviewees was: *How is it we see so many disenchanted Black young people getting into trouble* and yet these respondents seem to be quite satisfied with their opportunities so far. They responded by saying that they *"understand the system," "understand the hurdles,"* and know that *"the system is not perfect."* It seemed that it was the knowledge that *the system is not perfect* rather than the belief that *"the system is against you"* that was the basis of some of the respondents coping strategies.

Vanessa: ...I think that it is a much healthier attitude to say that the system is not perfect and needs work and work towards making the system better as opposed to the system is just against us. Otherwise, it is very easy to become disenchanted with the system and the system becomes the focus of everything bad and wrong as opposed to try to cultivate self.

The respondents who coped in this manner tended to be those who were responsible for educating or working with Black youth. Thus, they preferred to believe that there is justice so that their charges (e.g., students, team members) do not *"lose faith"* in the system.

But other respondents disagreed with this idea. They seemed to cope better by *"being realistic"* and worked with the knowledge that the system is imperfect in order to avoid *"burn out"* and *"frustration."*

> **Frank:** ...I can see that if you have the idea that the system is against you, you are going to go through a lot of frustration...and that in itself will lead you to burn out; that in itself could lead you to unproductive confrontations within the system. It might be a little bit "fairytale-ish" to believe that the system doesn't work against people because many of the social policies and many of the things that the system does, it does work against the people that it supposedly tries to serve so I think you have to keep that in the back of your mind.

I Know That I Am Qualified

It is important to note that while the respondents were prepared to use employment equity programs to obtain jobs, they believed that their qualifications, and not merely their colour helped them achieve access.

> **Frank:** ...I am not going to go take on more than I can chew. If I feel that I can do [the job] it and they give it to me, to hell with everyone else.

They perceived their qualifications positively and did not believe that colour was their *"only ticket in."* If co-workers labelled them *"employment equity employees"* they were confident that their *"demonstrated competence"* would be enough proof that they "were right for the job."

> **Anthony:** I am not there to say well, I'm the first Black... I am there to say that I am a qualified candidate and I can do the job if given the opportunity... They can always hire because of colour but you still have to do the job effectively because you are going to get pressure, pressure from all kinds, from your colleagues...

Respondents also believed that employers would be disinclined to hire unqualified person for fear of appearing "pretty devious, calculated," and engaging in "premeditated conspiracy." Such actions would "reflect on them for their ability to judge."

Be Realistic

Earlier, we discussed the respondents understandings of the limits to their achievement in employment — the *glass ceiling* concept. Here we focus on their coping strategy. A common response to how far they believed they would be able to go in the organization was captured in the following statements:

> **Anthony:** I don't want to get into management... I want to get more into community work. There are so many different levels; it is amazing.

They believed that *"the chances for promotion are good"* because they have the competence, education, ability and have done well in their jobs. But they were *"realistic"* about *hurdles* and that *"things are not always done correctly."* By declaring that their chances for promotion were good, they could remain confident in their skills and look to other areas of work in which they were interested.

This coping strategy was further exemplified by Judith, a law clerk and Brenda, a consultant, who praised the departments in which they worked by saying that they were *"recognized and appreciated;"* and that the people with whom they worked were *"a different breed of people."*

> **Judith:** ...The area I am in is unique. The corporate floor where people joke that you have to be White to even walk up there is a different story. It is very hierarchical and people don't cross boundaries, and you know your place and that kind of thing. At a lot of law firms, the lawyers are like that. They are very ignorant and arrogant... But the group that I am with is an exception. They are young lawyers... They are not conservative and treat us all as adults. I have been fortunate; I can't work under any other circumstances.

Believing that they worked in a respectful and supportive environment, they felt satisfied and justified in remaining in their positions.

I See Myself as a Crusader

Acknowledging the reality that their bosses and co-workers would be *"naive"* and *"ignorant,"* and knowing that they were *"pioneers"* and *"representatives"* within the workplace, many of the respondents cope by seeing themselves as *"change agents," "advocates," "educators"* and *"crusaders."*

> **Brenda:** ...I usually don't miss an opportunity to point out things that offend me or that I think are not right or that are only expressing a mainstream point of view... I know that one of the strengths that I bring to the team on that job is my sensitivity to minority issues because through my own personal experience and my involvement with community work, I feel that I should speak out in the context of the job...

> **Mervin:** At my current job...you get the odd person with a slight bit of racism. I think they are just naive. With most of the people I think that I have changed their minds. They have never known a Black person and don't understand them. There is just a big gap there that's my problem if I want to be some sort of crusader and want people to close this gap for them to see that I am just like them and vice versa...a human being. You have no reason to hate me because of the colour of my skin.

You Don't Have to Change Yourself

Dealing with loneliness was something that the participants, particularly the females, shared. Feeling lonely was largely a result of cultural differences based on class and racial and ethnic origin. For the most part, they coped by believing that they were "making space" for "other people of colour" — assuring themselves that they did not have to change their cultural habits and image in order to "fit in."

> **Brenda:** ...I remember taking an assertiveness training course where I mentioned my loneliness in a roundabout way...and it helped me to realize that you don't have to change yourself.

In so far as loneliness leads to feelings of alienation and disillusionment, the respondents seemed to cope by reassuring themselves of their own skills and abilities:

> **Tracy:** I have always been a survivor and I have always felt that the only way I have been able to get ahead is that I have been smart enough to know that you have to be smarter than them, and you have to know how to handle yourself.

And when they were *"offended and hurt,"* they concluded that tolerance was the best coping strategy.

> **Tracy:** ...There is nothing that you can do except bear the brunt and go on. You have to learn how to handle and get out of that situation without compromising your dignity.

Have a Support Network

However, a number of the respondents rely on friendship, especially same-race friends, outside and inside of the workplace for support and encouragement.

> **Brenda:** ...Every year we have to do a personal development plan for work indicating our goals and so on for the next year and along with a lot of other things I put down I joined the Congress of Black Women... Maybe because it is important to me, it gives me a balance and keeps me grounded in my community. The kind of upliftment and education I get from the community, I can't get anywhere else and I think that's one of the reasons why I was able to accomplish whatever I have accomplished... It is important for me to be connected with the community and it gives me a sense of security. Sometimes I use it to test my own views — like if I find myself reacting sort of sensitively to something that has been said or some policy in the workplace, it helps me to know that it's not just me, that other people see it that way and on several occasions I called Black friends of mine, and ask "What do you think about this?" — in reaction to something that has happened or some work that I am involved in, just to test — like, am I crazy or do other people feel that way. Is it the system or what?

> **Harcourt:** ...I get inspiration from my boss who has become a friend... He is African... And from the Black woman who works there. We're all family. We help each other, we talk to each other secretly. Sometimes a little bit in groups, but not on the job, and we coach each other. We make sure we are there for each other, and we would be nice to each other. We treat each other with respect, show that there is love. We do understand each other's point of view, whether it be good or bad.

Following up on the 1985 idea that sensitive and aware majority group members would give assistance, Vanessa pointed out that the network of supporters should also include Whites. Recalling her experience, Vanessa said:

> ...I think from the time I had my interview for that job, (the principal) liked what she saw, she liked my personality, and my resume said that I was capable, and after I got the job, she saw that I was capable... and she helped me. I still see this woman and still keep in touch with her... She works for the Board but comes around. I would like to keep in touch with her because I think that in time she might be able to help me some more and I think that she would be willing to. But I think Blacks have to set up that type of network as well, that type of contact network so that they can help a lot of young people and maybe that might help them to not feel so despondent, not feel so defeated.

Conclusion

The themes which emerged from the respondents' comments in 1984–85 and 1991 indicated that Blackness was constructed in accordance with its disadvantaged position in Canadian society. As a result, they believed that as visible minority individuals they would be labelled, stereotyped and discriminated against, and that their race would impact on their occupational experiences and opportunities. The young people perceived themselves in terms of the status quo and they sought ways to negotiate this reality — a reality for which they developed and utilized strategies. These strategies included: being self-confident, determined and hard working; being politically aware; making the right contacts; blaming the system; and networking.

Blackness seemed to be socially problematic and despite all efforts to disprove negative notions through individual modelling, the impact remained the same — being Black was a factor in social interactions. The choices in constructing oneself along lines of race seemed to be (1) to internalize and become to varying degrees the stereotype, or (2) to understand the stereotype, and construct oneself in opposition to it. Either option did not allow for a construction of self, independent of societal and structural racism, but it is the latter that was most evident in the perceptions and strategies of the respondents.

Work is not an isolated social experience, but rather an arena in which individuals' socialization, related to culture, minority status and class, influence social relationships and interactions. It was therefore understandable that these Black young workers experienced a sense of alienation in the majority culture of the work environment. Indeed, in the 1991 interviews, several respondents mentioned "feeling different" and "lonely" in their work settings and in their social relationships. Nevertheless, many of the respondents seemed confident in their ability to deal with racism. Rather than ignoring incidents of racism, many expressed a belief that those who hold racist attitudes are ignorant, uninformed individuals who have limited experience with Blacks. They contended that racism was systemic and based on stereotypic representations and the misinformation that is entrenched in Canadian society. Thus, they adopted an educator and a change agent strategy in which they informed their colleagues, and modelled exemplary behaviours that were designed to dispel misconceptions and make it possible for other Blacks and racial minorities to gain employment in the organization.

In summary, compared to seven years earlier, most respondents in 1991 seemed more aware of structural racism and the concomitant limitations and obstacles. Nevertheless, they refused to despair. They believed they would succeed because there were no other ways, psychologically, to retain their motivation to become successful workers and citizens. Most had found a safe space in which to work and felt that they were, or would be mobile *within that space*. However, many had lowered their career aspirations, possibly to avoid disappointment and to realize a sense of achievement. As Kai concluded:

> ...I just think that the system won't change so therefore we either deal with it, learn how to deal with it, or don't deal with it at all. For me, I am learning how to deal with it and I am getting experience that I need and want to excel in my career. I like what I am doing... But it's a challenge and I think it is something that you will always have to deal with in life. It is something that Black people have to deal with and there is no end to it... I think that we can make a difference, we should try to make a difference and we shouldn't give up because the system fails. We cannot make the system make you fail.

2
Gender Tracks: Male-Female Perceptions of Home-School-Work Transitions

Nancy Mandell and Stewart Crysdale

For the most part, sociologists agree that men and women experience family, school, and work life differently (Bernard, 1981) and unequally (Armstrong and Armstrong, 1990). Within homes, married women perform two-thirds of domestic labour and child rearing (Day, 1990) while also contributing approximately 40 percent of total family income. Most girls experience a "chilly climate" within schools, (Hall and Sandler, 1982) of sexist stereotyping of their abilities and sexist channelling of their futures. Moreover, the majority of Canadian women are clustered in nonprofessional, low paying clerical, sales and service occupations.

Clearly, some type of "gender tracking" appears to be at work in which extensive gender segregation of domestic labour, schooling, and workplaces means men and women live, work, and study in different areas. In high school, boys and girls are either streamed or put themselves, into different vocational and academic courses. These concentrations then prepare students for different types of job experiences and/or post-secondary education following high school. Despite our achievement of horizontal equity, that is formal equality of educational opportunity, vertical gender inequity, concentration within categories, still persists in high schools and in labour markets. Despite our now historic rates of higher female grades in high school, or higher female rates of high school completion and undergraduate university attendance, women are disproportionately found in the academic stream, in the humanities and social science, rather than the maths and physical sciences. In the vocational stream they are clustered in business courses rather than the technical areas.

What transpires during the home-school-work transition to produce gender tracks and divisions in high schools? Specifically, what gender messages are parents, teachers, and employers giving out and how are these perceived by our youth sample in their roles as children, students, and employees? Does this perception affect youth's transition from home to school and to work? Is transition a gendered phenomenon and if so, in what ways?

Two views of the genesis of gender tracking exist. On the one hand, structural accounts, such as social and cultural reproduction theories, focus on the agents of socialization, the content of their messages, and their manner of inculcation. This determinist line of research assumes an unproblematic and linear flow of information from agents to clients. As "empty" and "passive" receptacles, clients presumably internalize and then act on whatever messages they receive. Students, then, are cultural "dupes."

On the other hand, interactionist accounts emphasize the clients' or students' perceptions of the agents and their messages. They wonder what stories students hear, how students interpret these messages; how students account for and make sense of their choices in school and work; do students see their experiences as being gendered? Students are recognized as subverting, resisting, accommodating, belittling and ignoring the suggestions and manoeuvres of socialization agents. In this view, students are conceptualized as active participants choosing what appear to them as reasonable school and life paths from within a limited range of available options. While recognizing the influence of material and social circumstances in affecting student's choices, this perspective also acknowledges the diversity, richness and idiosyncrasy of individual behaviour.

This article focuses on vocational and academic students' perceptions of gender tracking, their accounts of its existence, its genesis, and its consequences. By following a sample of students from home to school and then to work, we are able to see the emergence of distinct gender tracks. By framing these perceptions against our current data on Canadian home, school, and labour market conditions, a portrait of distinct and unequal transitions emerges.

Method

The information is drawn from a series of questionnaires and interviews with young adults who graduated from high school in 1984–85. The goal of the larger study was to document the transition from school to work process as experienced by students five years after leaving high school.[1] Since this paper focuses on the particular influence of gender in transition, specifically the youths' perception of distinct gender tracks in their home and school environments, the data draw predominately from the interviews with youth.

Three hundred and twenty-four male and female youth were interviewed in 1989–90. In addition, 115 parents, 287 teachers, and 277 employers were also surveyed and interviewed. While occasionally the questionnaire data from the parents, teachers, and employers is referred to, this article is largely based on the qualitative responses of the youth. Quantitative data are mainly used for comparative purposes to indicate the seeming incongruence between youths' answers to survey items and their more in-depth explanations of these responses.

---

[1] This chapter draws on data collected from a larger study of the school to work transition funded by SSHRC and led by principal investigator Professor Stewart Crysdale. Professors Alan J.C. King and Nancy Mandell were co-investigators ("Towards a Resilient, Productive Generation").

Youth surveyed came from ten high schools in four Canadian cities: Toronto (Mississauga), Ottawa, Guelph, and Edmonton. As a whole, the sample consists of mostly white, Anglo, urban, middle-class, Ontario youth in their mid-twenties. Fifty-five percent were female; one-quarter were from working-class homes in which their parents were semi-skilled office workers, sales clerks, unskilled or low-skilled manual workers. One-third of these families came from Peel District in Mississauga. Eleven percent have fathers with upper middle-class jobs as senior managers, lawyers, engineers, doctors, and teachers, mostly from Ottawa. One-quarter had fathers with middle-class jobs as middle-managers, advanced technicians, and small business owners. Anglo-saxons comprise 60 percent of the sample with a few Ontario Francophones. Thirty-three percent were of other European origin and 7 percent were Asian/Oriental.

Fourteen percent of the youth sample did not complete secondary school (compared with 30% of all Canadian youth); 29 percent took some post-secondary training (this includes training programs or courses less than three years); 18 percent completed a college program (these last two categories should be compared with the 40% of all Canadians who attend community college or post-secondary training); and 38 percent took some, or are still attending or completed university (compared with 20% of all Canadians).

Occupationally, 7 percent of youth currently held professional positions, 21 percent were still attending college or university (11% attended university) and could be expected to hold above average positions in the future; 6 percent were unemployed; 31 percent had skilled jobs, and 35 percent had semi or unskilled jobs.

Egalitarianism: Myth or Reality?

Considerable research documents the strong influence families exert in their children's school and career choices (Moss and Rutledge, 1991). In particular, status attainment studies document the primary role of parents in helping children establish educational aspirations and accomplish their goals. For the most part, research on the home-school linkage focuses on how families facilitate or constrain their children's educational progress. This approach makes little reference to the work of mothers in its abstracted reference to "families" (Gaskell and McLaren, 1987: 21) nor is it concerned with children's interpretations of this work. Yet clearly, youth hear, see, and report gendered experiences within their families. Strong evidence to date (Lindsey, 1990; Richmond-Abbott, 1992) suggest girls do not receive the same messages as boys. After outlining youth's and parent's perceptions of gender role scripts, we are in a better position to speculate as to their effect on youth's formulation of educational and career aspirations.

Family sociologists have long acknowledged the class and gendered nature of family life which is at odds with widespread public endorsement of egalitarianism. Statistical findings in our study substantiate this variance while qualitative comments illustrate the differential treatment men and women receive in their family, school, and work lives. In the following section, these discrepancies are discussed by examining youth and parental responses to questions about gender, aspirations, and careers in an attempt to suggest the effect divergences have on gender tracking.

Equality of opportunity for both sexes in family, school, and occupational settings is generally shared. When asked, "How do you think people of each gender should be treated at home, school, and at work?" students enthusiastically endorse egalitarianism. This student's reply is typical of many.

> Equally in them all. Everyone should be given equal potential or opportunity in school or job. Individuals may be different but they should get equal opportunity.

This same woman, who so ardently supports egalitarianism also recognizes the lack of congruence between attitudes and behaviours. When asked what she dislikes most about her current job as a management trainee in an aerospace company, she concludes: "working in a male dominated industry in which it is difficult being accepted as a woman!"

Another woman articulates egalitarian ideology in some detail:

> Equally. At home they should share responsibilities like cooking, cleaning, raking leaves, and fixing the car. At work, promotions should be on merit. Hirings should be based on ability, experience, and education. At school, people should be judged on marks based on perfection and ability, not gender.

Statistically and qualitatively, youth and parents endorse a "level playing field." In order to elicit the extent to which youth and parents translate liberal principles to gender equity, five hypothetical questions about family, school and work life were posed.

The Gender Equity Scale consists of five questions:

(1) If family finances are a problem and one youth can be helped to go on in post-secondary education, which one should it be? The daughter or the son?

(2) Is a career more important for a man or a woman in a family?

(3) If both spouses are working full-time, who is to be responsible for household chores and care of the children?

(4) Are some courses usually more difficult for students of one gender?

(5) Who make the best employer? Men or Women?

Scores for each answer were added and a composite indicator of egalitarianism was computed. Overall, 23 percent of students, and 29 percent of parents do not support gender role equality and thus are labelled "traditionalists;" 18 percent of youth and 15 percent of parents scored high and thus are labelled "egalitarian." The bulk of respondents, 60 percent of youth and 56 percent of parents clustered in between these two poles, supporting egalitarianism in some areas but not in others. This group is labelled "quasi-egalitarian."[2]

---

[2] Quasi-egalitarian refers to marital roles that have moved from a traditional husband-as-breadwinner and wife-as-homemaker division to ones in which both husbands and wives earn wages, but the husband's work comes first in the amount earned, family influence, and location of family residence.

Table 2-1: Influence of Father, Mother and Both on Youth's Early Attainments (Zero-order Correlations)

Youth's Attainments	Father Education	Father Occupation	Father Help	Mother Education	Mother Occupation	Mother Help	Both Parents Education	Both Parents Occupation
Effort at School			.144*			.357**		
Self-help in Transition					.137*		.123*	.210*
Job Aspiration	.249***	.228***		.252***	.253*	.137*	.387***	.480***
Marks, Secondary School	.117*	.007	.123*		.171*	.175*	.204**	.354***
Educational Level	.308***	.223*	.169**	.245***	.308***		.350***	.468***
Present Job Level	.137*	.207*		.261***	.330***			.273**

* = R significant at the .05 level; ** = R significant at the .001 level; *** = R significant at the .0001 level

What emerges, then, is a statistical and qualitative display of quasi-egalitarianism among youth and parents. In answer to gender equity questionnaire items and in their in-depth elaboration of their responses, women and men of all ages and social classes endorse some combination of wage and domestic labour for men and women, somewhat equal responsibility for children, a little sharing of housework, and equal educational and occupational aspirations for women and men, provided no financial problems or other hardships are involved.

Quantitative data indicate no significant correlation between gender and aspirations for both parents and youth. In other words, a majority of parents want both their sons and daughters to achieve high educational and occupational success, as do the students themselves. As with other Canadian studies (Moss and Rutledge, 1991), the majority of parents are ambitious and interested in their children's success.

Researchers often interpret this finding as evidence of gender equity in parenting. But it may be that these aspirations merely reflect the instrumental appeal of schools as vehicles for social mobility. As post-secondary enrolments increase, and as Canadians live through continuing periods of economic dislocation, educational credentialing is reaffirmed as the major avenue to secure and stable employment. Both Canadian (Krahn and Lowe, 1991; Tanner, 1991) and American (Weis, 1990) studies note that, even when their dreams are hopelessly unrealistic given their marks or academic concentration, both boys and girls desire higher education.

Parental influence is felt to work indirectly through the assistance and encouragement parents give regarding school- work and career planning. Students in our sample identify parents, especially mothers, as significant supports (see Table 2–1).[3]

As one full-time male university student notes,

> The most important things in my life — my purpose, how I can serve my fellow man, how I should relate to people on the job or at home — were all learned at home, by example, from my parents, family and friends.

Yet the support parents give boys, (similar to that of teachers), apparently differs for sons and daughters and differs according to whether it is delivered by a father or a mother. It is only recently that regulating, monitoring and controlling children's schooling has been detailed as a constituent element of mothering. As Carol Smart (1990) suggests, fathers "care about" their children's well-being while mothers "care for" their offspring. The former entails verbal encouragement and articulation of high aspirations, while the latter involves the day-to-day work of assessing success and failure. Making sure the homework is completed, helping with school projects, interacting with teachers and school officials, hiring tutors, supervising children's friendships, and arranging after-school activities are just some elements of this mothering work.

---

[3] Table 2–1 compares youth's perceptions of their fathers' and mothers' help with the actual educational and occupational level obtained by both parents and their combined aspirations. A number of indicators of youth's attainments are included.

Table 2-2: Sex Role Norms, Youth and Parents (%)

Sex Role Norms	Parents			Youth		
	One Gender	Equal Chance	Both	One Gender	Equal Chance	Both
1. With limited funds in a family, which youth should continue past high school?	7	72	21	6	84	11
2. Is a career more important in a family for a man or woman?	15	44	41	18	56	26
3. If both spouses are working, who is responsible for household chores and child care?	3		97	3		97
4. Are some courses usually more difficult for students of one gender? *	19	30	51	12	27	61
5. Who make the best employers? Men or Women?	31	70		27	61	12
Composite Gender Equality Scale	Low 29	Middle 56	High 15 (66)	Low 23	Middle 60	High 18 (298)

* As replies to this question did not fit set categories, we recorded values as follows: 1= by nature, 2 = by practice, 3 = neither by nature or practice.
Total scores of 10 or under = Low, 11 - 12 = Middle, 13 - 15 = High

Recently, studies have investigated how this mothering work varies by social class. Griffith and Smith's study (1987) indicates how the discourse of the elementary school, its organization of time, and its reliance on parental participation assumes a stay-at-home mother, preferably a middle-class one. Walkerdine and Lucey's research (1989) documents the disjuncture between working-class and middle-class mothers' schooling knowledge. The middle-class mothers' knowledge of school rules, procedures and content makes their monitoring of their children's school work appear unproblematic. But in both classes, the task remains the mother's. Despite class differences in ways that mothers monitor their children's schooling, few studies have found mothers or fathers disinterested. The Crysdale study discloses that a substantial minority of parents are unhelpful.

Our youth feel their parents' intense concern. Over 80 percent read clear messages from their parents suggesting parents telegraph their ambitions distinctly. Parents wish their daughters, as much as their sons, to study hard, achieve good grades, and find secure and stable employment. Youth also wish to find intrinsically rewarding, financially lucrative, and permanent employment.

While clearly recognizing parental desire that they succeed academically, youth also report that their parents express different aspirations for sons than daughters. Sometimes students, mostly girls, describe a sexist home environment in which females are assumed to be different in personality and temperament than males.

> Men are easier to get along with than females. females tend to be moody. But on the other hand, females might be more sensitive.

In other homes, future child rearing is simply assumed to be women's work.

> Need a mother at home to have a family. Women have to have very steady jobs and day care to equally participate in careers like men.

At other times, students relay quite gender differentiated comments concerning women's abilities and future jobs.

> Math confuses girls, I don't know why. females are better at managing, better at interaction, better at solving problems without force, level headed.

There are no gender differences in the value of continuing education as a route to upward mobility or in the centrality of paid labour. But here the similarities end, as there are significant differences in labour market outcomes. While only speculative, we assume here that girls' and boys' experiences at home and school are sufficiently different to condition them both to define their futures in gender-distinct ways, and to act on these understandings in ways that lead to different social activities and to different interpretations of similar school experiences.

As part of the gender equity scale, two questions were designed to elicit more specific information about the relationship between aspirations and lived reality (see Table 2–2).[4]

The first question reveals contradictory trends. When pressed to elaborate on the question "If family finances are a problem and only one youth can be helped to go on to post-secondary education, should it be a son or daughter who is helped?" the majority of youth, (84%) and parents, (72%) provided putatively neutral, meritocratic answers saying, "the best student," or "the one with the most ability" rather than explicitly endorsing egalitarianism. Interestingly, 11 percent of youth and 21 percent of parents chose "equal chances for men and women" as their answer. Still a minority, 5 percent of youth and 7 percent of parents suggested that

---

[4] Table 2–2 compares youth's perception of their fathers' and mothers' help with the actual educational and occupational level obtained by both parents and their combined aspirations. A number of indicators of youth's attainments are included.

one sex ought to be helped and elaborated on traditional perspectives for the interviewers.

> Son is more likely to be the breadwinner so he should go to university. If something were to happen to the daughter, she could marry.

If forced to choose, a minority of parents find it less essential to send daughters to university than sons, noting that women get married and can depend on men for financial support. The traditional idea that women can fall back on male wages still lingers despite empirical evidence to the contrary (Armstrong and Armstrong, 1990).

The second question also reveals a discrepancy between expressed attitudes and actual experiences. When asked "Is a career more important for a man or a woman in a family?," the majority of youth, 56 percent, chose a quasi-egalitarian response noting that, "the person with the most aptitude should have a career."

Eighteen percent endorsed traditional choices and 26 percent supported egalitarianism. One young woman whose father is a baker and mother a retired movie theatre manager provided a common response.

> Careers are equally important for both. In my family, both parents had careers which were equally important to both of them and to the finances of the family.

While 26 percent of youth stated that careers are equally important for men and women, 16 percent said that careers are more important for men, and 2 percent cite women, too often youth commented on the discrepancy between egalitarian sentiments and lived experience. As one 80 percent average student with a B.A. in Social Work stated,

> Careers should be equally important for both of them but it depends on the family life. If a woman has children she has to leave work for a while. Women have to have very steady jobs and day care in order to have careers equal to men.

Still another female who graduated from high school with over 80 percent in Math and English comments caustically, "A man. It's still a man's world out there."

Youth and parents' sarcastic comments about the distinct occupational experiences of men and women are borne out in other questions probing the complicated link between domestic and wage labour. In response to the question, "If both spouses are working full-time, who is to be responsible for household chores and care of the children?" a bifurcated response emerges with youth and parents choosing either egalitarian or traditional answers. The majority of youth, 97 percent, and the majority of parents 97 percent felt both spouses should share household labour and childcare while only 3 percent expressed traditional views that one sex should assume responsibility. As one male student responded, "Equally done. It used to always be women."

Of all the gender equity questions, this last one received the highest egalitarian endorsement from both sexes, a finding consistent with other Canadian surveys, especially the Gallop Polls. This attitudinal subscription is fascinating in light of two apparent contradictions. The first comes from the well-known Canadian data collected by Statistics Canada in their general household survey, which indicates

Table 2-3: Youth's Perception of Decision-Making in the Family, at School and at Work

	Family	School	Work
Mostly by elders	33	22	34
Little guidance	22	52	21
Democratically with input from youth	45	26	45
Total %	100	100	100
N	(221)	(219)	(210)

that only half of Canadian husbands do any house-work at all. When they do, men perform one hour of housework each day while women do two and a half hours regardless of whether they work outside the home (Day, 1990: 36). Presumably our representative sample conforms to this national trend, suggesting our youth grew up in households where women assumed the bulk of domestic responsibility. As one parent articulated quasi-egalitarianism, "Women and men should do a 60/40 split of household work."

The second contradiction comes from our own qualitative data in which parents confirmed that domestic labour is not equally shared. As two different parents noted,

> The reality is, women do the household work. Most women do more than half the housework.

How are we to presume these contradictions affect youth's perceptions of their future responsibilities? We know that young women expect to take on a lifetime commitment to paid labour, as indeed most of their mothers have. Over 90 percent of 16 year old Canadian females surveyed recently (Silverman and Holmes, 1992) state they expect to have paid work in ten years. But is it realistic for young women to expect, as they seem to, that their young male partners will share child care and domestic labour?

While data from our study only allows us to comment on what youth think should happen, other research clearly outlines what is taking place. American studies reveal that today older and younger children participate only nominally in housework (Cogle and Tasker, 1982).

Contemporary youth are not being socialized into assuming domestic duties and presumably they arrive in shared living arrangements with little experience. Canadian data indicate women and men expect and desire marriage and children to fulfil a central role in their identity and energy. Again, over 90 percent of male

*Table 2-4: Consequences of Gender for Youth Attainment
(Significant R-Correlations)*

Marks in last secondary year	+.150*
Effort at school	+.122*
Teachers' aspirations for youth's education	+.159*
Consonance in democratic decision-making home, school, work	-.166**
Youth's education	+.108*
Intrinsic satisfaction with preferred job	+.132*
Pay, full-time job	-.147*
School's main purpose of education, teaching skills	-.116*
Training on the job	-.143*

+ Positive sign means a positive correlation with female gender; negative means a correlation with males.
* Significant at the .05 level. ** Significant at the .001 level.

and female adolescents interviewed by Silverman and Holmes (1992) agreed that family is important to them. We can speculate then that there may be an unspoken acceptance of quasiegalitarian behaviour in domestic labour in which husbands "help out" their wives. For example, Walkerdine and Lucey's study (1989) shows how middle-class mothers work strenuously to make childcare and domestic labour appear effortless and invisible by folding, in practice, one into the other. In contrast, working-class mothers clearly demarcate the two as "play" and "work" and subordinate the former to the latter.

Family research reports indicate Canadian women do not share power, workloads, or decision-making equally with male partners. In response to a series of questions regarding their perceptions of "democratic decision-making,"[5] young men are more likely to think that they experience democratic decision-making on a day-to-day basis within families than females (see Table 2–3). Young men from all social classes and ethnic groups grow up thinking their beliefs are listened to and acted upon, that they have control over their own ideas and the ability to

---

[5] Table 2–3 compares youth's perceptions of their involvement in democratic decision-making in family, school and work environments.

implement them. In contrast, young females report feeling their opinions and futures are less likely to be firmly in their control.

Other studies, (Porter, Porter, and Blishen, 1982: 133) correlate democratic decision-making with self-esteem. People who grow up thinking their views are listened to and acted upon in the family are likely to have high opinions of their own abilities. While 13 year old girls are nearly as confident as 13 year old boys, by age 16, females' sense of self-worth has plummeted (Silverman and Holmes, 1992). Coupled with this is our finding that women are less likely to report experiencing democratic decision-making in either home or school, and are more likely than men to think decisions regarding transition had been made for them (see Table 2–4).[6]

Yet, what we are able to capture of girls' emerging identity suggests a beginning challenge to the previous domestic code (Weis, 1990). Unlike young women of earlier decades who elaborated an ideology of romance and constructed fantasy futures around their roles as wives and mothers, Weis discovers that young women are now envisioning their lives very differently. They articulate that too many negative consequences result if they depend on men exclusively, so they do not envision part-time work combined with mothering as their ideal future. Similarly, in his Edmonton study of high school dropouts, Tanner (1991) notes that although women are slightly more inclined than men to envisage having a family of their own, this traditional domestic goal is not necessarily going to be pursued at the expense of success in the job world. This trend is confirmed in our study in which young women are slightly more likely to value future family roles than men while both envision work lives. What remains unsuccessful though are their strategies. Enrolment in "feminine" courses and employment in "feminine" occupational ghettos prohibits their financial independence, thus eventually making them dependent on male wages to support their dependents.

What conclusions can be drawn about quasi-egalitarianism, its behavioral manifestations, and its impact on gender tracking? First, men and women articulate individual, not structural or systemic explanations for their behaviour. While recognizing that the job and "real" world hold out different experiences for men and women, both sexes firmly believe that they alone are responsible for their fates. "It's up to the family and to the individual to realize their goals. Schools can't prepare you for the "real" world."

Other studies (Gaskell, 1987; Porter et al., 1982) confirm this individualistic, meritocratic assessment that individuals alone are responsible for their success or failure.

Second, what we have been able to capture of women and men's emerging identity suggest women are beginning to challenge the previous domestic code of husband-as-breadwinner and wife-as-mother in two ways: through their articula-

---

[6] Table 2–4 outlines significant relations between gender and transitional outcomes. Men are more apt to think that consonance in decision-making on a democratic basis has existed for them. Women are apt to think that decisions concerning transition have been made for them.

tion of wage labouring futures, and through their recognition of and dislike of unequal treatment in the workplace.

In contrast to twenty years ago, both sexes cite wage labour as a primary orientation and goal. While they eschew unskilled jobs as economically insecure and uninteresting, young women expect to work for wages throughout their adult lives. However, unlike men, they expect to assume the greater responsibility for domestic labour and childcare and track themselves into occupations that accommodate these designs. Educational and occupational aspirations for both sexes may be high, but they are also defined differently.

Gender Tracking in School

Students carry gender assumptions about personal worth, cultural importance, workplace segregation, and future careers into the schools. If, as we suggest, all of these are different for young women and men, do schools perpetuate or diminish these distinctions?

From both our statistical correlations and qualitative data, it appears that schools encourage the formation of distinct gender identities in three ways: through the creation and maintenance of separate identities; through regulation of access to skills, credentials, and ultimately the labour market; and through the taken-for-granted "hidden" curriculum which for decades has excluded and misrepresented women's experiences (Deem, 1980). This has come to be known as the "chilly climate" for women (Hall and Sandler, 1989).

Reproduction theory (Walker and Barton, 1983) proposes that gender differentiated identities, perceptions and cultural visions are legitimated by ideologies of male domination and reproduced and sustained by schools. Such a simple correspondence between the behaviour of school authorities and the behaviour of youth ignores data which suggest masculinity and femininity are constantly shifting and struggled over, not fixed or appropriated in schooling practices (Walkerdine, 1991).

Just as gender identity formation among youth in families is revealed as complicated and often contradictory, so too do youth in schools both accommodate and resist gender messages. Capturing young people's gender perceptions often involves recognizing the partial, ambivalent, and fragmentary nature of this identity process. Our analysis of both statistical and qualitative answers to our gender equity scale reveals the confusing and equivocal messages youth perceive.

A major contradiction stems from teacher's enactment of the official curriculum. This includes course offerings, school activities, and official proclamations on gender. Teachers, as front line carriers of school policy, are the most visible and most maligned of the school's agents. They are also assumed to be representative of the system's operations. For this reason, teachers were asked to answer the gender equity questions. They both espoused egalitarian attitudes and resoundingly criticized the questions as "out of date" and irrelevant" because "everyone knows that boys and girls are to be treated equally."

Table 2-5: Sex Role Norms, Teachers and Employers (%)

Sex Role Norms	Teachers			Employers		
	1 One Gender	2 Equal Chance	3 Both	1 One Gender	2 Equal Chance	3 Both
1. With limited funds in a family, which youth should continue past high school?	4	96		6	87	7
2. Is a career more important in a family for a man or woman?	6	88	7	25	44	31
3. If both spouses are working, who is responsible for household chores and child care?	1	99		25	44	31
4. Are some courses usually more difficult for students of one gender?*	8	15	77	10	31	59
5. Who make the best employers? Men or women?	3	96	1	26	65	9
Composite Gender Equality	Low	Middle	High	Low	Middle	High
Scale #	28	66	7	22	58	20

* We recorded values for Question 4 to fit replies, as follows:
1= by nature, 2 = by practice, 3 = neither by nature or practice
# Total scores of under 10 = Low, 11-12 = Middle, 13-14 = High

Teachers' criticism reveals the widespread acceptance of egalitarian ideology in general and gender equality in particular as morally and socially inviolate. For example, school officials fall back on these individualistic principles in explaining youth's selection of courses and academic concentrations.

Teachers' remarks also reveal the discrepancy between espoused egalitarianism and students' gendered reality. Students, especially females, experience schools as sites of gender conflict (Lindsey, 1990; Silverman and Holmes, 1992) through the bias in course materials, especially textbooks, through their tracking into particular subject areas, and through the lack of interventionist direction from guidance counsellors. Many females in a recent Canadian survey of adolescents said that even though school was a top priority for them, they were unhappy with "the way teachers treat us" and recorded strained teacher-student relationships (Silverman and Holmes, 1992).

One of the gender equity questions students, parents and teachers were asked was "Do you know of any recent instances of gender bias in course materials?" (see Table 2–5).[7] The majority of students, (67%), replied they were not aware of any gender bias while 22 percent said they were aware of a few cases. As in the family responses, a portrait of quasi-egalitarianism is revealed in youth's and teacher's replies suggesting incongruence between official egalitarian norms and students' experiences.

Students comment on the invisibility of women in textbooks.

> Male oriented novels are used, like *The Right Stuff*, with no effort to encourage females.

But for the most part, this question, designed to elicit comment on course topics, content, books, and evaluation process instead elicited critiques of teachers' attitudes and pedagogical procedures. As one youth stated, "Gender bias at school depends on the teacher."

Still others elaborate on the salience of teachers' attitudes and behaviour.

> Course materials were not biased but the teacher has made sexist comments about women.

One woman articulates the manner in which discrimination occurred.

> Materials were not biased but presenters were. My grade 10 geography teacher treated girls more severely. He made discriminatory comments and wouldn't allow girls on the wall mural team.

When teachers were asked about gender bias in courses, a fascinating trend was exposed. This question provoked considerable ambivalence as 46.5 percent of teachers suggest there are no incidents while 42 percent submit there are some. When teacher's responses were grouped according to their subject area, humanities teachers, especially English and History specialists, were far more likely to see gender bias against girls pursuing maths, sciences, physical education, and business. Yet teachers in these areas were themselves very unlikely to report any gender bias in their own academic area or in the humanities in general. Some teachers acknowledged the broad Canadian trend of male concentration in the so-called "hard" sciences and female congregation in the "soft" sciences, as an inequitable division that leads women to labour market segregation and centralization in poorer paying jobs. This economic reality subsequently makes it even more difficult for women with dependent children and male partners to maintain financial independence or to live above the poverty line without access to male wages.

We posed another question in order to discern gender concentrations in subject areas by asking, "Are some courses more difficult for one gender?"

---

[7] Table 2–5 compares teachers' and employers' responses to the gender equity questions.

Table 2-6: Final Secondary Marks and Education Attainment, by Gender (%)

Marks:	Boys	Girls
23-59	8	3
60-69	37	29
70-79	37	51
80-93	17	17
Total (%)	99	100
N	(145)	(174)

X 9.89, df 3, p .0195

Education Attainment:		
No diploma	21	9
Grade 12, 13	28	32
Post-Secondary (some or complete college)	19	24
University (some or complete)	32	35
Total (%)	100	100
N	(145)	(178)

X 9.05, df 3, p .029

Again, 61 percent of youth expressed an egalitarian view that courses are not more difficult for one sex, 27 percent expressed quasi-egalitarian views, and 12 percent supported the traditional idea that certain sexes do have more trouble with certain subjects. As one student confidently asserted,

No, it's a misconception. Men and women have the same intelligence.

Or, as another less confident student suggested,

So they say but I don't know if that's proven. May be learned.

How is the continued subject segregation by sex within high schools to be explained? When girls are steered towards careers, some students observe, in teacher's attitudes and interpretations of subjects, that women's careers may best lie in the more "feminine" occupations of education, social work, and more recently, medicine. As one male youth put it,

When I become a teacher, I'll encourage women as scientists and engineers. Gender bias in education is a problem that must be recognized. Of course, I'm more open-minded than most people I know.

Even though the majority of teachers (66.7%) denied that any course is inherently more difficult for students, this question elicited ample controversy among teachers.

Youth and teacher recognition of some gender inclination in course materials, academic streaming, and teachers' behaviour is often discounted as detrimental to women by statistical evidence that girls get higher marks and go further in education than boys. In our study, females obtained slightly higher marks than males, in both co-op and non co-op programs. They reported that they studied harder, and perceived teachers as having high hopes for their education (see Table 2–6).[8] Earlier studies (Hall and McFarlane, 1962; Porter, Porter, and Blishen, 1982) confirm this trend of females obtaining higher marks than males throughout high school. But, since these higher marks are mostly obtained in distinctly different areas from men, the long term consequences are minimal for women.

The final area of the official curriculum that could produce gender tracks in facilitating gender equity is the role of other school officials, especially guidance counsellors. When asked to remark on the counselling they received, most youth said they obtained little concrete help or assistance. Over 50 percent of youth report gaining little guidance at school in transitional decisions. School dropout studies report similar student alienation from counselling (Tanner, 1991). This includes little, if any, exposure to divergent career paths or to discussions of career consequences. As one female, former co-op student notes,

Most students don't have a clue when they leave school what's a good career, what the job market is like, you know.

This student goes on to voice a complaint heard repeatedly.

More time should be given for talking and listening to students about their hopes and fears, what their options might be, what the trends for job opportunities are.

Benign neglect of students by guidance counsellors essentially allows gender tracking to persist. By ignoring or paying insufficient attention to students' paid work and family "choices" (Duffy et al., 1989), students never confront or discuss what they consider their "important" concerns. Sociologists (Becker, Geer, Hughes and Strauss, 1968; Haas and Shaffir, 1977) have documented that students, administrators, faculty and parents have decidedly different perspectives on the value and content of what is learned in school. Our youth join a long line of student lamentations when they complain that teachers emphasize grades and good behaviour and neglect student's social and emotional lives. As one typical student commented,

School places too much emphasis on superficial things like homework and being on time. No real sense that anybody cares if you are prepared for the real world.

---

[8] Table 2–6 outlines gender differences in final secondary school marks and educational attainment.

Another complained,

> Schools never seem to make their purposes very clear. They focus too much on unimportant things like grades and attendance. They don't communicate enough with students....

Students question the school's official policies and rationales, arguing that they feel unprepared for the adult world of work since they are given so little opportunity to discuss their choices and little concrete assistance in making them. One youth explained her frustrations.

> Young people need a lot more support and encouragement regarding their transition from school to work — not only at school but at home and in the community. There is too little discussion about choices and options, too little guidance. Most people just let you struggle along on your own. If you make it, great. If you don't — oh well, too bad. We're the ones who suffer. Maybe students need to start asking for more help.

Aside from documenting that students and teachers differ in their construction and enactment of the school's goals, these accounts signify that teachers, by not actively challenging vertical gender tracking, a "personal" topic which students want to discuss, in fact, reinforce and maintain it through their silence.

The school's silence on gender issues reverberates throughout our teachers' and youth's qualitative elaborations. Since the early 1970s, psychologists and sociologists have underscored the salience of the hidden curriculum, that is, the covert ways in which teachers convey attitudes and expectations for groups of children at odds with the school's formal position. In particular, the gendered message students receive and experience from preschool (Serbin and Sprafkin 1986) to high school (Sadker et al., 1986) remains remarkably consistent. Girls receive less teacher attention, less time to participate in class, less praise and encouragement, less concrete guidance in their work, and fewer detailed instructions. Teachers and feminist educators alike, when shown videotapes of classroom discussions and asked to interpret these, found the opposite trends. It was only when researchers and viewers actually count male interruptions, male grabs for attention, and verbal feedback males received, that viewers overcame their stereotypes of women as "gossipy talkers" and declared that men received a quantitatively and qualitatively different form of teacher attention.

If a sexist classroom environment is hidden even from the teachers, it is perhaps premature to expect our direct questioning to reveal its nature. But in fact, students and teachers do characterize females and classroom practices in stereotypical ways.

When asked to rate how hard they studied in their last year of high school, females, of both co-op and non co-op programs, consistently admitted to studying harder than the males. Teachers also characterized female students as "hard working." In her study of elementary and high school classes, Walkerdine (1990) notes that "nice, kind, and helpful" are the three commonest signifiers posited as the most desirable qualities for girls to possess. As guardians of the classroom moral order, they help other children complete their work, discipline others, and are essential to the smooth, calm regulation of the classroom. Teachers also find them

*Table 2-7: Comparison of Youth's Marks and
Their Perceived Effort at High School (%)*

A.	Marks		B.	Effort at School	
	Under 60	6		Very little	25
	60-69	33		Less than best	23
	70-79	44		Moderate effort	37
	80-93	17		Great effort	16
	Total	100			101
	N	(319)			(310)

"boring" and lacking "brilliance," an adjective singularly reserved for males. Their academic success is due merely to their "hard work" (Walkerdine 1990).

While female youth rate themselves as more hard working, we have little teacher elaboration of this. But, interestingly, young women in our study were more likely to exhibit less self-confidence and to experience less democratic decision-making even though they obtained higher marks than young men (see Table 2–4).[9] Girls often seem unclear as to their abilities and the quality of their answers, while boys have a stronger sense of self-image and are more satisfied with their personal lives (Sadker, 1986: Lindsey, 1990; Richmond-Abbott, 1992). This "confidence gap" (Silverman and Holmes, 1992) increases as young women grow older.

Many myths exist about male and female high school performance.[10] Boys are presumed to "overachieve" while girls "underachieve." In fact, overall girls perform remarkably well, as do many boys (see Table 2–7). Another myth assumes girls' academic success is evidence of gender equity. In fact, girls' choices of careers do not reflect their educational success. As Whyte et al. (1985) noted, at all ability levels, girls tend to select from a narrower range of occupations than boys. Moreover, their post-school distinctions do not match their qualifications.

Why are girls' aspirations limited in relation to their qualifications? Whyte et al., (1985), Lindsey (1990), and Gaskell and McLaren (1987) suggested numerous structural and interpersonal dynamics. Undoubtedly, parents' attitudes and stereo-

---

[9] Table 2–4 compares male and female youths' perceptions of the effort they made at school.

[10] Table 2–7 combines male and female efforts at school and compares these with final marks obtained in their lat year. Almost half of all youth admitted to having coasted through high school.

typing play an important role (Whyte et al., 1985). Girls in our study entered high school from quasi-egalitarian homes in which men and women were portrayed as equal but distinct. Girls' experiences of the educational system seemed to reinforce, rather than challenge, these norms. Youth viewed teachers as equivocal in their outlooks. For example, although youth and teachers endorsed equal opportunities in education, teachers seemed, to youth and to some of their peers, less committed to equal opportunity in relation to future careers. Moreover, little attempt was made to widen girls' horizons about what job opportunities are available to them or to enlarge boys' horizons about what family opportunities they could grasp.

The literature suggests that much of this interpersonal behaviour is invisible to youth, teachers, and parents. Schools have yet to successfully intervene in the process of derailing existing gender tracks (Pratt, 1985).

Conclusion

Gender differentiates the transition process just as class and race do. The different destinations assumed for boys and girls structure how they enter it, the sorts of experiences and directions they encounter within it, and the manner in which they leave. These divisions produce, not one, but a whole variety of transitions. These distinct gender tracks bear on transition by locating individuals in different starting positions and, through the social division of labour, gender tracks determine different destinations to be arrived at (Clarke and Willis 1988).

Yet, educators remain perplexed by vertical inequity and by the incontrovertible fact that getting a good education has not improved women's position in the labour force in relation to men. Traditional models of status attainment and reproduction provide a partial explanation by focusing on the agents of socialization, teachers and parents, and the content of their messages, girls and boys belong in different worlds, and their manner of inculcation, lecturing and disciplining. Ironically, the structure of schools and traditional parent-child relationships reproduces gender inequalities even as school expansion is associated with women's struggles for greater equality and social mobility through education (Carnoy and Levin 1985).

But structuralist accounts of gender reproduction neglect the process by which students receive, interpret, and then act on socialization messages. By focusing on students' perceptions and actions, interactionists capture the multitude of experiences, contradictions, and responses they encounter.

Some youth succumb to traditional gender divisions by pursuing strategies such as enroling in female course-occupational ghettos that limit their prospects (Ogbu 1989). Others break free of customary scripts by pursuing non-traditional careers and egalitarian relationships. Still others resist by living outside the bounds of patriarchal culture within female-defined and organized settings.

Yet the majority do not behave in ways that maximize their equality. Surprisingly, or depressingly, while academic and vocational students are distinguished by class, by grades, and by occupational destinations (Gaskell, 1987), they embody similar gender stereotypes. Women, whether in professional-managerial or pink collar jobs, face double days as wage and domestic labourers. The higher wages of the professional group may grant these women more authority, autonomy, and paid household help (Duffy et al., 1989), but this does not alter the job requirements (Griffith and Smith, 1987). Similarly men, whether concentrated in professional jobs requiring math, science, or engineering, or in technical or business types of working-class jobs, both command higher wages and more domestic freedom relative to women. Schools are being asked to prepare men and women for a world in which employment patterns may become more fragmented, and men and women will have to share domestic labour (Orr, 1985). Yet, the strong possibility of such changes has not greatly modified the assumption made by some teachers, parents, and employers that women and men should be concentrated in separate areas for training and employment. As long as the work world remains so heavily stereotyped, it is difficult for schools to prepare pupils for flexibility in aspirations (Orr, 1985).

3
Interconnected Transitions and Their Costs; Gender and Urban/Rural Differences in the Transitions to Work

E. Dianne Looker

The study of the transitions from school to work, focuses on the *process* whereby individuals move into the world of work (Ashton and Lowe, 1991; Kerckhoff, 1990; Krahn, 1988; Mason, 1985). This research tradition compliments the extensive work on status attainment that emphasizes *outcomes* or attainments (Anisef, Paasche and Turritin, 1980; Blau and Duncan, 1967; Boyd et al., 1985; Campbell, 1983; Cuneo and Curtis, 1975; Looker and Pineo, 1983; Mackinnon and Anisef, 1979; Porter, Porter and Blishen, 1979, 1985; Sewell, Haller and Portes, 1969). Cross-national comparisons highlight the fact that the transition process varies in different national contexts (Ashton and Lowe, 1991; Kerckhoff, 1990; Pineo and Looker, 1983). This notion of "social context" will be extended to examine some variations in the transitions between school and work for a sample of Canadian youth. The analysis will focus on (a) gender differences and (b) urban-rural differences.

There is a growing recognition that gender is central to any discussion of both schooling and the world of work. There is considerable documentation of the extent to which Canada and other industrialized nations are structured along gender lines (Armstrong and Armstrong, 1975, 1978; Boulet and Lavallee, 1984; Cockburn, 1987; Hogan and Astone, 1986; Hunter, 1981; Statistics Canada, 1984). In many ways, boys and girls can be seen as living in quite different worlds. Certainly there are differences in their socialization experiences, the skills they are encouraged to develop, the expectations which they have for themselves and which others have for them (Porter, Porter and Blishen, 1982: 213). In other words, the social context in which the transitions between school to work are made differs considerably for young men and women. By highlighting these differences, the current analysis adds to the research that links gender issues and the transitions to work. It also serves as an introduction to the themes that will then be applied to a topic on which there is less research — the transition to work in rural areas.

Much of our knowledge about the transition from school to work in Canada is based on studies in urban areas or highly urbanized regions of the country (Anisef, Paasche and Turritin, 1980; Krahn and Lowe, in Ashton and Lowe, 1991; Martin and MacDonell, 1982; Porter, Porter and Blishen, 1979, 1982). While there is some information on how less urbanized areas differ from the large urban centres, little detailed information is available on the transition process in rural areas, especially rural areas in the less advantaged regions of the country. This paper will examine youth in rural Nova Scotia and highlight some of the ways in which the issues facing rural youth are quite different from those documented for their city cousins.

A life course perspective is taken (cf., Clausen, 1986; Dragastin and Elder, 1975, Elder, 1985; Hogan, 1981; Super, 1980) that focuses on the impact of social location on the various transitions that are made. Moreover, the relationship between the different "career paths" individuals take (Hogan and Astone, 1986) and the transition to work are examined. Of particular relevance to the current investigation are the connections between the transition to work, and marriage and parenthood plans for some youth, and the link to geographic mobility for others.

Life course analysis emphasizes the importance of the historical and structural context in which transitions occur (cf., Hubner-Funk, 1983). Kerckhoff insists that: "Any analysis of life course patterns must consider the social context within which the lives are being lived" (1990: 1). Building on this notion of social context, Elder takes issue with "assessments that are focused solely on adolescents and young people in society *as a whole*, that do not take ecological variation into account ... [and that] slight the uneven pace of development across sections of the country. ... Low income rural counties clearly represent very different socialization environments from those of affluent suburbs in metropolitan areas" (in Dragastin and Elder, 1975: 14). Furthermore, "young people do not live in the *total* society; they spend their lives in specified contexts, in neighbourhoods, schools, communities" (1975: 14).

This paper will examine some of the ways in which the social context differs for young women compared to young men, and for rural compared to urban youth. It will document some of the differences in constraints imposed by these diverse social contexts and will also discuss the social costs of the transition from school to work for the youth in these contexts.

Data and Measures

The data come from a 1989 study of 1200 17-year olds, 400 in each of three locales: Hamilton, Ontario; Halifax, Nova Scotia; and "rural Nova Scotia."[1] Names and addresses of 17-year olds were obtained from school lists in the relevant areas.[2]

---

[1] The rural Nova Scotia sample includes 100 respondents from each of the four economic regions outside the Halifax metropolitan area identified by the Labour Force Survey. These regions are approximately equal in size and were found by the Labour Force Survey to be relatively homogeneous in terms of a variety of economic and demographic measures.

These lists were supplemented with lists provided by the schools of school dropouts and graduates. A few 17-year olds who were already attending post-secondary institutions were approached through contacts with the post-secondary institutions in the sample areas.[3]

The decision to focus on a particular age cohort reflects a recognition of the importance of cohort effects in life course analysis. As Hogan states: " A cohort level of analysis is...an appropriate method of discerning the effects of social structural conditions on the transitions behaviour of individuals" (1981: 33).

The choice of 17 as the critical age was based on two considerations. The first was to maximize comparability with a parallel study of Hamilton youth done by the author in 1975[4] (see Looker, 1977 for details). The second, more salient consideration was that, in both 1975 and 1989, the focus was on educational and occupational plans. The research was designed to ensure respondents were old enough to give realistic responses to questions about their plans, but young enough that these were still "plans." That is, few of them would be in the full-time labour force. This is the stage at which, for many young people, several critical transitions occur when, as Greene and Boxer note, there is "... a pile up of role changes" (in Dantan et al., 1986: 128).

Once the names and addresses of seventeen year olds were obtained, random samples were drawn in each area. Face to face interviews were conducted with the approximately twelve hundred (1,209) youth who agreed to participate, and questionnaires were provided for both parents. The response rates for the youth, were: Hamilton, 78 percent; Halifax, 71 percent; rural Nova Scotia, 72 percent. Questionnaires were given to the parents only if the youth completed the interview; 74 percent of the mothers and 57 percent of the fathers completed their questionnaires; adjusting for mother and father absent households, the rates were 77 percent and 70 percent respectively.

The interviews with young people contained a number of precoded questions that dealt with their plans. The current analysis will focus specifically on those questions that addressed the transitions from school to work. These included questions on post-high school preferences and expectations, the type of job the

---

[2] In order to identify representative areas in rural Nova Scotia, labour force participation and unemployment rates for men and women aged 15 to 24 were examined to find communities that most matched the figures for county and the overall area. In each of the four economic regions, at least one "town" school and one school from an unincorporated rural area were included. Detailed occupational breakdowns (from special census runs) for each area were examined to ensure that the full cross-section of dominant occupations in rural Nova Scotia were covered by the sample and that the occupations in the towns and more rural areas accurately reflected the local economy.

[3] Registrars at the post-secondary institutions agreed to send the 17-year olds on their lists a request to participate in the study. This strategy resulted in sufficient volunteers to fulfil a proportional quota, that is, twelve out of 1209 respondents.

[4] Results from this earlier study inform some of the current analyses. One difference is that in 1989, but not in 1975, youth living in one parent families or on their own were included. A follow up of the 1975 Hamilton youth was undertaken in 1981 to obtain information on their attainments at that time.

youth expected to enter, as well as several questions about attitudes to work, school and other plans.

In addition to these coded items, there were a large number of open ended questions in the interview that elicited the respondents' perceptions and attitudes about why they want to do what they do and how they make sense of their world. As several researchers have argued, it is "...crucial to be aware of the 'subjective' experience of young people" (Ashton and Field, 1976: 13). "Human behaviour has its unconscious elements, but most of our actions are intentional, and the actor best knows the intent. To understand why a person married at a particular time, took or didn't take a particular job, we had best ask that person" (Clausen, 1986: 11).

Responses to the open ended questions were recorded by the interviewer in the respondent's own words. The file containing these verbatim responses were linked to the coded data (using the technique described in Looker, Denton and Davis, 1989). This linkage allows one to identify, for example, rural women who planned to attend university and their responses to the question "how would you feel about leaving?" A quantitative analysis revealed general patterns while verbatim responses fleshed out the quantitative description.

Some of the differences in the transitions from school to work reflect external pressures that are placed on youth (cf., Spenner and Rosenfeld, 1990). Other differences have more to do with the their perceptions, regardless of whether these perceptions correspond to "objective" experiences. Even external constraints such as occupational and educational opportunities, are likely to have an effect only when they are perceived by the youth. "Transitions in the life course...like job entry, are socially constructed" (Heinz, in Ashton and Lowe, 1991: 196). This analysis illustrates how youth construct their world and how these constructions constrain the transition from school to work.

Two themes emerged as we examined the responses given by women and men, and by rural and urban students. The first is the *interconnections* between the different transitions youth experienced. More particularly, the study revealed how plans for marriage and child bearing affect the timing and nature of the transition to work, especially for young women. Also, the social and emotional *costs* of the transition varied even for youth who achieved the same level of "attainment," or for those who viewed the transition process as being the same.

Gender and the Transition to Work

Central to any discussion of the transition from school to work is the recognition that both school and work experiences vary by gender. Labour force figures document the ongoing concentration of women in a few occupations (Armstrong and Armstrong, 1975; Boulet and Lavallee, 1984; Statistics Canada, 1984). Studies of young people's plans confirm that the gender stereotyping of occupations affects both men and women. Women are more likely to aspire to traditionally male dominated occupations than men are to female dominated ones (Looker, in I.S.E.R., 1985; Looker and McNutt, 1989), but both recognize gender segregation in the world of work. More than 90 percent of the respondents in the current study were able to name predominantly male and female occupations. Furthermore, almost half (49 percent) of the men and 20 percent of the women claimed that they would not enter an occupation that was associated with the other gender.

Even though many of the young women said that they would be willing to consider some male dominated positions (typically the high status, secure ones), the jobs they "realistically expect" to enter reflected considerable gender stereotyping.[5] Almost 60 percent of the women and over 70 percent of the men expect to enter occupations that are "gender appropriate" (occupations that are more than 55 percent female or male, according to current census data). We were left with a fairly clear image of occupations being segregated on the basis of gender, and of youth being well aware of this as they made their "realistic" plans.

The irony of gender segregation in the world of work becomes more pronounced when one examines the other side of the transition: the world of school. Several studies have shown that girls perform better than boys in school (Ambert, 1976; Baker, 1985: 14; Porter, Porter and Blishen, 1982: 162). Moreover, the long standing pattern that Canadian women are less likely to go on to university altered in 1981. While the proportion of women in higher education decreases dramatically when one considers graduate studies, women actually outnumber men in undergraduate study in Canada.

As the status attainment literature has documented, educational attainment is one of the main predictors of occupational attainment, although less so for women than men (cf. Turritin, Anisef and MacKinnon, 1983). The current data set allows us to address the extent to which young men and women *see themselves* as performing well in school. It may be that women fail to perceive their educational performance or downplay its significance.

Table 3–1 presents the responses of the men and women in the sample to a series of questions about their perceptions of their performance in school, and their attitudes to schoolwork. Girls were much more likely than boys to see themselves as having good study habits and were more likely to say they found schoolwork interesting. Boys were more likely than girls to say they found schoolwork boring, less likely to be enthusiastic about schoolwork, and more likely to report discipline problems in school.

In other analyses, not shown, there are other gender differences in the respondents' descriptions of their school experiences. Boys reported failing more courses and repeating more grade levels than girls. More girls than boys claimed to like

---

[5] The 1975–1981 Hamilton study indicated that while women's aspirations were more restricted than men's, women were more likely than men to fulfil their expectations. Thirty five percent of the women and only 13 percent of the men ended up in the same type of job in 1981 that they expected to enter in 1975 (coded to sixteen categories (cf. Pineo, Porter, McRoberts, 1977)). A third (32%) of the women aspired to clerical, sales or service jobs; 57 percent were located in such positions in 1981. Another third aspired to semi-professional positions yet only 23 percent attained them. The only concentration of preferences for young men related to skilled crafts and trades, to which 29 percent aspired and which 21 percent had entered by 1981.

Table 3-1: Gender Difference in Attitudes to School

Percentage of Respondents who:[a]

Attitude statements:		Agree	Neutral	Disagree	N	Sign. diff.[b]
1. I have good study habits.	M[c] F	37% 55%	24% 17%	39% 28%	547 626	***
2. I find school work really interesting.	M F	36% 46%	32% 25%	32% 30%	556 627	**
3. Most of the material I was taught in school is boring to me.	M F	43% 39%	24% 19%	34% 42%	555 628	**
4. I find it difficult to get enthusiastic about school work.	M F	69% 63%	17% 14%	15% 23%	554 629	**
5. I have had discipline problems in school during my last year.	M F	19% 9%	15% 8%	66% 84%	553 625	***

[a] Original categories were "strongly agree," "agree somewhat," "neither agree or disagree," "disagree somehat," "strongly disagree." The first two and last two were combined for this table.
[b] Level of statistical significance of gender difference where ** = .01, *** = .001 or more.
[c] Where M=males, F=females.

school. More young women believed they had a "very good" chance of successfully completing either university or some other post-secondary program if they tried.[6]

As Table 3–2 documents, the girls tended to translate their school performance and their interest in, and enjoyment of, school into educational aspirations. In all three geographic areas, the young women were more likely than the men to say they realistically expected to go to university. The men were more likely to say they planned to go directly into the world of work, or into an apprenticeship. Fully 85 percent of the young women said they realistically expected to invest in some post-secondary training beyond high school.

---

[6] The 1975–1981 Hamilton data document that young women were more likely than young men to attain their 1975 educational expectations by 1981. Sixty-six percent of the women and 54 percent of the men had aspirations that matched their 1981 attainments. This reflected the more modest aspirations of girls, but together with the previously reported occupational results (see footnote 5), suggest that women have a more realistic image of what they are likely to attain.

Table 3-2: Post High School Expectations by Gender and Area

Post high school expected path	Hamilton M[a]	Hamilton F	Halifax M	Halifax F	Rural Nova Scotia M	Rural Nova Scotia F	Total M	Total F
Work	18%	13%	22%	16%	26%	16%	22%	15%
Apprenticeship	11%	1%	5%	0%	4%	1%	7%	1%
Non-university post-secondary	30%	40%	14%	14%	32%	24%	25%	27%
University	40%	46%	60%	70%	38%	60%	47%	58%
N	188	210	208	188	159	225	555	623
Sign. diff.[b]	***		***		***		***	

[a] Where M = Males, F = Females
[b] Level of statistical significance of gender differences where *** = .001 or more.

Women, even more than men, seemed to value further education. Of course, one cannot simply assume that they were planning this investment of time, energy and money into post-secondary education as preparation for entering the labour force. They may have been postponing a decision or attending out of interest (or interest in meeting a potential future partner) rather than as job preparation. The data do not support these contentions. Only seven men and five women claimed to have no idea what they would do in terms of either education or occupation. Eleven percent of the women and 12 percent of the men were not sure what specific occupation they would enter. It appeared not to be indecision that accounted for girls extending their educational careers. As many women as men had a specific job in mind and, if anything, they were slightly more likely than men to say that they planned their education in light of their specific occupational aspirations.

Thus far we have an impression of young women doing well in school, and recognizing this in their descriptions of themselves. They recognized the connection between advanced education and occupational attainment, and aspired to relatively high status jobs. In fact over half these young women aspired to profes-

Table 3-3: Personal Priorities by Gender

	Percentage saying "very important" [a]		
Importance to you as a person	*Males*	*Females*	*Sign. diff.* [b]
1. Having a steady job	90%	87%	n.s.
2. Involvment in work or career	77%	81%	n.s.
3. Earning a lot of money	57%	36%	***
4. Developing friendships	77%	91%	***
5. Family relationships	70%	83%	***
6. Marriage or living together with a partner or companion	38%	43%	*
7. Having children	31%	43%	***
N	567[c]	638	

[a] The response categories were "very important," "somewhat important," "not very important," "not at all important."
[b] Level of statistical significance of gender differences where * = .05, ** = .01, *** = .001 or more, and n.s. = not statistically significant.
[c] Case base varies slightly by question due to missing cases.

sional level jobs and fully 50 percent of them realistically expected to attain them.[7] Another 21 percent of the young women expected to enter a semi-professional occupation, and only 17 percent listed some type of clerical, sales or service occupation as the one they expect. Thirty six percent of the men expected a professional position; twenty seven percent expected to be a skilled trades or craftsman. The other men planned to enter a range of occupations from managerial positions to unskilled labour.

The men and women surveyed seemed to share a similar commitment to occupational attainment. Both saw themselves planning their transition to work in order to maximize career satisfaction. When asked about the characteristics of the

---

[7] Many of the professional jobs to which women were aspired gender stereotyped. The most common choice was some form of teaching. Other frequently cited plans include social work, child care, psychology and law. The typical semi-professional fields chosen were nursing, physiotherapy and dental hygiene.

job that were of greatest importance, over 80 percent of men and women emphasized that it be enjoyable, interesting and secure. However, women were more likely than men to stress the importance of on the job day care facilities and the possibility of part-time flexibility.

When asked what "is important to you as a person," occupational issues were ranked highly by men and women and negligible gender differences were identified (see Table 3–3). Close to 90 percent said that a steady job was very important. Similarly, over three-quarters of men and women stressed "involvement in work or career" as very important.

Jobs seemed no less important to women (although money appeared to be less of a concern) while advanced education seemed more important. The gender differences I wish to emphasize relate to items four through seven in Table 3–3. The majority of both sexes stated that family and friends were very important, but their importance was significantly stronger among women that men. Similarly, more women than men emphasized the importance of marriage and children and few said that marriage or its equivalent was not important (less than 15%) or that having children was unimportant (less than 25% of both men and women).

In another set of questions (data not shown) respondents were asked to comment on some possible scenarios. Both men and women (but men somewhat more than women) said they would be "bothered a lot"[8] if they did not have a full-time job. Forty-four percent of the women and a third of the men stated they would be "bothered a lot" if they never married. Another third (37%) of the men and half the women (51%) said they would be "bothered a lot" if they never had a child.

In other words, both the young men and young women saw their educational and occupational plans as part of an overall picture that included marriage and child bearing. Given the high priority of children and family life for women, the life cycle linkages between the sets of transitions was more salient for them.

This is not new information. Several researchers have documented the importance of family and other relationships to women (Baker, 1985: 116; Day, 1990: 12; Kerckhoff, 1990: 180; Maizels, 1970: 287). Considering this priority in conjunction with an examination of their educational and occupational plans clarifies the implications of women's commitment to both family and work. Marriage and parenthood can be seen as "career contingencies," when they occur. This analysis shows that the young women anticipated these contingencies, but have not resolved the conflict they created. Their commitment to both family and work means that they will pay a heavier social price, whatever path they follow.

Table 3–4 gives youth responses to a series of questions that explicitly deal with the connections between work and family plans. Over 75 percent of both men and women, (but more men than women) said they would definitely work before and after marriage so long as there were no children. Given the number of women who planned some post-secondary education and the fact they planned to marry a year

---

[8] Possible responses were "bothered a lot," "bothered a bit," "prefer this somewhat," "very much prefer this," "don't care."

Table 3-4: Plans for Work at Different Life Stages by Gender

Life Stage:		Work Plans[a]			Sign. diff.[b]
		Percentage who will "definitely work"	Percentage who plan to work full-time	Percentage who "probably" or "definitely won't work"	
a. Before marriage	M[c] F	82% 76%	95% 92%	1% 2%	*
b. After marriage before children	M F	89% 80%	99% 90%	0% 2%	**
c. With preschoolers	M F	80% 18%	96% 31%	4% 37%	***
d. When all children are in school	M F	91% 64%	99% 75%	1% 3%	***
e. After all children have left home	M F	71% 69%	92% 87%	5% 7%	n.s.

[a] The question was in two parts: the first was asked if the respondent would "definitely," "probably," "probably not," or "definitely not" work in this life stage. Those who said "definitely" or "probably" were then asked if this would most likely be full time or part time.
[b] Level of statistical significance of gender differences where * = .05, ** = .01, *** = .001 or more, and n.s. = not significant.
[c] Where M = Males (n = 557), F = Females (n=634) with some minor variation in the case base due to missing cases.

earlier than the men, the small but statistically significant difference in the number of men and women who expected to work before marriage should not come as a surprise. However, other gender differences with respect to life cycle stages are apparent in Table 3-4.

Two points need to be made in examining the over all pattern of responses. First, when neither marriage nor children were being considered, women's plans were not that different from men's. Most planned to work, and to do so full-time. The second is the difference in plans to work when marriage and children entered the picture. Women saw marriage as having little effect on their plans to work. More men (especially those who planned to attend university, data not shown) saw themselves as moving into the work force (99 percent saying the full-time work force) once married. Women believed that the presence of children would affect their plans. There was a dramatic decrease in the number of women who planned to work at this life stage.[9] Whereas the vast majority of women stated they would work full-time before having children, less than 20 percent were confident that they would work with preschoolers. A third claimed they wouldn't. Even then, over two thirds of those who planned to work said they would work part-time. More intended to work once all children were in school, but an equal proportion of women and men visualized themselves as part of the labour force only at the empty nest stage, well into the future. A wealth of statistical data shows that childbearing does affect women's labour force participation (Boyd, 1982; Denton, Robb and Spencer, 1980; Spencer and Featherstone, in Wakil, 1975; Rossi, 1985). The data in Table 3–4 show that these young women recognized this impact and anticipated it in their plans.

These were women who tended to do well in school. Most planned major investments of time in post-secondary education and many wanted and expected high status, professional or semi-professional jobs, yet they intended to take several years out of their careers for child rearing. The men planned to both work and have a family. Combining the two was less of a viable option for the women (Armstrong and Armstrong, 1983; Byrne, 1978). In order to make a relatively permanent transition to work, the women stated that they either had to sacrifice their plans to have children or make major adjustments in their value system, within which full-time work was seen as incompatible with raising preschoolers. Such a sacrifice or value shift was not required of men. What is more, given the importance of children to women, it appears that either of these options would take a heavy toll on a greater number of the women than it would on their male counterparts.

The other side of these gender expectations places restrictions on the men. Male youth did not see themselves as having the option to stay out of the labour force. They felt that marriage and/or parenthood required them to get a job. Less than 15 percent of the men thought it would be a good idea for them to be the person who "looks after the home and cares for the children;" almost three times as many of the young women saw this as a desirable option. Women seemed to feel they would *have* to stay home while men believed they would *have* to work.

Responses to the open ended questions provided more details of how marriage and child bearing affected the transition to work differently for men and women. Virtually all the youth said the usual pattern is for one to finish schooling, get a job,

---

[9] Comparing the results in Table 3–4 with the data from the 1975 Hamilton study shows some shifts in the plans of young women across cohorts. Ninety percent of the seventeen year old girls in the earlier study said they definitely would work before marriage (fewer of them were planning post-secondary education). The corresponding percentages for the other life stages were: after marriage, before children, 65 percent; with preschoolers, 4 percent; when all children were in school, 42 percent; and when all children had left home, 55 percent. Another interesting finding from the 1975 Hamilton study was that only 5 percent of the girls' mothers thought it was a good idea for a woman to work with preschoolers, but over a third of them did so, 18 percent full-time and 19 percent part-time. These women apparently did not have the option of leaving the labour force.

get married, and have children, in that order. They also had a fairly clear idea of the age at which they planned to marry and start having a family.[10] The youth were asked how "out of sequence" transitions (getting married or having a child before they planned to) would affect their educational and occupational plans. Their responses provide insights not only into their attitudes to these out of sequence transitions, but also to their views of the relationship between the transition to work and other transitions.

While some youth were convinced that an earlier than planned marriage would have no effect on their plans (and some said it would never happen), many more stated that it would have quite an effect. Young men commented that this would "mess them up real bad"; "it would affect them badly"; "put quite a damper on it"; "it would destroy everything for me." Other men provided details on how it would affect their plans: "Probably would have to quit and get a job"; "probably have to quit education and find a job"; "I wouldn't go to school, I'd have to support a family"; "tied down; wouldn't be able to finish school, have to work"; "you would be held down too much with too many responsibilities"; "I'd have to start full-time work sooner"; "I'd probably have to take a job quicker." For these young men, marriage meant financial responsibility; once married, whether "on time" or early, they would have to have a job. If they were not already in the labour force, marriage would propel them into it.

The young women were less likely to see marriage as interfering with their plans. Many of them assured the interviewer that they didn't "think it would be a problem"; "it wouldn't affect them too much." Those who believed that an earlier than planned marriage would affect them, rarely mentioned having to get a job. They were more likely to contend that "it would complicate things; it brings another person into it"; "I wouldn't put them aside if I were to get married, I'd just have to rearrange how I'd go about it"; "you'd have more than just yourself to worry about, more pressures, distraction." The typical scenario for the young women seemed to be a possible delay or postponement of educational plans, but not an abandonment.

Almost all the youth perceived "earlier than planned children" as problematic. Comments by both the men and women included: "Terrible"; "I would be totally screwed up"; "It would ruin your career"; "It would demolish them." But the anticipated effect on men and women was quite different. Men perceived that it would destroy their plans for further education, because if they didn't already have one, they felt that they would have to get a job. Their comments to this question were similar to those for the question about marriage: "I'd quit school and go to work"; "Occupation would be labour instead of management"; "Find any job to support the family."

Women did not anticipate being pushed into jobs by the presence of children. Rather, they expected to be pushed *out* of the labour force: "I'd have to stay home and look after the child"; "I would have to stay home with the baby"; "I'd probably

---

[10] Very few (18 women and 2 men) said they already had a child.

have to stay home"; "I would quit my job"; "My education would have to wait until the children were older"; "I'd have to quit and look after them"; "You'd have to look after the kid, and you wouldn't have time for your own work"; "You'd have to be a full-time mother." Not only did they expect to stay home, but many of them used the phrase, "I'd have to." They apparently perceived this prospect less as an active choice than as a required social norm.[11]

To summarize this section, the youth in this study perceived work as important to them. Both men and women expected to work, mostly full-time, for much of their adult life. But they also viewed marriage and family relations as important. Their images of the ideal and expected transition to work took into account their marriage and family plans; the transitions were very much interconnected. However, family plans impacted on men and women quite differently. Family issues seemed to have higher salience for the young women when they envisaged their futures. What is more, the impact of marriage and family on educational and occupational plans was different for women than for men. Marriage and parenthood, but especially marriage, seemed firmly linked with the transition into work for men. Ideally they would have completed their desired level of education before marrying, but regardless of the timing, marriage for most men meant having to work. Marriage may complicate or delay some plans for the women, but it is child bearing that has the most dramatic effect on their planned involvement in the world of paid employment. Motherhood to most of these women meant staying home, with involvement in the paid labour force typically taking the form of part-time work. The cost of motherhood is the possibility of foregoing the kind of uninterrupted career that many men take for granted. Alternatively, the cost of pursuing a career path that parallels the typical male one is foregoing child bearing violating what appear to be strongly held norms about mothers' responsibility in child rearing.

Urban-Rural Differences in the Transition to Work

These two themes, the interconnections between transitions and the differential costs of the transition to work were also relevant to an analysis of rural versus urban youth. For many rural youth the transition from school to work was closely linked to decisions relating to whether or not to leave one's home community.

Rural areas differ from more urbanized areas in a number of ways. The ones that are of relevance to the current analysis deal with differences in the range of opportunities. Lucas (1971) describes what he calls limitations in choice in the rural, one industry towns he studied. "In urban areas, with a large population and an elaborate division of labour, the over-all offerings [of schools] are wide and varied. In the smaller community with a smaller school system and...a more limited

---

[11] They seem to adhere to this norm despite the fact that 63 percent of the young women "strongly agree" that "mothers and fathers should share equal responsibility for child care" (only 34 percent of the men strongly agree with this statement). Women may think the responsibility for child care *should* be shared, but they don't seem to expect that it will be.

division of labour, the types of training which go beyond the academic, university oriented course are restricted" (1971: 281–282). Hogan notes that "rural communities provide a social milieu with a narrower range of educational services than that found in urban communities" (1981: 160). Further, "small communities have less diversified labour markets than do large urban areas, and they offer fewer opportunities for employment and for occupational advancement" (Hogan, 1981: 121).

In a number of ways the current study reinforces these conclusions. The rural respondents were aware of fewer types of occupations than the urban youth. Rural youth had fewer jobs during the school year; those that were employed, had fewer jobs than those in urban areas, and they tended to start paid employment at a later age. In terms of their educational choices, rural youth listed fewer course options at their school than did urban youth. In a separate question, over 60 percent of the rural respondents (compared to 30 percent of the urban youth) agreed that there were "not enough course options at my school."

In terms of post-secondary educational opportunities, Hamilton (the urban Ontario centre included in the survey) boasts a university and a major community college, with several other post-secondary institutions within a 100 km. radius. While Nova Scotia has thirteen degree granting institutions, many of these are in or near the two urban areas of Halifax/Dartmouth and Sydney. There are some universities and vocational training centres in more rural regions, but they tend to have limited enrolments and are "nearby" to only a small percentage of rural youth. Nevertheless, the post-secondary institutions in small towns have two major attractions for rural students. First, they have a "small town atmosphere:" quiet, secure, and friendly, much like their home communities. Secondly, while they may be too far from home to allow for commuting, they are close enough to permit regular visits.

The teenage respondents were asked to describe what they saw as the main differences between an urban and a rural area. Both the urban[12] and rural youth described cities as places where there is *more* of everything: particularly "more opportunities" and "more jobs," as well as "more entertainment"; "more things to do"; "more people"; "more exposure to more things"; "more choices"; "more independence"; "more convenience"; but also "more pressure"; "more wild"; "more competition"; "more stress"; "more drugs"; "more crime"; "more violence."

The difference in occupational options was underlined by the responses to another open ended question: "How would you describe the job situation in your community?". The vast majority (90% or more) of the rural youth used phrases such as "Terrible"; "Not good"; "Poor"; "Very slow"; "Slim, very little choice"; "Minimal"; "There isn't any"; "Bleak"; "Scarce"; "Nonexistent"; "Pretty grim"; "Oh, it's very, very limited"; as one youth put it, "Not that good, I suppose "lousy"

---

[12] Hamilton youth seem to see "rural" as synonymous with farm living, whereas Halifax youth seem to be describing anywhere outside Halifax. One Hamilton youth summed it up saying the main difference is: "We don't milk cows, they don't have cable T.V."

describes it best." Those who believed that there were jobs available tended to qualify this observation by saying, "You have to take what you can get"; "There are jobs, but not enough for everyone"; "None for what I want."

The picture presented by Halifax youth is very different. There are jobs available, but "You have to look for them"; "There is a lot of competition" and, as one youth put it, "If you wanted a job you could get one — you might not get the perfect job you've been dreaming of." Overall, the job situation in Halifax was described as: "Adequate, but not great"; "Average"; "O.K."; "Medium."

Hamilton youth (in 1989) anticipated even brighter job prospects. Very few described it as bad, and most claimed it was: "Good"; "Very good"; "There are lots of jobs"; "Excellent"; "Quite promising"; "Kind of easy." Those who had reservations about job opportunities said that it "Depends on what field you are in." "It would depend on the occupation" and that "It's not as good as Toronto." The youth believed that there were jobs to be had, if not in Hamilton then in the nearby area.[13] These responses reflect the fact that, at the time of the survey Hamilton and the surrounding industrialized region of southern Ontario had some of the lowest unemployment rates in the country.

The unemployment rates in the city of Halifax were similar to those in Hamilton, but Halifax's situation was much different in relation to its surrounding area. Rural Nova Scotia had unemployment rates, especially for youth, which were among the highest in the country. In some parts of Cape Breton the youth unemployment rate was over 50 percent; in other areas the labour force participation rates for 15 to 24 year olds were less than 40 percent.

Given this description of the opportunities in their areas it is not surprising that, as the bottom row of Table 3–5 demonstrates, those living in rural areas were more likely to anticipate leaving their community than were those living in either of the urban areas. Seventy one percent of the rural youth said they planned to leave while a minority of the urban youth expected to leave.

Table 3–5 also shows the relationship between the transition to work and plans to leave. In all areas, those who intended to make the transition to work directly after high school more likely planned to stay in their home community, while those who planned some post-secondary training indicated they were more likely to leave. This difference is particularly pronounced in the rural areas. Over 80 percent of rural youth who planned to attend university and 69 percent of those who planned some other post-secondary education expected to leave. But the percentage of leavers was high (53%) even among the rural youth who intended to go directly to work after high school. This was higher than for any sub-group of the urban youth (cf. Anisef and Okihiro, 1982; Pollard and O'Hare, 1990).

The verbatim responses provide a clearer picture of "who leaves" in the three sample areas. Those planning to leave, especially those who intended to leave the rural areas tended to be those hoping to advance themselves. A few respondents

---

[13] It is important to note that this perspective might well have changed in light of the recession in southwestern Ontario in 1992.

Table 3-5: Plans to Leave One's Community and Post-High School Plans by Area

Post-high school plans:	Percentage who plan to leave				Sign. diff.[a]
	All areas	Hamilton	Halifax	Rural Nova Scotia	
Work or apprenticeship	40%	31%	35%	53%	p < .05
Non-university post-secondary	46%	33%	37%	69%	p < .001
University	56%	47%	43%	81%	p < .001
Total % of who plan to leave	50%	39%	41%	71%	p < .0001
N	1121	385	370	373	
Sign. diff.[b]	p < .0001	p < .05	n.s.	p < .0001	

[a] Level of statistical significance, examining the difference in plans to leave for the three areas.
[b] Level of statistical significance, examining the difference in plans to leave by post high school plans within an area.

suggested that those at the other end of the spectrum, the "dropouts" and "losers," also leave — they were perceived to have no options if they stayed and a possibility of some option if they were to leave. However, the ones leaving were most often seen as: "Independent"; "Motivated"; "Ambitious"; "Ones who want more for themselves"; "More interested in their education and their future"; "More determined." In rural areas the leavers were seen as those desiring more education and the chance for a job. In the urban areas, they were perceived to want a particular job or a better job, or, as one Hamilton youth phrased it, leavers were: "willing to risk throwing away a good thing for a better thing."

An interesting picture emerges if one asks "who stays." Some youth described those who stay as those who *don't*: "don't have any ambition"; "don't want to do anything"; "don't care about themselves"; "don't have the money to leave"; "don't have high goals"; "don't have as many choices"; "don't push themselves"; "don't mind where they are." But this is not the full picture. Many youth, especially the rural respondents (and to some extent the Hamilton respondents) described the "stayers" in more positive terms. They are "Kinds that are satisfied here"; "Those with close ties to their family"; "People that enjoy rural life ...and with a strong bond to home"; "Those that have a lot of relatives in the area"; "People who feel family is important." Family and community ties were seen as important to rural youth not only in their descriptions of why people in general stay, but also in their responses about whether and why they themselves would leave.

As we have seen in Table 3–5, the majority of rural youth were planning to leave. When asked where they would go, they responded "to cities," "to Halifax, Toronto," "out west," "big cities." Halifax and Hamilton respondents tended to say to "bigger cities." In choosing a particular city as a destination, the presence there of family, relatives, friends, or someone they knew was often a key factor, especially for rural youth.

When asked why they would leave, "job prospects" was a key decision for the rural respondents: "Have to go away for a job"; "There's no jobs here"; "Because I want to get a career and it wouldn't be worth staying here"; "There is nothing here." Urban youth would leave for "better opportunities," but unlike rural youth, they believed they could remain at home and still obtain a good job, if not the "perfect" job.

The discussion of urban-rural differences has thus far emphasized the connection between the transition from school to work and a move away from one's home community. This move involves more than a shift in geographic locale. It requires the severing of ties to the community, and usually also a disruption in relationships with family and friends.

There are social costs that youth in any area experience when they move. However, as Table 3–6 shows, the costs tend to be greater for rural youth. As the top three rows of the table indicate, the rural respondents were more likely than the urban youth to report strong community ties. Over half of the rural youth strongly agreed with the statement: "This place will always seem like home to me." Almost 40 percent predicted that "Even if I leave...I'm coming back someday." Rural respondents were more likely to agree that "Family matters a lot around here."

These strong community ties were linked with a desolate picture of the options facing rural youth. They were more likely than urban youth to agree that "The situation is pretty hopeless...around here"; "I'd be a lot happier living elsewhere"; and "Young people have a better chance of getting a good job if they leave..." Ironically, many of the same rural youth claimed *both* that, "This is home... I'll come back" *and* "I'd be happier living elsewhere."

The precoded responses and the verbatim responses to the open ended questions lead to the same conclusion. The rural youth were more tied to their communities, were more concerned about family relationships, but they were also more likely to leave. They perceived few, if any, options if they remained. The respondents planning to stay were those for whom family and community ties were more important than occupational advancement.[14]

---

[14] There is a danger of portraying the situation in the rural communities as so dismal that those who stay are seen as inherently disadvantaged. There are *some* jobs in rural areas, and there are rewards, in

Table 3-6: Perception of Community by Area

Perception of community:	Percentage who "strongly agree"[a]			Sign. diff.[b]
	Hamilton	Halifax	Rural Nova Scotia	
a. This place will always seem like home to me.	38%	37%	51%	***
b. Even if I leave this area, I'm coming back someday.	23%	28%	39%	***
c. Family matters a lot around here.	29%	25%	38%	***
d. The situation is pretty hopeless for folks around here.	3% (5%)[c]	1% (6%)	8% (18%)	***
e. I'd be a lot happier living somewhere else than here.	8% (17%)	8% (13%)	12% (21%)	**
f. Young people have a better chance of getting a good job if they leave home.	4% (14%)	4% (17%)	38% (35%)	***
N[d]	397	384	404	

[a] Response categories are "strongly agree," "agree somewhat," "neither agree nor disagree," "disagree somewhat," and "strongly disagree."
[b] Level of statistical significance of differences in response to each statement by area based on the full set of response categories, where ** = .01, *** = .001
[c] Percentages in brackets indicate those who said "agree somewhat" with the statement.
[d] Case base varies slightly by the question due to missing cases.

Other data, not shown, indicated that rural youth were more likely than urban youth to see seasonal work supplemented with unemployment insurance as a viable option.[15]

---

terms of maintaining important ties and traditions that should not be downplayed. Rita MacNeil (a rural Nova Scotian who maintains these ties and comes "home" often) points to these rewards in her song "You've Realized Your Dream."

[15] Seasonal and part-time work are a mainstay in much of rural Nova Scotia. The percentage of full time, full year workers is consistently below 50 percent of the labour force in the sample areas; in

Almost any work was acceptable if it would allow them to stay close to home. Day, in her study of young women in Nova Scotia, comments on "a general unwillingness to move from rural areas and an acceptance that they will 'take what they can get' when it comes to jobs, rather than making occupational or 'career' choices that involve moving" (1990: 13). Pollard and O'Hare note that, "Those who remain in rural areas face a scarcity of good jobs, while those who leave find themselves competing for employment against better educated metropolitan youth... With the relative lack of opportunities for young adults in rural areas, rural youth face the prospect of either leaving their home towns or staying and accepting these limited options" (1990: 2–3).

Their options are not likely to improve. In a recent study of employers in Nova Scotia, Grude et al. (1991) note "the substantial decline of employment opportunities that rural Nova Scotia has experienced in the recent past, and the likelihood of further substantial declines in the near future" (1991: 15). New employment opportunities tend to be in the service sector, but Grude et al. point out "...these are city jobs. The rural areas of Nova Scotia, like the rural areas of the rest of Canada, do not now attract service-based jobs and are unlikely to attract them in the future" (1991: 16). Their findings are consistent with the data reported in this study on those who plan to leave and move to the city: "Given the decline in employment opportunities in rural Nova Scotia, young people have continued to emigrate, as they have done for generations" (1991: 17). Grude et al. (1991) and Pollard and O'Hare (1990) note that migration depletes the rural areas of those with high levels of educational attainment, leaving those who opt instead for life in small communities.[16]

The Intersection of Gender and Urban-Rural Differences

It is clear from the above analyses that both gender and geographic locale influence the transitions between school and work. The interaction between gender and locale is complex, and merits further examination. Some preliminary observations are offered below.

We have already seen that the timing and nature of involvement in family commitments affect occupational plans quite differently for females and males. Some of these gender differences are particularly evident in rural areas. Rural youth, especially rural women, were more likely to stress the importance of family relationships. The kind of ties to the community that make leaving difficult, as described earlier, were particularly strong for rural women.

---

some areas of Cape Breton the figure is as low as 31 percent of the labour force (cf., Statistics Canada Cat. 94–106).

[16] The pressures on rural Nova Scotians to migrate to large cities have existed for decades. The parents in our sample are obviously those who chose to stay or return. Over 70 percent of the rural respondents (58 percent of the urban youth) had at least one grandparent who lived in the same community; 68 percent of rural (41 percent of urban) youth had a great grandparent who lived there.

In general, rural youth and their parents were more likely than others to espouse traditional gender roles and to stress the importance of family. They also seemed to endorse the gender stereotyping of occupations. They were less likely than others to say it would be a good idea for the teenager to consider an occupation that is traditionally associated with the other gender, and more likely to see entering a "gender appropriate" position as desirable. Whatever pressures are created by these traditional gender roles would be greater for rural youth. For males this would include pressure to get a steady, well paying job, a difficult prospect particularly in rural areas with high levels of unemployment. For females, combining family and careers would be difficult, assuming they could find jobs.

The few jobs available in the rural areas covered by the survey tended to be traditionally male jobs: skilled and semi-skilled positions, in the manufacturing industries, on farms and woodlots, or fishing vessels. Throughout rural Nova Scotia the labour force participation rates for men, especially young men, is higher than for women, by a margin of 10 percent or more.[17]

What is more, the *unemployment* rates for women in the rural areas are almost always higher than for men (except in Cape Breton where they are close to 30 percent for both). The labour force participation rates tell us that fewer women than men are looking for work; the unemployment rates indicate that, when they do seek it, fewer women than men find employment. This pattern is reflected in the employment records of the parental respondents. Unemployment among both fathers and mothers was higher in the rural areas than in Hamilton or Halifax; fewer rural mothers than fathers were in the labour force; more mothers than fathers were unemployed.

Few of the jobs available in the rural areas require post-secondary education. This might explain the relatively negative attitudes that rural males, in particular, hold towards schooling. Rural males, more than urban males and more than rural females claimed to find school boring. They were unenthusiastic about schoolwork, and reported that they had failed a course or repeated a grade. Fewer rural males liked school and were less satisfied with their schooling than the other groups.

The percentage of youth planning to attend university was high for both males and females in Halifax (over 60 percent), low for both in Hamilton (less than 50 percent). In rural Nova Scotia 60 percent of the women but only 38 percent of the men said they realistically expected to attend university (more men than women planned to attend some other type of post-secondary institution or to go directly to work).[18]

---

[17] For example, in Queens county, the labour force participation rate for men aged 15–24 is 67 percent, for women it is 51 percent; the corresponding rates for Cape Breton are 55 percent for men and 43 percent for women.

[18] Most (over 75 percent) rural and urban parents say they would very much encourage their *sons* to continue their education beyond high school. Rural mothers say the same of their daughters, but only 54 percent of the rural fathers say they would give the same level of encouragement to girls.

For all but the few youth who lived near a university, advanced education means leaving home. What is more, given the dearth of jobs in rural areas that require university training, leaving to further one's education usually means that one is unlikely to be able to return. As Grude et al. document, the jobs that are likely to develop in Nova Scotia are service sector jobs (traditionally women's jobs) primarily in the urban settings. Jobs are not likely to open up for either males or females in rural Nova Scotia in the near future.

Rural males have the "option" (which some perceived as a responsibility) of staying in their community and working, often in insecure, low paying,[19] seasonal jobs, or breaking their ties with their community in the search for more education and/or better job chances. Rural women have a similar option: staying or leaving, but for many of them staying would mean not working. Rural youth, especially the women, approach the prospect of leaving with very mixed feelings. When asked how they would feel about leaving their home community they answered: "I wouldn't like it, but I'd do it"; "I'd be disappointed, but I'd have to leave to get the job I want"; "If I had to I wouldn't mind, but I wouldn't want to."

An early marriage would tie both men and women to their home community. As documented above, men see themselves as forced into the labour force by marriage responsibilities; rural men would be limited to the jobs available in their area. Parenthood is the transition that most affects women; they expect motherhood to push them out of the labour force. Urban women believed that having a child might postpone or delay their educational plans; rural women were more likely to say children would destroy their plans for further education. Children, especially "earlier than planned" would tie rural women to their community and close off the few options they might have of getting *any* job, let alone the secure, interesting, enjoyable jobs so many of them desire.

Some of the characteristics found among rural youth in this sample could be expected in other rural areas: the close family and community ties, the traditional values, the lack of access to post-secondary institutions. Others derive from the fact that not only do these youth live in rural areas, but they live in a part of the country that has had chronic problems with its economy. The Maritimes has for decades experienced higher unemployment rates and less economic development than elsewhere in Canada. It may be that some of the dilemmas and limitations facing young men and women in rural Nova Scotia have less to do with their living in rural communities than with their living in economically disadvantaged areas.

---

[19] There are *some* well paying, secure positions in rural areas; unfortunately these are available to only a few. The rich farm lands of the Annapolis valley or the occasionally lucrative ownership of a fishing license are in small supply. More men than women seem to find the higher paying positions, as is evidenced by the fact that, even when considering only full time, full year workers, men report considerably higher employment incomes than women. Self-employment also seems to be more of an option for rural men than rural women (see Statistics Canada Cat. 94–106).

Conclusion

This paper has described some of the ways social context impacts on the transition from school to work. This transition can be quite a different process for women versus men and for rural versus urban youth. An examination of the educational, occupational and family plans of this sample of teenagers demonstrates that not only are there differences in expected outcomes, but the meaning of these outcomes and the social-psychological costs associated with them are affected by the social context in which the plans are made.

Two themes become evident when the data are examined. The first is the linkage between transitions. For women, the transition to work is particularly tied to when they expect to make the transition to parenthood. Men expect the transition to marriage to affect their entry into the permanent labour force. The critical link for rural youth is the connection between their educational and occupational plans and their intentions to leave or stay in their home community. Those who want to get ahead tend to leave. Those who choose to stay see themselves facing very limited options.

The other theme focuses on the apparent social cost of the transition to work for women and for rural youth. Women are more likely to place a high priority on their family plans, but they also aspire to secure, enjoyable, interesting jobs. They recognize the social norm that says they "have to" take primary responsibility for child care, especially with preschool aged children. Many of them plan to take time out from paid employment to do so. They want both parenthood and careers. Whether they opt for one, the other or both, they are likely to deal with pressures and expectations that differ from those faced by young men.

For rural youth the cost of having to leave to get a secure job becomes evident when one examines their degree of commitment to their home community. The characteristics of rural communities that make them attractive to these youth — the strong family ties, the close knit community, the security of "everyone knows you," the friendship networks, the family history — make it more difficult for the youth to leave. Bonds are set up that are painful to break, yet most rural youth see themselves as having to break them. Young people in urban areas perceive themselves as having more educational options, more job options, and the choice of staying or leaving. Rural youth, who can least afford to stay in terms of job prospects, are also those who can least afford to leave in terms of the social and personal costs of out migration.

The analysis focuses on the youths' plans, recognizing that these are very much social constructions. They are ways that teenagers make sense of their futures, in spite of the fact that the plans may change, some for better, some for worse. Young people see their various plans as very much interconnected; not as separate segments ("occupational plans," "educational plans," "family plans") but together as part of the future they would like to move into. Most of them want and expect advanced education, and a good job, and a family. Both the quantitative and the verbatim responses give us a clearer picture of the options these youth are considering and the costs that are likely to be associated with these options.

4

Transition of Adolescents into Science Career Pathways

John H. Lewko, Carol Hein, Rashmi Garg and Geoffrey Tesson

The career pathways of adolescents are of growing concern among various sectors of society. Science and technology fields in particular are expanding, and with this expansion comes the need for more workers in general and highly trained personnel in particular. In a recently published report from the Premier's Council on Technology (1990) the need for individuals with advanced knowledge in science and technology was directly linked to industrial competitiveness. Competitive advantage in the global economy is becoming increasingly based on the products of research, science and technology.

As a nation that sustains a high standard of living based on trade, Canada is facing a number of challenges to the future; the development of a skilled work force is of particular importance. An NSERC (1989) report cites a variety of studies that indicate that emerging technologies are bringing about a change in the occupational and skill structure of the labour force in industrialized nations. Many jobs that will be in demand in the 1990s will require employees with mathematics, science and computer skills. For high-technology intensive sectors such as computers, microelectronics, communications equipment, pharmaceuticals, robotics, aerospace and biotechnology, an adequate supply of personnel is critical (NSERC, 1989). Women and girls, in addition to minorities, are generally uninvolved in these areas.

In response to the debate regarding competitiveness, attention is increasingly directed to the young people who are now in university or are just leaving high school. Demographic trends indicate a decline in the number of people in the university entrance age group (ages 18–24) over the last fifteen years with a predicted continuation of the trend into the mid 1990s. The future work force dilemma is intensified by figures that indicate that while university enrolment increased by 20 percent from 1980 to 1989, the proportion of students enroled in physical sciences, engineering and mathematics fell from 18 percent to 15 percent (Premier's Council, 1990).

In order to understand the mechanisms involved for young people entering science and engineering careers, the dynamics of the career decisions merit investigation. Adolescents' entry into science careers might best be understood by examining students with highly focused interests and abilities in science, particularly those who are close to a transition point at which they are required to commit to a career pathway. In every secondary school in Canada, there exists a unique group of students who can be readily identified by their present commitment to science. These young people represent a unique resource since they have the potential to become the scientists and technologists of the future, if they so choose. Are these youth heading in the direction of science career pathways? What factors are affecting their career decisions?

Frameworks Explaining Career Choice

Several frameworks have been put forward in attempts to describe and explain the development of career pathways. Although limited empirical support is currently available to confirm their explanatory power, three frameworks (developmental — cf., Gottfredson (1981); psychological — cf., Holland (1985); sociological/status attainment — cf., Cuneo and Curtis (1975)) identify numerous variables that should be considered in efforts to elaborate on the choice of career pathways. These include: parental influence and support of a youth's educational and/or occupational choices; background characteristics of the family, such as parents' social class, level of educational attainment, occupation and involvement in science; personal orientations of youth, such as vocational interests, perceptions and knowledge of science; educational decisions (i.e., high school course selections and intended post secondary major); and gender.

Family Influence and Career Choice

For the past three decades, researchers have continued to demonstrate a strong link between 'significant others', particularly parents, and the educational and occupational choices of youth, especially females. In 1969, Sewell, Haller and Portes found that significant other influences, including that of parents, teachers and the college plans of their friends, directly affected the educational and occupational aspirations of senior high school males. The 1971 study of 9,000 grade 8, 10 and 12 Ontario students extended the family influence findings to Canada (Porter, Porter and Blishen, 1982). A high degree of parental influence was reported by students in grades 10 and 12, with girls more than boys indicating very high or high influence.

In another major Ontario study, Turritin, Anisef, and Mackinnon (1983) found that parental support played a key role in the decisions of their 1,435 grade 12 male and female study participants to pursue higher education, with males perceiving greater support from their parents than females. For both males and females "high educational aspirations were essential for completion of higher education" (Turritin et al., 1983: 415). While males were shown to be motivated to pursue post-secondary education based on their grades in school and level of educational aspiration, females were shown to be most influenced by encouragement from family and a strong self-concept of ability. Turritin et al. concluded that in order for men and women to enjoy equal educational opportunities, parents need to become more supportive of higher education for their daughters, and "significant others" including parents, teachers, guidance counsellors, and peers should make efforts to strengthen females' self-concept of ability (Turritin et al., 1983).

A number of studies on parental support have focused on females' choice of nontraditional versus traditional careers. Houser and Garvey (1985) studied a sample of females attending secondary schools, occupational centres and community colleges with the purpose of identifying which factors influenced the traditional versus nontraditional career choices of these women. The single dimension differentiating between choice of a traditional and a nontraditional career was the amount of encouragement and support that these females received from important others in their lives. females aspiring to nontraditional careers reported having received greater support from their friends, family, teachers and counsellors than did those with traditional career orientations (Houser and Garvey, 1985: 115).

Fitzpatrick and Silverman (1989) examined the effects of several background and motivational factors on the career choices of a sample of high ability college women majoring in engineering (n = 53, highly nontraditional), science (n = 29, typically nontraditional), and the humanities and social sciences (n = 31, traditional). Unlike most previous research, this study compared samples of females who were similar in ability and achievement, since past research has tended to represent "the traditional career orienters as the less educated and less achievement oriented women" (Fitzpatrick and Silverman, 1989: 267). The authors found that nontraditional women received significantly more support from both parents in their choice of career than traditional women. Sources of support appeared much more critical for women choosing careers in engineering than more typical nontraditional science majors (Fitzpatrick and Silverman, 1989: 275).

The Impact of Family Background Characteristics

The available research suggests that family background characteristics such as parents' occupation and educational attainment influence the movement of young people into career paths in indirect ways. From the earlier work of Blau and Duncan (1967) to the more recently reported longitudinal study by Sandberg, Ehrhardt, Mellins, Ince, and Meyer-Bahlburg (1987), a relationship has been demonstrated between parental educational attainment and their child's career choice. Higher educational levels of fathers and mothers have been associated with higher educational and occupational attainment of both sons and daughters. This general finding has been extended to adolescent female orientation to non-traditional careers (Sandberg et al., 1987) and to student preference for science-oriented careers (Tamir and Gardner, 1989).

Parental occupation has also been linked to adolescent's choice of a career. In a study of 900 grade 10 students from schools in Jerusalem and Israel, Tamir and Gardner (1989) found that students with one or both parents employed in science careers indicated a greater interest in becoming scientists. Fitzpatrick and Silverman (1989) examined the effect of background factors on the career choices of high ability female college students. The only significant difference that emerged on parental characteristics was that the girls majoring in engineering were most likely to have fathers employed in science or engineering as compared to females in traditional majors like the humanities and social sciences. These results are consistent with a Canadian study of final-year undergraduate students by Nevitte, Gibbins and Codding (1990). The sample consisted of 204 males and females from one of four academic disciplines; science, humanities, social sciences, and business/commerce. female science undergraduates were significantly more likely to have fathers employed in the sciences. Additional analyses using only the data for females revealed that father's occupation distinguished female students in the "quantitative sciences" from those in bio-medical sciences.

Personal Orientation and Career Choice

The influence of student interests and perceptions on their educational and vocational orientation to science has been reported in several studies. Perhaps the best known work is that of Terman (1954) who analyzed data gathered longitudinally over a thirty year period on a sample of 800 eminent men who had been selected in childhood on the basis of having scored in the top one percent on intelligence tests. In 1939–40 the Strong Vocational Interest Test (SVIT) was administered to 627 men in this sample. Terman reported that "the test scores from the SVIT differentiated the groups of science and non-science men more clearly than any of the variables examined in his study" (Terman, 1954: 17–18). In a study that also focused on eminent men, Roe (1953) obtained self-reports on a sample of American men selected for their eminence in research. She found that almost all members of the physical science group had expressed an early interest in mathematics, physics, chemistry or gadgeteering. Very few of the subjects had indicated that they were ever interested in literature or the humanities.

Educational Decisions and Career Choice

Hackett (1985) has maintained that inadequate preparation in mathematics and science results in the premature foreclosure of scientific and technological occupations. Reflective of this is the study by Lee (1987) which examined the effect of students' choice of subjects on their choice of a science versus non-science career. Lee analyzed data collected at three separate times (sophomore and senior years of high school and two years after graduation) on subsamples of the 10,739 American students in the High School and Beyond (HS and B) study. She studied how students' choice of course taking in mathematics and science influenced their decision to switch from a declared non-science major in their sophomore year of high school to a major in science in their senior high school year. Lee noted that although the courses taken in mathematics and science at the introductory level appeared similar for both non-science majors and "migrants," students who decided to change their major from non-science to science, a significantly different pattern was observed between the non-science declared majors and the migrants. The "migrants" had taken significantly more advanced courses in chemistry, calculus, and physics. In a study of Australian youth, Baker (1987) also reported that the science versus non-science career orientation of a sample of grade 10 students could be distinguished, with participation in science courses being greater among science career oriented students.

Gender Considerations

Hackett (1985) noted significant sex differences in student enrolment in science and mathematics, a trend which has acted as a "critical filter" severely restricting the career options of females. A Canadian study conducted by Erikson and Erikson (1984), which analyzed data collected in 1978 from samples of grade 12 students in the province of British Columbia, also reported a gender difference in course enrolments in mathematics and science. The grade 12 female students were largely underrepresented in physics courses: only 5.6 percent of the females indicated they were either taking or had completed a grade 12 physics course. In his study of australian youth, Baker (1987) found no significant gender differences in the number of math and science courses that his sample of grade 10 students intended to take in grades 11 and 12. However, he noted a greater likelihood among males to indicate an intention to take more advanced level mathematic courses.

Grandy's (1987) analysis of top-scoring SAT examinees in the U.S. from 1977 to 1986, revealed rather large differences between the sexes, particularly in the choice of fields that are highly quantitative. Females were more likely to choose social sciences, life sciences and psychology, whereas males were more likely to choose engineering.

Current research suggests that males and females typically aspire to occupations that are considered "appropriate" to their gender. Some individuals do choose to deviate from this pattern, selecting occupations that are identified more highly with members of the opposite sex. However, the available literature suggests that males and females differ in their choice of occupations based on their interests and that their interests are influenced by occupational sex-typing. For example, in a study of 249 junior high school students, Shemesh (1990: 32) reported a general tendency among boys to prefer science, math and technology while girls evidenced a decline in interest in these areas and tended to lean more towards social studies and humanities.

Based on the analysis of data gathered on a sample of American high school students two years after graduation, Lee (1987) found a sex difference in student enrolment in the quantitative and nonquantitative education fields. She noted a higher representation of females in the nonquantitative sciences (i.e., life and health sciences) and a greater representation of males in the quantitative sciences such as engineering, math and computer science. Lee speculated that underrepresentation of females in quantitative majors could be due to their perception that enrolment in courses leading to quantitative majors are not important to their future careers.

After examining math and science course enrolment of a sample of male and female college graduates in both high school and college, Deboer (1984) concluded that the higher enrolment of males in math and science courses reflected a greater emphasis on the importance of these courses in the future careers of males. Benbow and Stanley (1982) also examined the perception of course importance using a sample of intellectually and mathematically talented grades 7 and 8 students who had scored in the top three percent on a standardized math test in a 1976 National Talent Search. They found that while females considered biology to be of most importance, males perceived physics as most important to their future careers.

Schulenberg, Vondracek and Crouter (1984) proposed that different socialization practices employed by parents with their sons and daughters explained in part the sex differences observed in their vocational choice development. In a similar vein, Kelly (1988) proposed that parental influences may affect the choices of girls and boys in different ways. For example, if parents encourage their sons and daughters to consider different types of jobs, it is possible that they will take different subjects in order to prepare for these jobs (Kelly, 1988: 9).

Approach to the Study

Sample

The data used in the current report were collected in the summer of 1990 as part of a larger study of science students in Northern Ontario. One hundred and seventy nine students from the Northern Summer School for Excellence in Science at Laurentian University participated in the study. There were 104 females equally divided on the basis of language (Francophones and Anglophones), and 75 males of whom 34 were Francophones and 41 were Anglophones. Each student had been nominated by their school principal and science teacher and then chosen by a selection committee to attend the summer school. Two main attributes were required of the candidates — keenness and ability in mathematics and science and a positive attitude to learning. Students had to be enroled in grade 11 or 12 and be graduating from high school no sooner than January, 1991. Each high school in the northeast sector of Ontario was guaranteed at least one place in the program regardless of the size of the institution, and some schools were permitted to select two students to attend the summer school on the basis of enrolment.

An important criterion for selection into the NSSES program was high performance in science courses. Thus, it was not surprising that 99 percent of the students indicated that they were enroled in an advanced or enriched high school program. Most of the students (80%) stated that their grades for the past year had been mainly A's and 71 percent described their grades as among the best in their class.

Procedure

The students completed a self-administered questionnaire during an evening session of the program. They assembled in two separate groups, based on language of instruction (French and English), and language appropriate forms of the questionnaire were distributed to each group. The nature of the study was explained to the students by senior members of the research team who also informed the students that their participation was voluntary. Members of the research team were available to answer questions throughout the data collection period. Students required an average of 40–50 minutes to complete the questionnaire.

The Questionnaire

The variables employed in the current analysis were taken from a larger questionnaire used in an ongoing multi-panel, longitudinal study of science students in Northern Ontario. In addition to original items developed by the team, questions had been adapted from the instrument used in the Three City Study of the school to work transition (Krahn, 1988) and the work of Breakwell, Fife-Schaw and Devereaux (1988) in Britain on youth, science and technology.

Classification of Science and Technology Occupations and Career Pathways

Each student was asked to indicate the kind of occupation that he or she was hoping for eventually. Gottfredson's (1981) perspective was adopted in viewing the variable as the individual's best response at that particular time. No effort was made to distinguish between realistic and idealistic or short- or long-term choices as these dimensions have been shown to relate to one general dimension (Haller et al., 1974). Occupations were coded according to *The Canadian Classification Dictionary of Occupations (1989)*, the classification system that is standard for both Canadian industry and education. Using this classification structure in conjunction with Statistics Canada (1988) *Enrolment in Universities in Canada*, and the educational major fields developed by Grandy (1987), in accordance with the American National Science Foundation, occupations were further classified as science or non-science. Occupations in science were further identified according to type of science: quantitative or nonquantitative. The groups were as follows.

1. Occupations in medicine and health, occupations in life sciences: nonquantitative
2. Occupations in natural sciences, engineering and mathematics: quantitative
3. Non-science: education, humanities, managerial, administrative and related occupations, clerical and related occupations, sales and service, manual labour, occupations in social sciences and related fields.

Key Independent Variables Used in the Study.

In this report we set out to examine the extent to which high performing science students were moving towards careers in science and to develop a better understanding of factors that are associated with alternative pathways at the critical transition point out of high school. Basic to this search was the attempt to identify a set of factors that differentiated between those students who were intending to pursue a career in nonquantitative or quantitative science and those who had aspirations for a non-science career. The following variables were examined to this end:

Parents' Education; Parents' Occupation; Socioeconomic Status (SES). Parental occupation(s) were coded using the occupational prestige scale developed by Blishen, Carroll and Moore (1987). For descriptive analysis, parental occupations were recoded into high, middle and low SES using the mean and standard deviation of the scale.

Educational Decisions Regarding Math and Science Courses. The number of advanced math and science courses students had taken or intended to take before graduation from high school was determined by two questions. Separate summed scores were calculated for science and math courses. Only the advanced math and science courses (the Ontario Academic Courses) were included in these variables.

Perceived Family Influence. Students' perceptions of family influences were measured separately for mother and father. The respondents were asked to rate on a five point scale agreement or disagreement with five statements, first for their mother/stepmother and then for their father/stepfather. These include: Expects me to do well in science; Expects me to do well in math; Would like me to become a scientist, doctor, engineer; Is good at math; Knows a lot about sciences.

Perceived Family Support. Parental support of the students' career aspiration was determined by asking the respondents to indicate the reaction of their mother and father to their choice of occupation.

Interest and Motivation in Science. Student's interest and motivation in science was determined by rating two questions on a five point scale.

Images of Scientists. Students' perceptions of scientists were assessed through responses to a twenty-four item scale developed by Breakwell, Fife-Schaw and Devereaux (1988). Subjects indicated yes, not sure or no to twenty-four statements about the characteristics of scientists and their work. Responses were summed to obtain a single score.

Views of Science. A second scale measuring views of science and scientists, developed by the authors required respondents to rate six statements using a five point scale. Responses were summed to obtain a single score.

Attitudes to Science and Technology. Students' attitudes to science and technology training, and change resulting from science and technology were measured by an eleven-item scale developed by Breakwell et al. (1988). Students were asked to rate each statement on a five point scale. Responses were summed to obtain a single score.

Scientific Knowledge. A nineteen-item quiz developed by Breakwell, Fife-Schaw and Devereaux (1988) was included to obtain a measure of student's factual knowledge of science. Students responded to each statement by indicating true, false or don't know. Responses were summed to obtain a single score.

Science Activities. Students were asked to indicate, using a five point scale, how often they did the following: read science magazines, read computer magazines, watch science programs on TV, write a computer program, attend a club to do some scientific activity, conduct a piece of scientific research or experiment outside of

Table 4-1: Comparison of Parents' Educational Attainment with Canadian Adult Labour Force, 1988*

	*Adult Canadian Labour Force	*Subjects' Mothers*	*Subjects' Fathers*
Secondary school or less	57.4%	42.2%	39.8%
Some post-secondary	8.6%	19.5%	15.4%
Post-secondary certificate/diploma	16.5%	16.2%	8.4%
University degree	17.6%	22.1%	36.4%

* Source: Statistics Canada, Labour Force Annual Averages, 1988

school. Responses were summed to obtain a single score reflecting involvement in science activities.

Results and Discussion

Family Background

A comparison of the educational attainments of the subjects' mothers and fathers with those of the adult Canadian labour force indicated that the parents of students in the NSSES program tended to be more highly educated than the general employed population. As Table 4–1 shows, fewer of the subjects' mothers and fathers were in the lowest educational category and more of them had attained university degrees than the general adult labour force. In particular, the proportion of fathers who had attained a university degree was more than double the proportion of those in the general population.

Study participants were more likely than the average Canadian youth to come from dual income families. The majority (89%) of subjects' mothers were employed outside the home, (56% full-time; 33% part-time; 11% unemployed/not seeking employment). Ninety percent of the fathers were employed full-time, 5 percent part-time and 5 percent unemployed. Study participants were virtually all from middle or high social class backgrounds. A majority of the employed fathers were in occupations with high (39%) or medium SES (52%). Thirty-two percent of mothers were in high, and 58 percent in medium status occupations.

Parental occupations were classified as science or non-science occupations to provide an indication of the extent to which parental field of employment may

Table 4-2: Parental Influence and Encouragement

	Percentage of Negative Responses	Percentage of Positive Responses
Mother encourages me to do well in math	7.9	78.5
Mother encourages me to do well in science	7.4	81.3
Father encourages me to do well in math	10.9	75.9
Father encourages me to do well in science	10.9	74.7
Mother knows a lot about science	50.3	17.3
Mother is good at math	33.7	29.2
Father knows a lot about science	32.8	42.0
Father is good at math	26.0	54.9
Mother's reaction to choice of job	7.7	82.2
Father's reaction to choice of job	8.5	78.2

influence occupational interests and aspirations. Few of the parents (mothers — 9%; fathers — 12%) were employed in science-related occupations, suggesting that parental employment in a science-related field was not a critical factor influencing high performance and interest in science for most students in the sample.

Analysis of questions dealing with family structure showed that the majority of the study participants (87%) came from intact families (3% — mother/father had died). In the remaining 10 percent of cases, students came from homes in which the parents had divorced, with most of the students (76%) maintaining some contact with the absent parent.

Parental Support and Knowledge

Overall, parents of these students were very supportive and encouraging. As Table 4–2 shows, more than 75 percent of the sample perceived both parents as encouraging them often or very often to do well in science and math, with a slight trend towards mothers being perceived as offering more support than fathers. Both parents were also seen as being very supportive of their adolescents' occupational choices (Table 4-2).

Students were also asked to rate the level of their mothers' and fathers' knowledge of and ability in science and math. As demonstrated in Table 4-2, fathers were perceived to be somewhat more knowledgeable about science than were mothers, and were also seen as being higher in mathematical ability. However, most students did not perceive either of their parents to be very knowledgeable about science nor good at math.

Interest and Motivation in Science

Most students in the sample reported being very interested in, and strongly motivated to do well in science (interest: strong — 37%; very strong — 55%; motivation: strong — 26%; very strong — 67%). A majority of the students (82%) indicated that their interest in science had developed before entry to high school (30% before grade 7; 52% between grades 7 and 9). The remainder (18%) developed an interest in science during the high school years, between grades 10 and 12. Analysis of subjects' descriptions of how they became interested in science showed that the single most important influence was encouragement from other people, mentioned by 66 percent of students. Teachers were perceived by the greatest numbers to be a source of influence, followed by family members and friends. Approximately one quarter of the students also reported one or more of the following as inspiring their interest in science: experiencing science as an interesting subject at school (27%), performing well in science as a school subject (26%), or being involved in science fair experiments (26%).

Thus, from the students' perspective, the two major factors that stimulated their interest in science were: encouragement and support from other people (most notably teachers) and positive experiences with the subject in school. The fact that a majority of these students reported becoming interested in science during their elementary years suggests that elementary teachers and schools have an important role to play in stimulating interest in this subject area.

Occupational Pathways

Student's occupational aspirations were classified into three groups: non-quantitative science (NQS), quantitative science (QS), and non-science (NS) occupations as noted above. Crosstabulation of students' aspirations by gender (Table 4-3) indicated that females were significantly less likely than males to choose occupations in the quantitative sciences and more likely to choose occupations involving non-quantitative science as well as occupations not involving science (chi-square = 15.35; df = 2; p <.001). The finding is not surprising given that careers in the quantitative science traditionally have been dominated by males. Nevertheless, the small number of "elite" female science students aspiring to quantitative science

Table 4-3: Percentage of Females and Males in Three Career Groups

	Females	Males
Nonquantitative science group (Non-Quantitative)	47	28
Quantitative science group (Quantitative)	13	39
Non-science group	40	33

careers suggests that the proportion of females in these occupations may not change dramatically in the coming years.

The responses of students regarding attitudes to science and scientists, science knowledge and involvement in science activities were examined for students in each of the three occupational pathways. While the group differences were frequently not large, the overall pattern of responses suggests some consistent differences between the occupational groups. Students in the QS group had the highest scores on the science knowledge test, more positive views of scientists, more favourable attitudes towards science and technology and tended to participate more often in activities involving science.

Level of interest in science varied between students with science versus non-science career aspirations, with more than two thirds of those in the science pathways (QS — 72%; NQS — 68%) reporting high interest in science compared to slightly more than one third (37%) of those in the NS career pathway reporting this level of interest. However, all groups showed a high degree of motivation in science, with students in the NQS pathway reporting the highest overall levels (80%) while students in the NS and QS groups reported similar levels (62%) of motivation to succeed in science. While one might expect students in the NS group to indicate a lower level of motivation in science than students with aspirations in science, it is possible that the similar levels of motivation noted for QS and NS groups resulted from perceived differences in the level of effort required to succeed in science. Those who do not hope to pursue a career in science may feel that greater effort and thus motivation is required to do well in science, particularly when they are less interested in science as a discipline. The lower levels of interest in science noted amongst the NS group provide some support for this explanation.

Moderate ratings emerged across all three groups for the 'science attitude' variable with the QS group being most positive/highly involved, followed by the NQS/NS groups that were more similar: Views of Science (QS — 49%, NS — 28%, NQS — 21%); Images of Scientists (QS — 46%, NS — 43%, NQS — 39);

Table 4-4: Significant Gender Differences on Science Attitudes, Knowledge and Activities

		Females	Males	Chi-Square Value	DF	p
Images of scientists	% Positive	51	32			
	% Negative	15	36	10.4	2	.005
Views of science	% Positive	43	20			
	% Negative	21	39	12.13	2	.002
Science/ technology attitudes	% Positive	40	21			
	% Negative	25	43	9.26	2	.01
Science knowledge	% High	53	26			
	% Low	20	34	13.99	2	.001
Science activities	% High	51	20			
	% Low	15	30	18.89	2	.0001

Science/technology attitudes (QS — 31%, NQS — 29%, NS — 23%); Science activities (QS — 54%, NQS — 34%, NS — 23%). While group differences were not dramatic for some of these variables, the variation supported their inclusion in the discriminant analyses that are described below.

Gender Differences

Cross tabulations of all variables in the study with gender indicated significant differences between males and females in a number of areas (see Table 4–4). A greater proportion of males than females held positive views of scientists and science/technology. Males were also more likely to have higher scores on the science knowledge test and were more likely to engage in science activities. There were no significant differences between males and females on the other variables;

thus, females and males perceived similar levels of parental support, had similar perceptions of their parent's knowledge of math and science, and had similar levels of interest and motivation to succeed in science. While the differences were not significant, females were slightly more likely to take a greater number of science courses than males.

It seems probable that traditional gender role socialization accounts for differences in the attitudes and behaviours of the male and female students in the sample. It is somewhat disturbing, however, that many female students who excel in science continue to possess negative views of the discipline and those who work in related fields. It also seems reasonable to assume that there is a link between attitudes and behaviour, and that females who hold more negative views of science will be less inclined to participate in science activities. The data support this idea since similar proportions of female students had negative views of science/scientists, had low scores on the knowledge test and reported low levels of participation in science activities.

Prediction of Occupational Pathways

A series of discriminant function analyses was performed to determine whether a set of variables could be used to discriminate between subjects in the three occupational pathways. Initially, a discriminant analysis was performed employing the total sample and all variables. One discriminant function was found to be significant, with seven variables predicting group membership: interest in science; motivation in science; involvement in science activities; views of science; images of scientists; number of science courses; and scores on the Science Knowledge test. The overall proportion of students correctly classified was 61 percent. Given the reported gender differences on a number of these variables, discriminant function analyses were performed separately for females and males.

Table 4–5 shows the results of the discriminant analysis for females. As in the analysis on the total sample, one function was significant, but the set of variables discriminating between female subjects in the three pathways was somewhat different from those of the total sample. Interest and motivation in science did not emerge as significant variables differentiating between the groups of female students, while several family influence variables were important. Students' perceptions of mothers' and fathers' math skills and fathers' reactions to the students' occupational aspirations were entered into the analysis as significant discriminating variables.

Examination of group responses to these variables showed that females in the QS pathway were more likely than the other two groups to agree that their mother was good in math but a smaller proportion than the other two groups felt that their father was good in math. females in the QS group were most likely to say that their father supported their career aspiration, while the NS group was least likely to indicate that their father was pleased with their occupational aspiration. As in the total sample, the number of science credits, involvement in science activities, and images of scientists were significant predictor variables. females in the NS group

Table 4-5: Discriminant Function Analysis for Females in Three Career Groups

Variables	Wilk's Lambda	Significance
1. Number of science credits	.88	.006
2. Science behaviour	.81	.003
3. Mother is good at math	.77	.002
4. Images of scientists	.73	.002
5. Father's reaction to job choice	.69	.002
6. Father is good at math	.65	.001

Overall: Eigenvalue .40, Wilk's Lambda .65, Significance .001

Classification Results: Nonquantitative Science Group 72%
                              Quantitative Science Group 36%
                              Non-Science Group 71%
                              Overall 67%

generally had more negative images of scientists and were less likely to participate in science activities. female students in the QS group were most likely to take a greater number of science courses but more of the NQS students indicated high levels of participation in science activities. The classification results were slightly better than those for the overall sample, correctly classifying more than 70 percent of NQS and NS groups. As in the analysis for the total sample, prediction of the QS group was least effective (36%).

One function was significant in the discriminant function analysis for males, with a combination of motivational, family influence, and behavioral variables predicting group membership (see Table 4–6). In contrast to the results for females, interest and motivation in science were entered into the prediction equation for males. Group differences on these variables reflected the greater interest and motivation in science reported by NQS males, intermediate levels by the QS group, and the lower levels of interest and motivation by the males in the NS group. Somewhat surprisingly, the family influence variables (father's knowledge of science and math) reflected the greater likelihood of QS males to disagree with the

Table 4-6: Discriminant Function Analysis for Males in Three Career Groups

Variables	Wilk's Lambda	Significance
1. Father is good at math	.90	.05
2. Strength of interest in science	.81	.02
3. Science behaviour	.70	.003
4. Number of math credits	64	.003
5. Number of science Number of science credits	.57	.001
6. Strength of motivation in science	52	.001
7. Father knows about science	.50	.001

Overall: Eigenvalue .59, Wilk's Lambda, .50; Significance .001

Classification Results: Nonquantitative Science Group, 75%
           Quantitative Science Group, 61%
           Non-Science Group, 50%
           Overall, 61%

statement that their fathers were good at math and science, and for the NQS group to agree with this statement. With regard to math and science credits, males in the NQS group were more likely than the other two groups to take a greater number of courses. A greater proportion of the male students in the QS group indicated a high degree of involvement in science activities. The classification results were somewhat different for males than females, with a higher percentage of the male QS group (61%) correctly classified. The set of discriminating variables was least effective in classifying the male NS group (50%). As in the classification results for the females, prediction of membership was most effective in the NQS group (75%).

The separate gender analyses indicated that the factors discriminating among the three career groups are very different for males and females. Only two common variables entered into the prediction equations for males and females; decisions regarding science courses, and involvement in science activities. It is noteworthy that different patterns of responses emerged for males and females on these two common variables. Among the males, the QS group was more likely to engage in science activities, while among the females, the NQS group was more likely to do so. In regard to science courses, QS females were more likely to take a greater number of science courses, while NQS males were more likely than the other two groups of males to do so. It may be important to note, however, that females were, in general, slightly more likely than males to take a greater number of science courses and that this trend was accounted for by the greater likelihood of females to take biology in addition to other science courses. The fact that females in the QS group were more likely to take a greater number of science courses may indicate that they are not foreclosing on opportunities in the non-quantitative sciences and that their plans to pursue a career in quantitative science may be more tentative. With regard to this issue, it is of interest that the classification results for females showed that all except one of the QS females who were incorrectly classified were misclassified as belonging to the NQS group. Thus, as measured by variables in this study, there were few overall differences between females in the quantitative and nonquantitative science groups.

The separate discriminant analyses also showed that certain variables were important gender-specific predictors. Family influence variables were particularly important for females. The perception that mother is good at math and that father supports one's career aspirations were particularly predictive of group membership for QS females. On the other hand, the perception that one's father is good at math was more relevant for a greater proportion of NS and NQS females. Images of scientists was a predictor variable for females but not males, with positive images of scientists being predictive of membership in a science group.

The motivational variables (strength of interest and motivation in science) were significant for males but not for females. The inclusion of these variables in the prediction equation for males reflected lesser interest and motivation on the part of NS students and higher levels on the part of NQS students. Membership in the QS group for males was not dependent on the same-sex parent having expertise in math as it was for females, but males in the NQS group were most likely to perceive their fathers as knowing a lot about science.

In general, the discriminant analyses suggested that external factors are more important for predicting science versus non-science group membership for females while internal, motivational factors are more important for males. Encouragement and support from family members represent critical factors discriminating females in the two science groups from those in the non-science group. In particular, it appears that positive influence and support from family members is important for females who are members in the QS group. On the other hand, since the quantitative sciences have traditionally been an occupational domain for males, family support and influence may be less important as a determinant of career choice for males who chose to pursue occupations in this field.

Conclusions

Knowledge of the characteristics of students who have demonstrated interest and ability in science can assist in our understanding of how adolescents come to pursue science education and careers. The current sample of high performing science students had come from very advantaged backgrounds characterized by high socioeconomic status, a high degree of marital stability and very high levels of support and encouragement from parents. The overall high levels of familial status, stability and support evident in this sample are somewhat surprising given that students represented very diverse communities in Northeastern Ontario and also represented every school in this area of the province. The lack of variation in the background characteristics of the sample is somewhat disturbing if taken to mean that students who do not come from similarly advantaged backgrounds may be less likely to succeed and excel in math and science.

Previous research on the status attainment process has documented the importance of family influence on educational and occupational attainments in general. In the current study, students with fathers who had attained some college or graduated from college were more likely to pursue careers in science in general and careers in the physical or quantitative sciences in particular. This is consistent with the findings of Blau and Duncan (1967) who found that father's level of education operated indirectly to influence the occupational attainment of males in their sample, and Sandberg et al. (1987) who found that adolescent females who aspired to nontraditional science educations and occupations were more likely to have fathers who had attained significantly more education than traditionally oriented girls. It is possible that parents who have attained higher levels of education may be less traditional and generally better informed of a wider range of career opportunities available to their children.

Family influence also emerges through the support and encouragement that parents offer regarding the educational and occupational plans of their adolescents (Fitzpatrick and Silverman, 1989; Houser and Garvey, 1985; Porter et al., 1982; Noeth et al., 1984). The high levels of parental support that were evident across all three career groups could be read by these students as an unconditional signal to excel. The message might read "I support you in whatever career path you choose." If true, such a message places the directional control for entry to science careers more in the hands and mind of the individual adolescent.

Despite being relatively homogeneous in terms of background characteristics and academic ability, slightly less than two thirds of the students in the sample reported that they had aspirations for an occupation in a science-related field. Cross tabulations revealed that females were more highly represented in the nonquantitative sciences and most underrepresented in quantitative science. Males were more evenly distributed across the three groups. Consistent with earlier studies (Grandy 1987; Lee 1987; Wilson and Boldizer, 1990), our results indicated that females were more highly represented in nonquantitative/health or life sciences than in quantitative post secondary science education (82% versus 18%). It is clear that very few females in our sample intend to pursue post-secondary programs in quantitative science.

We had expected females in this sample to be somewhat more likely to pursue education and occupations in quantitative science since they represent an academically superior group in this subject area. Hackett (1985) has argued that career choices of females are often limited because they take fewer advanced mathematic and science courses, which are needed to prepare for scientific and technological careers. Results of research conducted by Erikson and Erikson (1984), which observed a serious underrepresentation of grade 12 Canadian females in physics courses, lend support to this assumption. Baker (1987) and Deboer (1984) also observed a gender disparity in course-taking patterns with males being more likely than females to pursue more advanced mathematic and science courses. In contrast with findings from the earlier studies, females in the present sample had taken or planned to take a higher number of advanced math and science courses as compared with males. Unlike those in the Erikson and Erikson (1984) study, females in the present sample were represented as highly as males in the number which had taken or planned to take OAC physics. Representation was, however, observed to be considerably higher among females than males in the number planning to take OAC biology. Benbow and Stanley (1982) found that the females in their sample were most likely to identify biology as the course most important to their future careers. The higher number of females planning to take biology also provides support for the idea that most females are preparing for post-secondary majors in the non-quantitative health sciences by taking the necessary high school prerequisites.

Gottfredson's (1981) theory of career development offers a possible explanation for the underrepresentation of females in physical science. According to Gottfredson, children between six and eight years of age have already classified occupations according to their perception of gender appropriateness. Consequently, occupations perceived as inappropriate to their gender are eliminated from the range of occupations from which they later choose. Gottfredson maintained that once occupations are eliminated at this stage of a career development, it is unlikely that these will be reconsidered in the high school years. Despite the fact that they possess the aptitude to pursue education and occupations in science, females may not do so because they have already eliminated these occupations from consideration at an earlier stage of their career development. It is of considerable interest, however, that many of the females in our sample had taken, and planned to take a large number of science courses (including maths and physics) but had no intention of pursuing a career in quantitative science. Hence, it is evident that course-taking and interest in science are necessary but not sufficient to ensure that youth will pursue careers in science. If young women were less restricted in their career choice by traditional gender stereotypes they might be more likely to consider education and occupations in science, particularly young women who possess the ability to do so. Sandberg et al. (1987) also proposed this link between gender role socialization and occupational choice, reporting that adolescent girls aspiring to nontraditional careers appeared somewhat subjected to less stereotypic sex-typing than those oriented to traditional careers.

In addition to examining the career orientations of male and female students in the sample, a goal of the study was to identify the combinations of key factors that jointly operate to influence choice of occupation in science (quantitative versus nonquantitative). The results of discriminant function analyses indicated that a combination of motivational, attitudinal, behavioral and family influence variables are significant in the prediction of career aspirations in quantitative, nonquantitative and non-science fields. These analyses also underscored the differences between male and female students in terms of factors related to career choice.

Family influence variables appeared to be of particular importance in the predication of career choices for females. This finding is consistent with previous research (Fitzpatrick and Silverman, 1989; Houser and Garvey, 1985) which found that females aspiring to nontraditional careers were more likely to have perceived more support from their parents in regard to their educational and occupational choices. The probability of females pursuing quantitative or physical science careers in the present study increased substantially among females who perceived high levels of support from their fathers in their choice of career.

Contrary to Fitzpatrick and Silverman's finding, the importance of mother's "support" was not fitted in an equation predicting choice of nontraditional career in our study. Gecas and Schwalbe (1986) offered a possible explanation for this occurrence. In their study of parents and adolescents aged (seventeen to nineteen years) they found that father's influence was stronger than mother's in the development of young people's self-esteem. They speculated that the greater (perceived) influence from fathers could be attributed to the "greater power and authority" typically exercised by fathers in families. Alternatively, Gecas and Schwalbe reasoned that the lesser involvement of fathers, relative to mothers, in their children's socialization makes the fathers' involvement more influential in the minds of their children. It is also possible that a student's perception of father's support (as found for females in this study) may reflect the stereotypical notion that careers in physical science are appropriate for males and not females, which might explain why father's support would have a greater impact, particularly on a daughter's choice of nontraditional science careers. Youniss and Smollar (1988) found that adolescents were more likely to seek their fathers' advice on career matters while youth relied on their mothers in matters of a more emotional nature. Possibly, mothers' advice on career matters may be subordinated to that of fathers, or perhaps mothers are perceived to support their husbands in the career information that they offer their children.

Our results have provided evidence that many of the female students who do not wish to pursue a science career possess more negative, stereotyped views of scientists. These images may be generated through the media, which often projects a disturbing image of the "mad" scientist. Although the female students in the sample indicated that they were interested in science and wished to do well in science classes, their negative views of science and the people who work in science-related fields appear to discourage them from pursuing activities in science during their high school years and, in the long term, from pursuing careers in science. The lower scores of females on the science knowledge test may also be related to more negative views of science and a lack of participation in science-related activities. This may be an area in which schools can play a role by actively promoting more accurate and positive images of science and scientists.

The findings of the present study supported the view that interest in science and science-oriented vocations influences aspirations, particularly for the males. In the current study, 64 percent of all students, and 67 percent of the males indicated that they had chosen a science career, offering support for Gottfredson's (1981) theory. Gottfredson has argued that in stage four of the theory (beginning around age fourteen), personal identities expressed by jobs are an additional criteria by which individuals further distinguish among their acceptable alternatives. Choices that seem most compatible with the type of personality one wants to project and develop are valued more highly. The pattern of changes in adolescents' aspirations in the fourth stage suggests that they are recognizing the interests and competencies required for pursuing different fields of work. This may explain why teenagers aspiring to the same fields of work form increasingly homogeneous groups as they get older. The fact that interest and motivation were significant factors predicting career group membership for males but not for females suggested that males may be less constrained in expressing their interests and competencies in their career choices in fields traditionally dominated by males. Females appear to be more influenced by external factors such as parental influence and societal gender scripts as noted above.

Implications for Future Research

It is important to understand how students' interest in science and science related vocations develops. The influence of "significant others," most notably parents, was found to be an important factor influencing the decision to pursue a science career. It was also evident that interest in science is promoted through an early and favourable exposure to science in an educational setting. Over half of the students in the present sample identified grades 7 to 9 as the period in which their interest in science had been most inspired in school. This also coincides with the age at which children's cognitive development progresses from a concrete towards a more abstract ability to reason. It is possible that cognitive developmental changes may be operating at this time to better prepare youth to digest and interpret subject matter in science. It might be argued that the development of abstract reasoning skills is necessary for success in performing scientific tasks. Further research should be directed towards understanding the interaction between developmental changes and curriculum practices (i.e. method of instruction and presentation) occurring during the time frame in which most of the students developed an interest in science, and how these may operate to promote a greater interest in science.

In addition to promoting awareness among school personnel regarding the need to develop effective methods to inspire interest in science, it is also important to consider the role of parents as principle agents influencing the future educational and occupational pathways of their children. Numerous researchers have identified the family as a major source influencing the developing interests of youth (Holland, 1985; Tamir and Gardner, 1989). The number of youth choosing to participate in science might be increased if family and school systems worked cooperatively to realize this common objective by promoting interest in science-related activities and by supporting educational and occupational decisions leading to science careers. Results of this study clearly indicate that particular attention must be paid to encouraging the participation of females in science, especially in quantitative science. Greater effort must be aimed at halting the perpetuation of traditional sex-typing of occupations. If Gottfredson's assumptions are valid, females will continue to be underrepresented in physical science as long as the vast majority continue to perceive occupations and education in this field as inappropriate to members of their gender.

Both school and family could be instrumental in changing this belief by dispelling negative stereotypes about science and scientists and acquainting students with the various careers in science from which they may choose. If females could be persuaded to believe that education and occupations in science are as appropriate to them as they are to males, then females may be less likely to view science as unimportant to their future careers. Turritin et al. (1979) also recommend that if males and females are ever to enjoy equal education opportunities, parents, teachers, peers and guidance counsellors will have to become more involved in strengthening females' self-concept of ability in pursuing higher levels of education in sciences, which is also the door to many careers in physical science. The influence of a strong support network, particularly in a female's choice of a nontraditional science occupation, is also echoed in the research findings of Houser and Garvey (1985) and Fitzpatrick and Silverman (1989) who have reported that females aspiring to nontraditional careers perceived greater support from family, friends, and various school personnel. Both earlier research and the present findings suggest that a strong support network appears crucial to females choice of career in a nontraditional science.

It is clear that there are fewer barriers to male entry into quantitative science careers. Males in our sample were more likely than females to have chosen a career in science, and were more likely to have chosen a quantitative science career over a nonquantitative science career. A smaller proportion (one third) of the males chose non-science careers. Motivational factors were key variables predicting male membership in a science versus non-science career group. The indication that internal factors were important variables influencing career decisions for males suggests that efforts directed to stimulating interest in science among male students may prove fruitful. As noted above, students who had chosen non-science occupations generally had more negative views of science and scientists, were less likely to participate in science activities and were less knowledgeable about science. In conjunction with the evidence regarding the important role of positive elementary school experiences with science and science teachers, this pattern of results clearly suggests that if the goal of securing skilled scientific and technological personnel in this country is to be realized, efforts to recruit science students should consider: 1) dispelling negative stereotypes and perceptions of science and scientists; 2) emphasizing the positive aspects of quantitative careers for all students; 3) developing collaborative school-family strategies for encouraging and inspiring student interest in science at an early age; 4) removing barriers to female participation in science activities and in the pursuit of careers in the sciences, particularly in the quantitative sciences.

5
Lifelong Education and Chronic Underemployment: Exploring the Contradiction[1]

D.W. Livingstone

"Lifelong education, fundamentally, belongs to the history of education of all countries, it is not, therefore a new idea. It lies in the Chinese tradition, in Indian Buddhism, it lies within Greek philosophy and within the spirit of the European Renaissance. The real revolution today lies in the *popular demand* for lifelong education, not in the idea itself, and this demand is very difficult to accommodate. We can begin removing the obstacles by eradicating this idea that lifelong education is just something that belongs to developed or highly industrialised societies, and by encouraging new approaches to the concept."

Ettore Gelpi, Director, *Lifelong Education Division, UNESCO*[2]

"The impact of technological change upon our life patterns is only now being recognized. Skills are learned behaviour. The useful duration of any skill—whether it relates to employment, family life, leisure, community affairs, or spiritual development—is rapidly becoming shorter. The sole exception may be the ability to learn. This factor of skill obsolescence suggests that our society must cease to pay mere lip service to the concept of lifelong learning. Our individual and collective future will depend upon implementing lifelong learning, breaking the lockstep between learning, earning and retirement."

Canadian Association for Adult Education[3]

"European industry, as well as the cost structure of its products, has become more knowledge intensive. Therefore, a competitive advantage can be gained by raising employees' level of education and thus their competence. Skilled and well-educated people are vital for success. Europe allows and even encourages its young individuals to take the liberty of pursuing 'interesting', not directly job-related studies, which in

---

[1] Revised version of paper presented at the Transition from School to Work Conference, Toronto, October 4–5, 1991. I am grateful to Kari Dehli, Doug Hart and Peter Mayo, as well as other conference participants, for comments on a previous draft of this paper.

[2] E. Gelpi, "Lifelong Education and International Relations" in K. Wain (ed.) *Lifelong Education and Participation* (B'Kara: University of Malta Press, 1985), p. 18.

[3] Canadian Association for Adult Education, *From the Adult's Point of View* (Toronto: CAAE/ICEA, 1982), p. 1.

many cases have little prospect of practical application. At the same time society is expected to provide full employment for everybody...The technical and industrial development of European industry clearly requires an accelerated revitalisation of education and its curricula. It also requires new opportunities and new models for updating and upgrading the skills and competence of Europe's working age population.

The concept of work is continuously changing. An individual not only has several jobs in a lifetime, but may also have several careers. Therefore, everybody needs a continuous updating and upgrading of skills and competence throughout working life...Lifelong learning should become an attitude and a practice. Present attitudes to education will have to change. Companies should generate an atmosphere in which competence and education are esteemed and supported. Education has to be viewed as an investment in line with corporate strategy. Competence and education are an individuals' assets. It is up to individuals themselves to update and upgrade this capital in order to preserve their personal competitiveness and develop to meet the new demands of the working environment.

Dr. Kari Kairamo, Chairman,
Standing Working Group on Education,
Round Table of European Industrialists[4]

To be honest, I am a bit anxious about my prospects. Today, a liberal arts education is undervalued. Instead, technical skills are sought by many companies. I've received letters that say I have an impressive educational background, but without the necessary technical skills, I cannot be considered as a candidate for a job. I am beginning to think I am an anomaly. Perhaps a higher education as an end in itself is anachronistic. If true, I shudder to think of the consequences.

Jillian Cohen, Unemployed
Liberal Arts Graduate[5]

The notion of "lifelong learning" has become one of the most hackneyed clichés of public discourse in advanced capitalist societies during recent times. We all now tend to agree on the necessity for continuous learning, in some generic sense, in order to deal effectively with changing aspects of our economic, political, cultural and physical environments. But the term actually has starkly different application to the different basic types of education as currently construed by adult educators, namely informal, formal and non-formal education.[6]

Informal education refers to all those learning activities that we do beyond the authority or requirements of any educational institution. It has been documented that virtually all of us undertake at least a few major self-directed learning projects

---

[4] K.Kairamo (ed.), *Education for Life: A European Strategy* (London: Butterworths Scientific Limited, 1989), pp. 1, 12, 13.

[5] J. Cohen, "Is an education, for the sake of it, passé?" *Toronto Star*, September 11, 1991, p. A25.

[6] For discussion of these "three main approaches," see G. Selman and P. Dampier. *The Foundations of Adult Education in Canada* (Toronto: Thompson Educational Publishing, 1991), pp. 11–12.

a year throughout our adult lives (Tough, 1978, 1979). In contrast, formal education has been defined as *full-time* study within state-certified educational institutions. Modern formal schooling has been restricted almost exclusively to young people who have been expected to proceed through extensive graded curricula in lockstep fashion prior to achieving full adult status (Illich, 1971). Non-formal education is everything in between, that is, all other organized educational activities offered by any social agency. It is these systematically organized educational programs offered mainly to adults on a part-time basis by diverse authorities that have been the primary reference point in recent calls for increased lifelong learning.

The distinctions between these three types of education are becoming blurred. Self-directed learning projects increasingly involve standardized packages of learning materials designed and sold by large corporations. Both high school and post-secondary formal educational institutions are more attentive to mature part-time credit students who are the major growth potential in their enrolments. From the vantage points of both independent adult learners and formal education authorities, there is clearly a growing attraction to rely on expanding non-formal programs to address lifelong learning needs.

This paper will focus upon assessing recent growth in the demand for non-formal education in general, with particular attention to recent labour force entrants. The basic argument is that the creation of a genuine "permanent education culture" continues to face the twin obstacles of enduring *educational discrimination* against poor people and the chronic *underutilization* of many people's actual educational attainments by their employers. The contradiction between this growing popular demand and the limited opportunities for people to apply and develop their educational competencies within their present workplaces is leading to increasingly *complex transitions* between educational institutions and labour markets. This is particularly true for young people in pursuit of either better jobs or enhanced personal development.[7]

The Popular Demand for Adult Education

Throughout the post-World War II era, Canada has been one of the two most highly schooled societies in the world. It has continued to become more so, with the average years of schooling of the population over fifteen increasing from 9.6 in 1960 to 12.2 by 1986, and with post-secondary enrolment ratios closely rivalling those of the United States in recent years (Nobert, 1990). Conversely, Canada and the United States both have lagged behind many European countries in the provision of non-formal adult education programs (e.g., Rubensen, 1989; Kerckhoff, 1990). All evidence indicates that general annual participation rates in Canadian adult education have increased greatly from about 4 percent in 1960

---

[7] See A. Thomas's chapter in this volume for a fuller conceptual treatment of these transitions and some of the mechanisms, such as Prior Learning Assessment Procedures, that can facilitate greater re-entry into educational institutions from other work places.

Table 5-1: "*In the past year, have you taken any of the following types of adult or continuing education courses?*"

	1986 %	1988 %	1990 %
Have taken a course	20	25	31
Job retraining	5	4	5
English as a second language (ESL)	<1	<1	2
Basic reading, writing and number skills	<1	<1	1
Courses toward a high school diploma	1	2	5
Courses toward a community college certificate or university degree	5	9	10
French as a second language (FSL)	2	2	2
General interest courses	9	10	11
None of the above	74	72	67
Not applicable—Still in school/university	3	3	3
N	1042	1011	1032

Source: Livingstone, Hart and Davie (1991)

(Selman and Dampier 1991: 80) to 20 percent in 1983 (Devereux, 1985: 4) with further steady increases since then (Gallup, 1990).

The recent increases in Ontario are summarized in Table 5–1.[8] There has been about a 50 percent increase in general participation in adult education between 1986

---

[8] It should be noted here that the OISE Survey of Educational Issues from which the data presented in the tables in this paper have been drawn relies on standard Gallup Poll weightings for age and sex in its published reports. The figures presented here have been reweighed to correct for an underrepresentation of the least educated, and therefore differ slightly from those in the survey reports.

5 / Lifelong Education and Chronic Underemployment

Table 5-2: Participation in Adult Education by Background

Have taken a continuing education course	1986 %	1988 %	1990 %
All respondents	20	25	31
Age			
18-24	27	42	49
25-29	27	35	39
30-44	25	32	38
45-59	13	14	19
60+	6	7	12
Education			
Elementary	3	6	8
High school incomplete	10	17	27
High school diploma	28	31	36
Community college certificate	27	37	41
University degree	37	39	46
Occupational class			
Corporate executives	20	28	26
Small employers	35	28	33
Self-employed	19	20	24
Managers	35	40	23
Supervisors	26	37	26
Professional employees	39	43	55
Service workers	26	35	43
Industrial workers	14	19	30
Unemployed	7	16	30
Homemakers	5	13	18
Retired	11	4	15

Source: Livingstone, Hart and Davie (1991)

and 1990, from 20 percent to 31 percent of the population over eighteen years of age. Most of the growth was found in diploma/degree credit courses which now constitute about half of all adult education courses. It is also notable that, despite widely publicized government job training initiatives, participation in job retraining programs appears to have been quite stable at around 5 percent throughout this period.

Further insights into the social composition of adult education programs are provided in Table 5–2 which presents the most significant differences by social background of participants. As in all prior surveys, there are marked inequalities by age and formal schooling, with the oldest and least schooled much less likely to participate. Professional employees continue to have higher participation rates than other occupational classes. But is also true that recent participation has increased in nearly all age and formal educational groupings as well as most occupational classes. The most substantial recent gains have been among high school drop-outs and those working people who tend to have the *least* formal education, namely service and industrial workers, and the unemployed. In addition, by 1986, over half of the adult population of Ontario were planning to take a future adult education course, more than doubling the proportion with such plans a decade earlier (Livingstone, Hart and Davie, 1986, p. 7; Waniewiez, 1976). Clearly, there is growing popular demand for non-formal education throughout nearly all sectors of the population.

People's motives for participating in non-formal education also seem to have changed. While general personal development goals were the predominantly expressed reasons in prior surveys, during the 1980s *employment-related objectives* became at least equally important motives (CAAE, 1982; Waniewicz, 1976). Such motivational shifts are in accord with a widespread public perception that recent technological changes have served to increase the skill and training requirements for both individual types of jobs and the labour force generally (Livingstone, Hart and Davie, 1987: 14–15; Myles, 1989). An overwhelming majority now believe that workers will have to take further education courses in order for the country to remain competitive in global markets (Angus Reid Group, 1990). Ontarians now generally expect that only jobs requiring post-secondary credentials will increase in the foreseeable future, and increasingly see post-secondary education as very important (Livingstone, Hart and Davie, 1987). While there continues to be little enthusiasm for narrow job-specific retraining programs, a "permanent education culture" is emerging in which most adult workers expect to rely on some sort of non-formal education in order to get along in both the workplace and other spheres of a changing technological society.

Participation in and popular demand for non-formal education have continued to grow in spite of *persistent barriers*. At an institutional level, the history of adult education in Canada is replete with periodic efforts by progressive educators to develop programs for working people only to be undermined by the indifference or resistance of dominant class forces, as well as by immense distances, ethnic diversity and jurisdictional politics (Welton 1987; Selman and Dampier, 1991).

Table 5-3: Educational Attainment-Job Requirement Matching,*
Employed Ontario Labour Force, 1982-1990

Social Group	Year	Under-employed (%)	Under-qualified (%)	(%)
Total workforce	1982	17	59	24
	1990	20	55	26
18-29	1982	21	61	18
	1990	29	58	14
30-44	1982	18	58	25
	1990	22	54	25
45+	1982	13	60	27
	1990	10	53	37
No diploma	1982	-	74	26
	1990	-	47	53
High school diploma	1982	29	39	32
	1990	22	60	18
Community college certificate	1982	30	50	20
	1990	42	49	9
University degree	1982	24	76	-
	1990	36	64	-

*Based on level of educational certification: less than high school diploma, high school diploma, community college certificate, or university degree.
Source: Livingstone and Bowd (1991)

More specific obstacles include very limited financial support from either employers or governments, lack of accessible information about or coordination between educational agencies, and restrictive admission and scheduling practices (CAAE, 1982: 11–12). From the perspective of individual non-participants, particularly the poor working people, the major barriers have continued to be prohibitive costs of programs and lack of time (Waniewiez, 1976; CAAE, 1982). In light of such sustained constraints, the steady growth of adult participation is doubly impressive.

Chronic Underemployment

At the same time, and in stark contrast to the growing demand for both advanced formal education and non-formal education, there is a chronic underutilization within the paid workplaces of advanced capitalist societies of the education that many people have previously obtained (see Rumberger, 1981; Livingstone, 1987). Researchers have extensively documented a tendency for many employers to inflate required entry credentials beyond the education actually needed to perform job tasks (Berg, 1970; Collins, 1979; Blackburn and Mann, 1979; Hunter, 1988). A substantial portion of the labour force continues to get higher educational credentials than their employers require. Table 5–3 summarizes the patterns of underutilization of credentials or "underemployment" found in Ontario over the last decade.[9] The most notable findings here are the persistent underemployment of about one-fifth of the entire employed labour force (including substantial proportions of older workers well along in their employment careers), the increasing underemployment of post-secondary graduates,[10] and the increasing localization of underqualification for their jobs among older workers without high school diplomas. At least one third of all workers under twenty-five and more than a third of all workers with post-secondary credentials are now underemployed in Ontario.

There may be a slowly growing sense of underutilization of their formal education among the Ontario work force. During the late 1970s, slightly less than half the labour force expressed the view that their schooling had been very useful for their work; by the mid 1980s, this proportion had declined marginally. But the majority of post-secondary graduates continued to believe that their schooling had been very useful, as opposed to slowly declining minorities of those with less formal education (Livingstone, Hart and Davie, 1987: 10–11). Thus, chronic underutilization of education generally and increasing underutilization among

---

[9] It should be noted here that the measures of "underemployment" that are used in this paper, in terms of educational certification that exceeds job requirements by at least one credential, produce *quite conservative* estimates. There are many other workers who have one, two or even three years of schooling beyond the credential their job requires. It may, in fact, be even more important to address the issue of whether underutilization of educational credentials in employment is associated with underutilization in broader political and cultural spheres. This issue is beyond the scope of the present analysis.

[10] Canada-wide surveys of recent post-secondary graduates have detected the same trend using different measures. (See Clark and Zsigmond 1981; Nobert, 1990: 32.)

post-secondary graduates in particular have not dramatically altered most peoples' sense of the value of their own formal schooling, to say nothing of their faith in the value of and need for further education.

Explaining the Educational Contradiction of Advanced Capitalism

Educational theorists have explained this contradiction between growing popular demand for education and chronic underutilization within workplaces in terms of the opposed aggregate educational needs of employers and prospective employees within the advanced capitalist market economy (see Livingstone, 1983; Carnoy and Levin, 1985). Employers are under the general compulsion to continually modify their production systems in order to efficiently produce and/or competitively realize profits on their enterprises' goods and services. For most firms, this now entails retaining a significant number of highly educated managerial, professional and specialized technical employees to ensure the efficient and/or profitable coordination and design of production systems. But employers must generally hire other workers from whom they only need a more basic range of skills to actually operate, adapt and execute productive activities. They must also encourage sufficient standardization and simplification of any new production process, so that most employees' productive control and wage demands remain limited by the possibility of replacement by the general (or "abstract") labour capacity of others. Thus, capitalist enterprises must continually demand educated workers to develop and run more advanced production systems, at the same time as employers try to ensure profitability and their overall control via the systematization and continuing replaceability of their employees' competencies. This entails the reproduction within capitalist firms and labour markets of a hierarchy of educationally advanced, intellectual labour and basic skilled, manual labour.

Any advanced industrial society has a generic need for a versatile, technically knowledgeable labour force. In any such complex society undergoing continual change, there is an experiential requirement of more fully socialized access to accurate information and knowledge for all people so they can live fulfilling lives as well as work productively. This is one of the bases of the popular democratic demand for more advanced education and useful knowledge of all types. Within capitalist labour markets, there is also the inherently ambiguous imperative of gaining sufficient educational skills and credentials to meet competitive job entry conditions without becoming too overqualified to be considered eligible for available jobs.

As I have observed elsewhere (Livingstone, 1985: 38):

> For the schools to respond to these contradictory requirements, they must first offer free access and thus provide basic skills (along with diffuse cultural orientations). But then they must attempt to restrict opportunities, in terms of the political and technical scope of the curriculum and of the numbers who are permitted to achieve their educational aspirations. Moreover, if the class structures of paid work, household consumption, and civic participation are to be reproduced effectively, the schooling process must continue to play these contradictory roles while maintaining a relative

autonomy from capitalist enterprises and without drastically upsetting such popular aspirations.

The fact that the educational reproduction of the labour force in most advanced capitalist societies is now mediated through both free, if segmented, labour markets and a liberal democratic state, guarantees only a loose correspondence between the aggregate job requirements negotiated within workplaces and the actual qualifications of the prospective work force. In particular, these mediating conditions ensure that there are consistently more people trying to attain advanced education than capitalist enterprises are prepared to employ at that level. Secondly, they imply that underqualification of some employees also persists both because of the genuine cumulative growth of technical knowledge combined with a restrictive educational system, and because employers continue to inflate credential requirements to select from an increasingly educated labour pool.

In the context of a protracted capital accumulation crisis and consequent fiscal constraints on the state (see O'Connor, 1984), the funding and accessibility of advanced formal education are under increased threat. There is a growing strategic appeal for both employers and governments to rely more on non-formal educational programs to meet both democratic demand for education and short-term training needs. The most immediate issue here is how the popular aspirations of those in the labour force whose current educational attainments are deemed to be "mismatched" with their job requirements are actually responding to non-formal education opportunities.

Underemployment and Adult Education Participation

Prior research has not detected any major radicalizing effects of underemployment status on political consciousness (Burris, 1983; Livingstone and Bowd, 1991). But, if employment-related objectives are among the important motives for learning, it might seem reasonable to postulate that underemployment generally diminishes interest in further non-formal education, whereas an underqualified status in one's job tends to encourage further education. The basic results of our investigation, drawing on recent Ontario surveys of the active labour force, are summarized in Tables 5–4 and 5.

As Table 5–4 shows, the simple relationship postulated between underemployment and adult education participation must be rejected. Between 1986 and 1990, the gross participation rate for the underqualified remained quite stable, at about one quarter. Participation rates for the underemployed, as well as for workers with matched attainments/requirements were comparable to the underqualified in 1986 but subsequently have actually *exceeded* these rates. Clearly, the general condition of underemployment has not recently dissuaded workers from seeking further adult education.

However, since participation rates are known to have been closely related to both prior educational attainment and age, and underemployment/underqualification statuses are highly interactive with attainment levels, it is probably more informative to look at the employment status-adult education participation rela-

Table 5-4: Adult Education Participation Rate by Educational Attainment-Job Requirement Match, Employed Ontario Labour Force, 1986 - 1990

	Annual Participation Rate (%)		
Employment Status	1986	1988	1990
Underemployed	25	37	37
Matched	26	30	35
Underqualified	28	25	27

Source: Livingstone, Hart and Davie (1987, 1989, 1991)

tionship while controlling for both age and educational attainment. As Table 5–5 indicates, those with post-secondary credentials have generally maintained high participation rates in adult education regardless of their employment statuses. There is no indication that highly qualified workers who are underemployed are losing their interest in further education.

On the other hand, for those under thirty and with high school diplomas or less, *there is a rapidly growing positive relationship between underqualified status in one's job and participation in further education.* That is, young people without post-secondary credentials who are underqualified for their jobs are now more likely than any other category of workers to take further education, about *two-thirds* of them were enroled in courses during 1990. In fact, most young drop-outs now do not stay drop-outs but go back to school within several years (see Thomas, in this book). For both older and more highly schooled groups, the effects of mismatched employment statuses are more mixed.

But there is little indication in any of these sub-groups that underemployment status has become a substantial disincentive to participation in adult education programs. Thus, while young underqualified workers with few credentials are increasingly being drawn into adult education programs, the underemployed in most age and educational levels are continuing to participate in comparable proportions to most others. Further analysis also indicates that participation rates are unaffected by widespread perceptions of a surplus of current post-secondary graduates for commensurate jobs (Livingstone, Hart and Davie, 1987). Hence, the pattern of chronic workplace underutilization of the education of highly qualified workers shows little sign of abating through their diminishing use of non-formal adult education programs.

Resolving the Contradiction

There *are* alternatives to continuing toleration of the gap between popular educational demands and chronic workplace underutilization of working peoples'

Table 5-5: Adult Education Participation Rate by Educational Attainment-Job Requirement Match, Controlling for Age and Educational Attainment, Employed Ontario Labour Force, 1986-1990

	Adult Education Participation Rate(%)											
	Less Than High School			High School Diploma			Community College Certificate			University Degree		
Age Group	86	88	90	86	88	90	86	88	90	86	88	90
Total Labour Force												
Underemployed	-	-	-	19	30	21	35	41	47	23	40	48
Matched	10	21	19	33	28	39	26	41	46	54	46	45
Underqualified	16	16	24	40	46	35	48	29	44	-	-	-
Under 30												
Underemployed	-	-	-	17	30	25	32	47	62	27	36	36
Matched	14	31	29	31	39	45	27	28	55	54	62	62
Underqualified	17	38	65	33	46	76	*	*	*	-	-	-
30-44												
Underemployed	-	-	-	21	20	23	43	37	48	24	52	53
Matched	14	22	26	22	36	45	27	48	44	46	43	42
Underqualified	13	16	19	34	41	34	*	*	*	-	-	-

* N < 5 cases.

Source: Livingstone, Hart and Davie (1987, 1989, 1991)

competencies, other than the incremental expansion of non-formal adult education. We could break the still dominant lockstep mentality in formal education. For example, adult workers could be given much greater opportunities and support to engage in short-term, full-time formal studies, while co-operative work-study programs for school-aged youths could expand correspondingly. More radically, we could consider dismantling portions of the compulsory formal school system and allocating the resources on an equitable per capita non-profit basis, to be used when needed in community-based non-formal education networks.

The central point here is that dominant modern economic and educational institutions must be fundamentally transformed in order to respond to the growing need for *multiple substantial transitions* between education and employment, a need which the increasing demand for non-formal education partially demonstrates.[11] To give governmental priority to more lockstep "stay-in-school" initiatives is to ignore this reality. For example, the extraordinary recent increase in the adult participation rate of underqualified young workers with few credentials expresses an almost desperate plea for another real chance at formal education.

Workers' increasing qualifications, popular educational demand and the growing centrality of information technologies in production systems are intimately related within current "neo-Fordist" and "post-Fordist" economic restructuring initiatives. A central preoccupation of nearly all these emerging models of organization is to more fully address human learning potential within the workplace (e.g., Lojkine, 1986; Mathews et al., 1988; Streeck, 1989). Whether the dominant new form of enterprise is an economic democracy based on worker self-management, genuine versions of participatory management and workplace humanization, or merely the introduction of "team" methods within established hierarchies of corporate power, a more active discretionary use of many workers' knowledge is likely to be needed. If authorities simply maintain the lockstep formal school system while condoning the ad hoc growth of non-formal adult courses, this is unlikely to satisfy the related popular demand for genuine lifelong education.

---

[11] For brief illustrations of alternative design principles that can be used to build an authentic permanent education culture, see Reed (1981) and Curtis et al., (1992).

6

Universities, Graduates, and the Marketplace: Canadian Patterns and Prospects

Paul Anisef and Paul Axelrod

To many proponents of liberal education, the identity, self-image, and mythology of the university are bound up in the academic mission of "pursuing knowledge for its own sake." Yet outside the institution, and often within, the "relevance" and utility of higher education are continuously in question. Throughout this century, universities have been expected to promote economic and/or social goals, and the support they elicit from governments, employers, taxpayers, and "consumers" is frequently tied to general perceptions of how well they fulfil these functions.

Research Problem

In a recent report, based on interviews with twenty-one provincial treasurers, education ministers and their deputies, and prepared for the Commission of Inquiry on Canadian University Education, universities were the subject of a number of criticisms (Deverell, 1991). In particular, it was alleged that universities have done almost nothing to assess the career performances of their graduates as an indicator of university performance. This paper will address this issue by reporting on findings from a survey of institutional researchers and academic vice-presidents in sixty-five degree granting institutions in Canada (Anisef, and Baichman-Anisef, 1991). A total of thirty-eight universities responded to this survey, constituting a 58 percent response rate. The sample distribution by region closely approximated that for all sixty-five universities, meaning that we can have confidence that the findings adequately reflect beliefs and values at the national level (Anisef and Baichman-Anisef, 1991).

Institutional researchers and academic vice-presidents were asked to evaluate the position of their university with respect to monitoring employers' and graduates' satisfaction with the skills acquired by graduates. Intensity of concern; variation in concern by department or faculty; whether and how monitoring occurred; what obstacles hindered the use of employer/graduate surveys; and the uses of survey information, were among the issues addressed in this study.

Before reporting on the findings of the institutional research survey, it is instructive to place the problem into historical perspective. What have been the (changing) demands on Canadian universities since the mid–19th century in terms of the relationship among universities, employers and university graduates? Why has "relevance" become a popular buzzword during the 1990s? How have students' orientations altered with respect to university education? In addition to developing the historical context, it is also important to document the employment experiences of university graduates.

Historical Context

Society makes material demands upon universities, but the substance of these demands, and the environment in which they are issued, has changed over time. In the mid–19th century, university students were steeped primarily in religious and classical teachings. In the early 20th century North American universities enhanced their utility and broadened their public appeal, particularly among the middle classes, by becoming training grounds for aspiring professionals whose educational and cultural values befit their social backgrounds and anticipated vocations (Axelrod, 1990: 160–5). In the 1940s, universities further served "practical" needs by providing manpower and research for the war effort, and then by enroling on an emergency basis, thousands of post-war veterans (Pilkington, 1983).

During the 1960s, a period of sustained economic growth, universities prospered from the widespread acceptance by economists, business, and government agencies of the human capital theory: the belief that heavy investment in human resources, including education, would contribute to economic development and higher standards of living. Notably, business leaders defended "investing" in general education and the liberal arts in the expectation that broadly trained graduates would make valuable employees (Axelrod, 1982: ch. 1–2). The expanding public sector played a particularly important role in recruiting university degree holders into social service positions in such areas as school teaching, and health and welfare (Novek, 1985; Department of the Secretary of State, 1990). It was assumed as well that by extending educational opportunities to an increasing percentage of the population, universities would serve as instruments of equity and social justice (Anisef, 1985). The unprecedented support for the expansion of higher education was thus sustained by the popular belief that educational spending would contribute to economic growth and social progress.

During the recessions of the 1970s and 80s, this unqualified faith in the value of higher education was undermined by the legacy of student uprisings, by a growing concern with the level of public expenditures and deficits, and by further questions, sometimes from academics themselves, about the quality of teaching and learning in the university (Axelrod, 1982; Rea, 1987; Bercuson et al., 1984). In addition, surveys began to document either the 'overeducation' or 'underemployment' of university graduates. Overeducation was considered a consequence of education systems not adjusting to new job realities, while underemployment was primarily seen as a result of the job market not keeping pace with labour market supply.

Universities survived during this period, increasing their enrolments significantly, but they were supported at levels far below their real needs. According to a 1990 report by the Ontario Council on University Affairs, if "the future were the past" with respect to university funding, "by 1995–96, deficits within the system will mount to such an extent that to balance the combined budgets of the universities within this grant and tuition structure, two universities [in Ontario] the size of Western and Ottawa would have to be closed" (Ontario Council on University Affairs, 1990).

As the funding problems of universities intensify during the 1990s, the "relevance" of higher education is a continuing, indeed, growing preoccupation. The 60s rhetoric celebrating the ideal of universal accessibility to post-secondary education has given way in some quarters to the more limited notions of "selective" accessibility and restricted enrolment. While the public is apparently reluctant to limit access to higher education, a number of educators, businessmen and politicians have questioned the principle — and the affordability — of universality (Livingstone, Hart, Davie, 1991: 16–17).

University programs and research projects too are increasingly drawing selective as opposed to general support from public and private sector sponsors. Academic activities designed to enhance the country's competitive position in the global marketplace appear especially favoured. State supported funding agencies — even those in the arts — like the Social Sciences and Humanities Research Council, now provide "strategic" research grants in areas of so-called "national importance," such as "education and work in a changing society" and "managing for global competitiveness." Newly established "Centres of Excellence" on university campuses similarly elicit special funding because of their perceived contribution to economic and technological development (SSHRC, 1990; and *CAUT Bulletin*, Dec. 1990: 14).

According to recent surveys, students too, are especially concerned with the investment value of university training. Facing an uncertain economic climate, they want to ensure that their university experience will provide a gateway to secure and lucrative careers. There is some evidence that the more academic and esoteric dimensions of university life hold less sway for students today than was the case for previous generations (Levine, Riedel 1987: 274).

From a purely academic perspective, this selective interest in the marketability of the university "product" can be intellectually and culturally limiting. Potentially, it devalues the importance of the "non-monetary" dimensions of the university mission, including the cultivation of "pure" research, of critical thinking, of aesthetic sensibilities, and of cultural breadth (Neilson and Gaffield, 1986). Nevertheless, recent developments suggest that the preoccupation with the economic function of higher education, particularly its job-training capacity, is unlikely to diminish in the years ahead. Employers, governments, students, and the public at large appear interested in fostering even closer links between post-secondary education and the marketplace, and university policy makers are likely to find these views difficult to ignore in the years ahead.

University Graduate Surveys: Findings and Issues

In this section we review findings pertinent to the employment experiences of university graduates in varying fields of study. Included among the experiences are degrees obtained, unemployment rates, and part-time employment rates. Most information concerning the employment experiences of university graduates derive from national (and some provincial) graduate surveys, the methodologies of which have varied through the years. The most comprehensive graduate surveys were conducted by Statistics Canada in conjunction with the Department of the Secretary of State. These include: a 1978 survey of 1976 post-secondary graduates (all fields and levels, excluding graduates from Quebec); a 1984 survey of 1982 post-secondary graduates (all fields and levels); a follow-up survey in 1987 of the 1982 graduates and a 1988 survey of 1986 university graduates (all fields and levels) (Department of the Secretary of State, 1990). After reviewing the findings we will explore the policy implications of using different indicators for monitoring the employment experiences of university graduates.

University Degrees and Fields of Study

In 1988, 143,700 university degrees were granted in Canada, an increase of 39 percent since 1975. Almost 86 percent or 132,000 of the degrees were at the Bachelor's level. This represents an increase of 29 percent over those graduating in 1975.

The major fields of study in which a degree may be obtained include: Humanities; Social Sciences; Business/Commerce and Administration; Agricultural/Biological Sciences; Health Professions; Mathematics/Physical Sciences including Computer Science.

Bachelor's level graduates include those earning undergraduate degrees in the above areas and first professional degrees in Law, Medicine, Dentistry, Education and Theology. While the scope of our study emphasizes the undergraduate level, it also includes a consideration of first professional degrees.

The three most popular fields of study among 1975 university graduates were Education (25%), Social Services (20%) and Humanities (13%). By 1988, the largest group of graduates earning degrees was in the Social Sciences (24%). The proportion of graduates earning degrees in Education decreased substantially to 16 percent. This decline is generally attributed to the anticipated drop in demand for elementary and secondary school teachers that followed declining birth rates in the 1970s and 1980s. Graduates in Computer Sciences quadrupled since 1975 while the proportion of graduates in other fields remained stable.

Unemployment Rates

University degree holders experience levels of unemployment significantly below the national average. In the 15 to 24 age cohort, the unemployment rate for secondary school graduates in 1989 was 14 percent while university graduates in the same age group experienced an unemployment rate of only 4.8 percent. Results of the 1988 National Survey of the Graduates of 1986 show that only a fraction of graduates experienced chronic unemployment with Fine/Applied arts graduates experiencing the highest level (10% were unemployed 7 months or more). In contrast, graduates in the Health Professions experienced the lowest level of unemployment (only 2% were unemployed 7 months or more after graduation).

A similar study of 1985 Quebec Bachelor's level graduates showed that 92 percent of graduates in the labour force were employed in 1987. Again, Fine/Applied Arts graduates were the least likely to find employment (78%) while Health Services and Mathematics graduates experienced the highest level of employment (98%) (Audet, 1989). A 1986 Ontario government employment survey of 1985 Ontario University graduates showed that the average unemployment rate across fields of study for those who were in the labour force one year after graduation was 7 percent. Health professionals enjoyed the lowest rate of unemployment (2%) while graduates in Fine/Applied Arts had the highest rate (13%) (Denton, et al., 1987).

Care should be taken in drawing conclusions about the relationship of degrees to the success of finding employment, particularly when examining the unemployment rates of graduates at the Bachelor's level a short time after graduation. Data from the 1988 survey of 1986 graduates, and 1987 survey of 1982 graduates allows us to compare university graduates with a maximum of two years in the labour market to those with up to five years experience (Department of the Secretary of State, 1990: 33–36). The figures show that unemployment rates decline as time in the labour market increases. While 1986 Social Science graduates showed an unemployment rate of 12 percent in 1988, the 1982 Social Science graduates rate of unemployment was only 5 percent in 1987. Fine/Applied Arts graduates showed an even higher discrepancy with 16 percent of 1986 graduates not having found employment in 1988 while the 1982 cohort only experienced a 4 percent rate of unemployment in 1987.

Part-Time Employment Rates

While the level of unemployment decreased with time spent in the labour force, overall part-time employment rates for all graduates remained stable. Thus, the proportion of graduates employed part-time two years (in 1988) or five years (in 1987) after graduation was 10 percent. There are however major variations by field of study. By way of illustration, graduates of the 1987 survey in Engineering and Business were almost universally employed on a full time basis whereas Fine/Applied Arts graduates had the highest level of part-time employment even five years after graduation. In the 1988 survey two reasons were equally mentioned for part-time employment — the inability to find a full-time job and the fact that they were attending school on a part-time basis. In the 1987 survey, the inability to find full-time employment was given most frequently.

Methodological Issues and Policy Implications

In assessing the match between education and jobs attained by university graduates, researchers have employed a variety of indicators. These include: a ranking by graduates of how important it was that their jobs be related to their field of study; whether in the view of graduates, their jobs related, partly related or did not relate at all to their programs of study; whether, in the opinion of graduates, the program they had taken was necessary for the job; whether graduates' educational qualifications were required by employers for performing the job; and whether graduates would repeat their program of study.

Our review of graduate surveys — their methodologies and findings — lead to a number of observations (Department of the Secretary of State, 1990: 37–45). First, there has been a change in the perspective taken in doing graduate surveys. Initially, university graduates were followed up as early as six months after graduation. But it was subsequently recognized that the articulation of higher education and employment experiences of graduates was subject to change over time. A careful reading of substantive findings reveal that with time, the subjective definition of educational relevance by university graduates, particularly in some major fields of study vary — sometimes substantially. For example, classics graduates fared poorly on employment measures two years after graduation — only 50 percent stated that they would do the same program. But five years after graduation, 86 percent claimed that they would repeat their program of study — the highest score in the humanities.

Care must also be taken in drawing conclusions about the relationship of degrees to success in finding employment, particularly when examining the unemployment rates of graduates at the baccalaureate level a short time after graduation. Data from two follow-up surveys of graduates two and five years after graduation reveal that unemployment rates decline as time in the labour force increases. This suggests that a systematic monitoring of graduates requires the use of short, medium and long-term perspectives depending on what one is trying to learn.

Second, the issue of selecting an appropriate mix of educational relevance indicators needs to be resolved. As Teichler (1989) indicates, a number of European studies cast doubt on the value of establishing any single index of appropriateness. The facets of appropriateness are simply too heterogeneous and any one job may be considered appropriate on one level (e.g., knowledge utilization) but inappropriate on another (e.g., position held). Teichler concludes that:

> Obviously, a broad range of indicators has to be taken into consideration in any analysis of the relationship between education and work that tries to establish how many graduates do have 'appropriate' work? From a comparison of various research approaches, no criteria emerge as particularly suitable. Obviously, the difficulties in choosing a limited set of clear criteria for analyzing which work is 'appropriate' to

one's abilities relates to the diversity of the links between higher education and work (p. 235).

It would appear that insufficient attention has been paid by Canadian researchers to whether available indicators provide valid measures of the match between higher education and jobs.

Employers

(i) Nature of Concern

Institutional research officers were asked how much concern there was at their institution with respect to employers' satisfaction with the skills acquired by Bachelor of Arts graduates. A majority expressed either very strong or strong concern (51.6%) while a minority (25.8%) felt little concern about employers' satisfaction.

Those institutions expressing concern employed a number of strategies to address this matter, including: sponsoring an all day conference to discuss issues related to university accountability; undertaking a communications survey which asked employers to assess the quality of the university's graduates and education; and introducing into the curriculum (by one university) ten internship options, which included two-to-four month work terms following students' second and third years of study. It should be noted that some universities that felt compelled to consider employers' views of graduate employability also believed that such concern could inappropriately narrow the scope of undergraduate education.

Institutions indicating little concern with employers' satisfaction expressed the view that training for the workplace should not take precedence over the university's responsibility to provide a high quality undergraduate education. One spokesperson claimed that by its very nature, undergraduate work will provide students with the skills that employers are looking for. Another noted that the skills acquired by graduates are varied, used in different time spans, respond to changing perceptions of their utility, and are thus difficult to measure.

(ii) Variation of Concern by Faculty or Department

Over half of the researchers/academic vice-presidents (57.1%) claimed that the level of concern varied by faculty or department. Those that perceived such variations generally agreed that more concern with employer satisfaction existed in professional and quasi-professional departments and programs than in Arts and Science faculties. On some campuses with professional and co-operative programs, structural arrangements are made with business organizations that allow for feedback on employers' satisfaction with skills acquired by graduates. Some Social Science departments, such as Geography, Sociology, and Political Science take into account the applied value of their degrees, more so than do departments in the Humanities. Certain program variants, like the Bachelor of Community Studies, are by nature vocationally oriented. One respondent noted that students' chances of finding employment depend on market forces over which the universities have no control.

(iii) Institutional Methods for Monitoring Satisfaction

Only a minority (22.6%) of institutional researchers indicated that their institutions monitor the satisfaction of employers with the skills acquired by their B.A. graduates. Strategies mentioned by researchers for assessing satisfaction include: informal (as opposed to systematic) feedback from employers; the use of co-operative program coordinators who visit students at their place of work and report back to the relevant departments; monitoring graduates at various stages of their careers through a joint longitudinal research project designed to assess the match between employee skill development and workplace requirements as perceived by the employer. One institution has adopted an evaluations' policy that takes into account the opinions of outside experts in analyzing course content. Another institution invites employers to comment on the potential for job opportunities arising out of new academic programs, and encourages ongoing employer assessments.

Researchers were also asked whether their institutions assessed the satisfaction of employers with the skills acquired by baccalaureate graduates other than B.A.s; 48 percent indicated that their institutions did such evaluations. These surveys are generally conducted in professional faculties. Frequently universities depend on professional bodies such as professional engineering associations, business councils, the College of Physicians and Surgeons, and accounting organizations to obtain information on employer satisfaction. Faculties of Education receive feedback from various boards of education. At one institution, detailed program evaluations in a variety of areas are conducted by advisory committees, which include external representation from professional bodies and employers. Efforts are made to examine societal needs, academic quality, and financial viability.

(iv) Utilizing the Information

All universities that monitor employer satisfaction subsequently use the information collected. Major uses include: feedback to the department for curriculum planning purposes; direction of graduates to specific companies where it is expected they will be most welcome; university fund-raising; data input for institutional analysis; career counselling; and enrolment planning.

(v) Obstacles in Monitoring Satisfaction

Nearly 75 percent of all institutional researchers/academic vice-presidents claimed not to use measures of employer satisfaction. A major reason for this was insufficient financial and human resources. In addition, a variety of institutions expressed the view that the Bachelor of Arts degree is seen as a general education rather than as a professional or job training program. Others noted that employers have not been very vocal about wanting a voice in academic planning. Beyond complaining generally about the literacy level of graduates, most employers have not specified how they would place their concerns on the university agenda. Some institutions questioned the value of such information even if it could be elicited.

At the same time, when asked whether their institutions would employ measures to monitor employer satisfaction with the skills acquired by B.A. graduates, should obstacles to their use be removed, the vast majority (82.6%) responded affirmatively. According to institutional spokespersons, such studies could provide one of several indicators of institutional success. They could help the university plan and recruit effectively, and increase its sensitivity to society's needs. If adequate resources were supplied, the university could hire staff to research and track placement results. It was also suggested that these studies could encourage employer participation in university life. An Employer Advisory Group might serve as a consultant to the university on a continuing basis.

Baccalaureate Graduates

(i) Nature of Concern

Concerns expressed regarding the satisfaction of B.A. graduates by institutional researchers include: the ways in which graduates' career decisions match their interests, skills, values and goals; the degree of satisfaction expressed by students with respect to the teaching skills of their professors; the degree to which B.A. graduates meet the institution's learning objectives and are able to transfer that learning throughout their lifetime; the degree to which graduates have learned how to think critically, write well, and analyze logically; the difficulty faced by students who are undecided about their futures; and the ability of the university to serve students, the region, and society as a whole.

Concerns expressed pertaining to the satisfaction of graduates other than B.A.s include: the ways in which academic training is relevant to the practical and technical skills required in the work environment; the degree to which professional training and laboratory facilities remain current; and the degree to which the institution is able to meet the demands for graduates from specific professional areas.

(ii) Monitoring Satisfaction Through Existing Surveys

Researchers were asked to indicate whether existing provincial, federal, management consultant or other kinds of surveys were employed within their institution for the purpose of assessing the educational relevance of university studies for baccalaureate graduates. Provincial surveys were the most frequently mentioned type of survey employed (44.7%), followed by federal surveys (28.9%) and management consultant surveys (15.8%).

(iii) Institutional Methods for Monitoring Satisfaction

Researchers were asked whether their institution employed strategies for monitoring the satisfaction of B.A. graduates; a minority (34.3%) responded affirmatively to this question. We asked this latter group how their institution assessed the satisfaction of graduates, to comment on the timing of surveys and why these assessments are performed.

Many institutions monitor their graduates' satisfaction by informal rather than formal means through such vehicles as alumni associations, and career and placement centres. A number of institutions employ more systematic assessments. One surveys all of its B.A. graduates one year after graduation. Another surveys all of its graduates two years after graduation, polling them on their subsequent education, employment, income, and satisfaction with their employment. They are also asked to assess the contribution of their university education to specific areas of personal and skill development.

Researchers were also asked whether their institution assessed the satisfaction of graduates of other faculties at the baccalaureate level. The majority (57%) indicated that efforts to monitor the satisfaction of other than B.A. graduates were in place at their institution. The faculties/departments mentioned most were: Engineering, Nursing, Physical Education and Recreation, Science, Business Administration and Education. These surveys are conducted both by Alumni Affairs offices and program departments. The data on the success of graduates might provide insight into the perceived relevance of education to career experience.

(iv) Utilization of the Information

Institutions employing such surveys assessing the satisfaction of graduates pointed to their use in student career planning and in placement counselling, and in planning student services. This information is also provided to university and departmental planners, and may aid the process of curriculum development and revision.

(v) Obstacles to Monitoring Satisfaction

Most researchers (72.7%) indicated that there are obstacles to employing measures of satisfaction of graduates in their institutions. It should be noted that all researchers identifying such obstacles claimed that it would make sense to use measures of satisfaction, if the obstacles were to be removed.

A major obstacle mentioned by researchers and academic vice-presidents in measuring the satisfaction of graduates was the difficulty of defining an appropriate measure of satisfaction. Students and faculty frequently have different expectations with respect to educational outcomes. For students, short-term outcomes (e.g., professional job-related and professional training) are valued while faculty and programs stress broader and longer term educational needs. Satisfaction measures must reflect both of these perspectives. Another obstacle included the lack of resources available to collect and use such studies. Systemic budget constraints further diminish the priority of this activity.

Conclusions

Our review of findings of the institutional research survey conducted in the spring of 1991 should serve to place in perspective the impression of universities as being indifferent to the assessment of career performance of graduates. Institutional researchers are not at all opposed to such evaluations. Indeed, they strongly endorse the use of regular assessments of both baccalaureate graduates and their employers, emphasizing that such surveys should take place one and five years after graduation.

Researchers also voiced a concern, supported by our literature review, about the lack of consensus on appropriate measures for evaluating graduate satisfaction or satisfaction by employers with graduates. Exclusive concern for short-term outcomes such as professional training makes little sense. Rather, satisfaction measures should include both a broader range of indicators and span an extended period. Because their perspectives on the value of their education may change as they mature, graduates should be surveyed several years after they leave university.

It should also be stressed that the level of concern with monitoring employer and graduate satisfaction varies significantly by faculty, department and program. Professional faculties are consistently more concerned with the vocational destinations of their graduates and the satisfaction of employers than the typical liberal art faculties where the academic content is deemed to be less directly related to work experience.

While fewer than a third of universities have a system in place for monitoring their own graduates and even fewer monitor employers of university baccalaureates, the benefits derived from gathering this type of information are considered to be significant. Nevertheless, there are serious obstacles both to collecting and applying such data. Some are financial — universities lack the resources to undertake these tasks. Others are methodological — researchers confirmed the conclusion arising out of our literature review: that there is a lack of consensus on appropriate methods for evaluating both graduate and employer satisfaction. Still other obstacles are ideological — there are concerns about how this instrumentalist focus might distort the academic mission of higher education.

It should be stressed that the degree of interest in monitoring employer and graduate satisfaction varies significantly by faculty, department and program. Professional faculties are consistently more concerned with the vocational destinations of their graduates and the satisfaction of employers than the typical liberal art faculties where the academic content is deemed to be less directly related to work experience.

The tension between the cultural and utilitarian orientation of higher education has a long history (Axelrod, 1990: ch. 3–4), and the sustained financial restraint experienced by universities over the last two decades has served to sharpen the perceived contradictions between these values. Proponents of market-driven efficiency favour research, teaching, and training programs that reflect the changes and demands of the global economy. Critics contend that universities following this course risk losing their academic integrity and institutional autonomy (Axelrod, 1986; Newson and Buchbinder, 1988; Sanayal, 1990; Bell, 1990).

If employer and graduate surveys are to be of value to universities attempting to respond to community concerns about the "relevance" of higher education, then the following conclusions bear consideration. First, such surveys must be methodologically more sophisticated than has generally been the case. Because graduates' views about the value of their education may change the longer they are out of school, surveys should be developed in ways that elicit long-term perspectives. Furthermore, researchers should encourage respondents to comment broadly on the value of university education, with respect to *both* cultural and economic factors. Measures of "satisfaction" that are crude and simplistic are of minimal value and are likely to be ignored. In addition, it is important to acknowledge the ideological and political tensions that such surveys might well elicit within the academy. Evaluations of university education that are perceived to privilege professional and graduate training over undergraduate studies and "pure" research could exacerbate conflict over the allocation of scarce resources. Finally, survey researchers and planners must be sensitive to the perceptions, needs, and changing nature of the student constituency itself as it negotiates the school-work transition.

PART II
PERSPECTIVES AND RESEARCH METHODOLOGIES

7

Transitions: From School to Work and Back: A New Paradigm

Alan M. Thomas

This paper contains some challenge to the dominant theme of the collection of which it is a part. For that reason it seems appropriate to begin with some reflections on the language commonly used in discussions of the relationships of "school" and "work."

There is some historical innocence surely, in the implications of the title, not peculiar to this collection by any means, that "school" is not "work." Recalling such familiar terms as "home-work," and "school-work," suggests why most students would or should respond to the implication with some indignation. What exists here is the confusion of the terms "work" and "employment," a common confusion, which is probably a deliberate phenomenon of labour-market economies. However, if we are to make sense of the principal topic, it is essential to resist that confusion, by making clear that what we are talking about mainly is employment, work or effort that is valued, and therefore rewarded by the same labour market economies.

In addition, when this confusion is combined with the word "transition," used in the singular, we are further ignoring the fundamental realities with which we are trying to cope, or at least, to understand.

The substitution of the term "employment," gets us closer to the truth, though not all the way. A glance at the lives of older students, particularly graduate students in Canada, with their legitimate "educational trade unions," and more particularly at the lives of such students in other societies, makes it difficult to distinguish many aspects of student life from those arising from employment. However, it is arguable that the roles are distinguishable, and that we will gain greater clarity by talking about "from student to employee" in place of "from school to work." Indeed the word "from" is perhaps misleading, suggesting only one direction. The word "between" will, in our opinion, reflect more clearly the series of exchanges that increasingly characterize the behaviour we wish to understand.

That is to say that what is involved is the interchange between roles defined and created by two large systems, education and employment. The relationships between these two systems and the indigenous roles have been changing relentlessly, and are not as the dominant theme suggests, clearly understood. It is wise at this stage to remind ourselves that these interchanges are basically human rather than predominantly conceptual or technological.

For example, the use of the word "transition," in the singular, distorts the actual circumstances. If we wish only to address ourselves to one transition, that is the first formal movement of a young person (increasing numbers can be described as young only out of formal courtesy) from uninterrupted, full-time, student life, to full-time employee life, then a great many realities will have to be ignored. On the one hand a great many students, not all of them young, even in the academic secondary schools in this province, are part-time employees. They are engaged, much earlier than current educational or employment discourse allows, in the concurrent exchange of the two roles in question. On the other hand, Canada, unlike Japan, for instance, is already characterized by the repeated interchange of student and employee roles, both concurrently and consecutively, by increasing numbers of older individuals. For example, there are the increasing numbers of women who exchange domestic (surely to be included in work), student, and employee roles, concurrently and consecutively. The thrust of this paper is to acknowledge and, with some qualifications, welcome these developments, and to argue that even the classical "transition" can neither be understood nor made to function, efficiently or equitably, unless it is understood, and accepted, as one among many in individual life times.

The Limits of Education

Under the heading, "Building the System Around Lifelong Learning" the recently issued Federal Government Discussion Paper *Learning Well...Living Well* states:

> Finally, and perhaps most importantly, learning cultures are built around the notion of lifelong learning. Much of Canada's educational arrangements are still based on the antiquated notion of "the three boxes" (the childhood and adolescent years, the working years, and retirement) in which nearly all formal learning occurs in the first box. A learning system for the 21st Century must operate on the assumption that learning, training, and education, is a continual lifelong process (1991: S–4).

While motives may be suspect, the use of the concept of learning muddled, and the perspective about twenty years behind the times, the document remains the first official, formal commitment by the Canadian Federal Government to what would be better called "continuing education." While the report is depressingly ignorant of the extent of participation in lifelong learning by Canadians, it does serve to underline, that in terms of "system," "continuing education" in Canada is haphazard, inefficient, and largely inequitable in its present form. From another source:

> Our present education system is an archipelago with universities constituting one island, high schools another, primary and elementary schools another, and community colleges yet another. The ferry service between these islands is infrequent and unpredictable. What we shall need for the 21st century...is a series of fixed links between the islands in order to mobilize and coordinate all of our considerable educational resources in the interest of the people and the society we serve... (*People and Skills in the New Global Economy*, 1990: 79–90).

Both reports reflect not only the current difficulties of movement by individuals within the system of education, but the equal difficulties of gaining access to it in any other role than that of the conventional student.

The outstanding characteristic of any formal educational system has been its self-containment. Success for students is based upon achievement in terms of experience provided by the system itself, that is in terms of the "form" of learning promoted by that system. While the education system has assumed the status of providing all formal education, in fact it provides only the dominant one. There are other forms of education and learning as every learner knows. As long as the formal system, with its formidable "certifying" power, was concerned only with the young, and the classic one-time transition from student to employee prevailed, we did not fundamentally contest its self-absorption. But that limited concern is no longer the case. The age of students is rising at all levels of education, and the certifying power of the system has come to be accepted ever more widely throughout the affairs of employees and employers, in fact throughout the entire society.

The situation in Canada, in this respect, is markedly different from Japan, where a system of what might be called "multi-educationalism" keeps these two sectors much more separate (Thomas, 1991). These developments combined with the steady growth of learning opportunities and demands outside the educational system lead us to be less and less willing to accept the intellectual "hegemony" of the schools. It is apparent that there has always been learning outside of the dominant culture and its teaching agencies (Ginzburg, 1976). A prominent source of the modern growth of external learning, and in some cases extensive teaching, can be traced to the rise of the oil companies in the twenties and thirties, the glamour industries of those years, where internally sponsored research produced specialized knowledge not generally, or even academically available (Clark and Sloan, 1958; Eurich, 1985).

The willingness of North American employers to support the certification functions of the schools has stimulated the increasing demand for "employable" graduates, and for the opportunity of multiple entries and exits. Basically there are two forms in which this relationship manifests itself in varying guises. The most familiar examples are found in the rapidly growing co-operative education movement (Ellis, 1987) and in the more traditional system of apprenticeship. In the first case, the school reaches into employment in order to meet its objectives; in the second, employment reaches into the schools. An examination of the political, economic, and intellectual problems associated with each of these means of interchange can be very revealing. The need for more thorough comparative analysis than the two practices have received, so far, is compelling. However, it is in the less structured forms of exchange that we meet the more interesting problems and opportunities.

The logic of the formal system requires that progress through it be undertaken basically on its own terms. Formally, a person who leaves the system at any point, must reenter at the point of departure, and complete the ritual process. Anything other than that is regarded, oddly enough by authorities and students alike, as less than ideal. The notion that the alternative experience might be more effective than the idealized one, for some learners, has so far received little sympathy. However, just as in the sixties and seventies, experiments within the system concentrated on student roles (Gould, 1974), in the eighties and nineties there has been experiment with various means of gaining access to that system in a way that does not discount external learning, thereby demeaning the learner, and that promotes the more efficient use of formal resources by eliminating the need to teach what has already been learned in other settings.

Almost every one in education is familiar with the range of devices that have become increasingly prominent in recent years. Transitional years, challenge exams, maturity credits at the secondary school level, CLEP, and the evaluation and acceptance of whole programs, as in the case of the American Armed Services, are all means to account for learning objectives achieved outside of the formal system of education. In general, these activities are lumped under the term *Prior Learning Assessment* (PLA).

They can be classified in two primary ways. The first is on the basis of whether they are "program" evaluations, where learning programs provided systematically by large non-educational systems are regularly evaluated by representatives of educational agencies, (American Council for Education, 1976) or whether they are individual evaluations arising from the unique experience of each individual applicant (Council for Adult and Experiential Learning (CAEL), 1977). The second is based on the nature of the evaluation procedures, that is, whether they are essentially indigenous to the formal educational system such as the written examination or whether they are drawn from other areas of experience, such as the celebrated individual "portfolio" used extensively in the United States and the United Kingdom. We are, of course, dealing with a continuum and therefore an enormous range of combinations. While we intend to concentrate on one area, Prior Learning Assessment, which emphasizes individuals and predominantly non-formal procedures, other practices are proliferating and demand systematic investigation and public recognition.

To recapitulate, the exchange between student and employee role is a frequent and multiple phenomena, beginning with the first part-time employment entered into by the secondary school student, either after school or during the summer, continuing throughout the whole of adult life in a great variety of forms, and perhaps concluding at retirement. Some individuals abandon or escape the employee role forever, but combine the role of retiree with the student role in such manifestations as the Chinese universities for the elderly, and the growing North American agencies, the Seniors' Institutes and Elderhostels. A common phenomenon is that these exchanges are both concurrent, as reflected in the steadily increasing numbers of part-time students, (Canadian Association for Adult Education, 1982) and consecutive, as reflected in the numbers of secondary school "stop-outs" who return several years later to complete their programs, or the growing numbers of middle-aged women returning to university on a full-time basis. The demand for such unconventional use of educational resources on the part of the Canadian public has grown steadily since the end of the second world war, even though educational authorities have for the most part exhibited a benign indifference (Livingstone, 1992).

These developments, as Livingstone demonstrates, produce their own ironies, not uncharacteristic of large systems trying to cope with fundamental changes. For example, while secondary schools and universities are developing various forms of "co-operative education" with enormous enthusiasm, a development openly supported by the Federal government, in word and deed they continue to ignore, if not deplore, learning achieved by students who find their own jobs. So much for the nurture of self-reliance and personal autonomy. Similarly the Federal government, with its "Stay in School Campaign," which promotes uninterrupted early education, has steadfastly ignored the fact that the Ontario Ministry of Education has reported that since it began counting "re-entrants" in 1986, more than half the stop-outs have returned to secondary school (Statistics, Ontario, 1986). An equal, more widespread anomaly, relentlessly supported by the press, has been to ignore the changes in age among students in Canada, at all levels of education. The CBC television program *Degrassi High* may be popular more because most of its audience is enjoying the nostalgia, than because it is a reflection of contemporary reality.

If we accept the reality of and need for multiple exits and entries for more than half of the population that now engages in them, then we must maximize the ease of these exchanges, while at the same time maintaining the integrity of the learner and of the certifying system. Both learners and providing agencies have a right to know what is available in terms of access and what might be tried. In addition, they have, from the moment of the very first exchange of these roles, the right and the obligation to learn and to teach the skills associated with such exchanges in order to maintain the most extensive freedom of access possible.

Prior Learning Assessment

Prior Learning Assessment (PLA) has been pioneered in the United States by the Council for Adult and Experiential Learning (CAEL, 1986), in the United Kingdom by the Learning from Experience Trust (Evans, 1984) and by other agencies in other countries. Sweden has experimented with and completed more research about PLA than perhaps any other country (Abrahamsson, 1986).

In 1986, CAEL reported:

1200 post-secondary institutions using one or more of the following means of granting credit for prior learning: national standardized examinations; the Military Guide (American Council for Education); the Guide to Training (American Council for Education); advanced placement, assessment by portfolio, challenge examinations; oral interviews; demonstration of competencies. Of these 527 had 25 or more students who entered the program by one of these procedures... Most recently CAEL has entered into a series of joint ventures in which formal agreements between large employers, large labour unions, and post-secondary institutions, have resulted in the identification of new and substantial bodies of potential students (Thomas, 1989a: 7).

Developments in the United Kingdom have stemmed in part from the introduction of the Council for National Academic Awards, which separates the achievement of a degree from the venue of study, and have been concentrated largely among the polytechnics.

In Canada, the most systematic development has been in the Province of Quebec, sponsored by the Federation of CEGEPS, and funded by the Federal and Quebec Governments (Isabelle, 1984). While that particular mechanism was discontinued in 1990, the practices seem well rooted at least among the CEGEPS. British Columbia has introduced a system of "credit-banking," somewhat comparable to that of the United Kingdom, and is experimenting with other means of admission. What all of these developments have in common is the separation of certification from specific teaching agencies, a development that immediately introduces greater flexibility, if not clarity, with respect to entrance and exit from the student role.

Two studies have been conducted in Canada with respect to large scale utilization of these practices. The national study (Thomas, 1989a) revealed the following patterns of development:

> More than half of all the respondents report the use of practices of granting admission to students who do not meet the conventional standards. However, more than half of those, with the highest number among the universities, the lowest among the Ministries, require some form of "in-house" academic achievement as a basis for confirming admission.

> Fewer than half of the universities, but nearly three-quarters of the colleges, and half the ministries, make provisions for granting advanced standing on the basis of the assessment of prior learning. There is considerable variation in the way this is done, ranging from exemption from some prerequisites for admission, to specialized programs, to granting full credit for particular courses.

> For all levels of education, these practices began to appear in Canada in the 1950s, with the Ministries making changes in admission, until the late 1970s, when the rate of introduction declined.

> There is almost no systematically gathered information regarding the numbers or characteristics of students who apply or are accepted under these procedures.

> With respect to informing potential students of the availability of these procedures, most agencies depend first upon their conventional instruments of information, and second upon word-of-mouth (Thomas, 1989a: 13–17).

The conclusion seems to be that these practices have been and are being introduced more widely than might have been supposed, but their availability is not widely advertised or apparent, and their usage is entirely at the pleasure of the teaching agencies. Only in Quebec and British Columbia do students have rights to such alternate assessments.

The second more limited study is essentially an evaluation of the policy of granting what are termed "maturity credits" in secondary education in the province of Ontario (Thomas, 1989b).

While this policy represents a somewhat blunt instrument for PLA, nevertheless it functions, according to the report, as a major instrument in facilitating reentry to secondary school.

> The "Equivalent Credit Policy" is in use in Ontario by almost all Public Boards of Education. ...it has grown steadily in terms of applicant volume since the early nineteen-eighties. Total numbers of applicants and recipients are difficult to obtain...
>
> The number of "maturity" or "life-experience credits outstrips the other two classes of "equivalents" (apprenticeship and other formal courses) by a considerable proportion. The assessment on which the award of these credits is based requires the greatest amount of individual judgment on the part of the assessor.
>
> Women outnumber men by about three to one in applying for and receiving equivalent credits, and in completing their programs.
>
> The bulk of the applicants are to be found in the 25–45 age groups. Applicants under twenty predominate in a few Boards, and everywhere present particular problems (Thomas, 1989b: 5).

There is, therefore, evidence of the growth of multiple exchanges of these roles, that is of transitions, throughout the lives of Canadians, and of a slow, and not much acknowledged growth of practices designed to facilitate them. There can be little doubt that the system(s) of support are halting, even grudging, and inequitable. For example it is now widely established in most industrial societies, including Canada, that the primary users of resources for the adult sector of continuing education, are those who have done well in their initial schooling (Waniewicz, 1976; Devereaux, 1985). The middle class, who originally introduced compulsory schooling, has been extremely successful at using most of the available public resources for adult education for itself. Information on "part-time" adult students reveals, in general, backgrounds of lower socio-economic standing than is characteristic of full-time students (CAAE, 1982). Those who are not successful in their initial schooling, for whatever reason, rarely find their way to greater educational achievement in their later years. To be sure they are offered increasing opportunities for training, but they seldom get the opportunity to return to the "educational" mainstream, except by means of some form of prior learning assessment. Despite its welcome affirmation of the value of lifelong learning, the Federal Discussion Paper reveals little acknowledgement of this situation or interest in alleviating it (Prosperity Secretariat, 1991).

Unresolved Issues

The underlying assumption is that Canada will need, and ought to support, if only for humanitarian reasons, the development of a better educated population in any future we can imagine. The trend in recent years to lower birth rates and steadily declining number of children and youth — the traditional source of better educated generations — means that more and more of the better educated, skilled, and highly trained population must come from existing and future generations of adults. The exchange of student and employee roles can only increase in frequency and occasion. Expectations and skills associated with managing these exchanges must become much more wide-spread among individuals and teaching agencies.

These developments raise some particularly urgent questions. First, to what degree should Canada depend upon its formal educational agencies for the provision of these opportunities (Livingstone, 1992)? While the present thrust of the PLA movement, particularly in the U.S., is exactly in that direction, the present thrust of the Canadian federal government is not. Instead it appears to be turning in the direction of reaching learning goals, in this case very narrowly conceived occupational skills, by other than educational means. However, as Livingstone demonstrates, Canadians have in the past indicated a profound belief in the dominant value of "formal education" as distinct from training and continue to expect increased access to educational providing agencies. The result has been that we have used our formal agencies for increasingly extended educational purposes, that is, extending it to older members of the population, while at the same time progressively maintaining an essentially class-based access throughout the system. All the evidence suggests that this is no longer supportable. It may be that with the declining numbers of young people there will be sufficient space in post-secondary providing agencies to accommodate the increased demands from older students. However, there is not much reason to believe, based on present and past experience, that these same agencies will demonstrate much enthusiasm for that development.

If that is to be the case, then we shall have to examine more closely the experiences of the American System, where the growth of PLA has been and remains driven by the existence of large numbers of small, private, post-secondary providing agencies. Their energies and hunger for students have fuelled PLA to a considerable extent. While it would be easy to be cynical about lowered standards and all the usual academic protective cover, there is no clear evidence in the U.S. that that has been the case. Instead, one can argue, that the movement has revealed and released talent and ability that the initial system was incapable of identifying and nurturing. The curious fact is that Canada is maintaining, and in fact encouraging, at the elementary and secondary level, the kind of mixed system of educational provision that it has systematically, over the past forty years, eliminated in post-secondary education. The emerging question is whether we can continue to do so with any hope of reaching the "learning culture" envisaged in the Federal document. The demand for the admission of private providing agencies to the post-secondary system may have to be evaluated in terms of the absolute limits of the public treasuries to meet all the vital learning objectives that must be met.

Whatever we decide, it is apparent that exchanges of student and employee roles will increase. A great many of them, those for example that take place entirely within the precincts of employers, will be less publicly visible, but they will be there. Studies of the development of Paid Educational Leave (Learning a Living in Canada, 1983) indicate that even with time and money made available by statute, individuals still have to learn the skills of interchange.

Second, what are the demands made by PLA on skill, time, and money? The most characteristic, or perhaps the most appealing procedure associated with PLA, is the compilation of the learner's "portfolio" of achievement. The guiding phrase arising from American experience in particular, is that it is not the experience itself or its length that is critical, but evidence of what has been learned from that experience. And there is the rub; to gather and demonstrate that evidence is demanding and time-consuming, requiring careful judgment on the side of both producer and consumer. Many U.S. providing agencies now offer something like a course, the purpose of which is to help the learner develop such a portfolio, which is then used for determining future admission and placement. Many of these portfolios are extremely moving testaments of individual lives, and one comes to the conclusion that the production of a portfolio itself is a useful educational enterprise for both learner and providing agency. It is clear that there is a need for educators to develop skills of assessment that go beyond grading papers, setting examinations, or assessing foreign credentials.

The reported research indicates that those skills have already been developed to a degree in Canada, but that they are rarely shared and little appreciated. Simple strategies such as inviting assessors at various levels to share their experience could be extremely valuable in the next few years. Any form of PLA is an intervention in the present forms of academic evaluation that extend over time, and less efficiently, over space, but have been thoroughly integrated into the financial structures of providing agencies. PLA makes new and novel demands on those imbedded practices. In the U.S., at least in some of the earlier years, the development of new procedures was funded by extra external money. That seems to be declining as more stable sources of funding such as the "portfolio-course" are found, and the new practices become more acceptable.

There is no point in denying the emergence of these extra costs, just as there is no point in allowing them to become excuses for avoiding the issues involved. We can draw upon the experiences in Quebec, the U.S., and elsewhere.

Third, it is clear that the surest way to reform a teaching agency is to alter the character of the student body. It may be slow, and painful for some, but it is inexorable. Formal education is a culture and its admission procedures are carefully designed to admit only those who have been properly prepared for that culture. The development of the use of PLA ensures the introduction into conventional providing agencies of students with quite different backgrounds than those they are used to. It may be that some of the cultural clashes will turn out to be unreconcilable, though there is not much evidence to that effect so far. We must be careful to acknowledge the likelihood of those clashes and not pretend they are something else, to be dismissed under the guise of lowering standards. Teaching agencies do function to release and nurture intelligence and human growth, but of particular kinds, more particular than we are often willing to admit. Students admitted by means of PLA are precisely those students who have learned in different "forms." It is possible to argue that in fact the careful use of PLA will engender the type of educational reform that is long overdue.

A certain amount of scepticism about the claim of threats to academic standards has been present throughout this paper. While the alarm often disguises an unwillingness to change anything, the issues involved cannot be easily dismissed. It is interesting that the research reported earlier (Thomas, 1989a) revealed that the most powerful support for utilizing PLA in Canadian universities and colleges came from administration, while the greatest hesitancy in their acknowledged use came from professors. It is undeniable that the "certifying" power that uniquely distinguishes "formal" education from other kinds is a matter of public protection. This appears to be a purpose that is valued by Canadians, and perhaps accounts for our inordinate use of the formal system for so many functions. The integrity of that function deserves protection, but not at all costs.

The closest comparison to the challenge presented by PLA might be found in the practice of the medieval Catholic church in granting indulgences. They were in fact prescribed learning programs designed to reduce the likelihood in the sinner of repeating the sin. Church history tells us all too clearly of the corruption of that practice by the wealthy and powerful to the extent that it became a major factor in the Reformation. There has always been, particularly in the U.S., the suggestion of the threat of the corruption of educational certification, symbolized by so-called "degree mills" and the like. But given the size and scope of the educational enterprise, not only in the U.S., but throughout the world, it has been surprisingly minimal. PLA goes to the heart of the educational enterprise since it separates teaching from evaluation. Maintenance of standards within the utilization of PLA is crucial. The slightest breath of corruption would destroy its potential, and injure too many innocent students. It is notable that CAEL in the U.S. has been assiduous in its protection of the standards of the PLA with which it has been associated. There is a good deal to learn from them about the training of assessors, and the careful supervision of assessment. The potential of the practices is far too great in facilitating these exchanges to allow it to be destroyed by our own carelessness.

A group of scholars at OISE has developed a proposal for longitudinal research that would allow comparisons between students admitted to formal agencies on the grounds of some form of PLA with students admitted on conventional grounds. As well as providing the only kind of evidence that, in the long run, the academic establishment will and should accept, it would allow us to identify more clearly the skills and other factors involved in the necessary assessments.

Conclusions

The argument of this paper has moved from a consideration of transition from school to work, to transitions from school to work and work to school. In addition, we have argued that the terms are somewhat misleading, and that better ones would be those of exchanges between the role of student, and the role of employee. Further we have tried to demonstrate that these exchanges are already, for about one half the population, multiple in time, and increasing in variety. That those conditions and opportunities must be extended to the other half of the population is clearly apparent in the arguments of the dominant institutions in this society primarily associated with the economy. To effect this, with the greatest degree of equity and efficiency, is the most pressing and interesting challenge before us. It involves a major transformation of the educational system and the public attitudes that support it.

There is considerable evidence that large segments of the Canadian population have already come to that conclusion, and are bringing about these changes in the most practical and promising way, that is by offering themselves as unconventional students, and gaining admission, in one way or another. The foundations for the maximization of these exchanges is already in place. What is needed now is encouragement, monitoring, and informed support. There is no way we can return to the state of the three boxes described in the Federal Paper. But there is equally no guarantee that we will realize the potential that lies in the greater liberation and nurture of the intelligence of all our citizens that PLA, among other developments, promises.

What we are addressing is the matter of how two major institutions of contemporary Canada, indeed of any existing society, education and employment, can best be related. We have been accustomed to that relationship applying only to the earliest stages of life, to defining childhood, youth, and adult status. Many of our most basic assumptions about education are derived from those expectations. All contemporary evidence points to the contrary. Factors that define learning, student characteristics, teaching, and all of the associated educational activities, now effect entire lifespans. Class, employment, income, citizenship, the exercise of political power, to identify only a few basic roles, are affected not just in their beginnings, but in their daily manifestations, by their relationships to learning and education. Movement between student and employee is no longer the subject of a single concern, but, since it defines more and more areas of every citizen's every day life, requires all of our intellectual instruments and perspectives if it is to be understood.

8

Education and Employment in Quebec: A Review of the Literature[1]

Pierre Dandurand and Roland Ouellet

This chapter is part of an attempt by the two authors to illustrate research trends in the field of sociology of education in Quebec between 1976 and 1986. The study was based on a systematic analysis of some twenty specialized magazines and a number of research reports published by public organizations. The authors would like to point out, however, that this is not an exhaustive inventory of all the works published in Quebec during this period in the field of sociology of education.

The works focus on five themes: access to education, school and employment, school policies, the impact of school organization on socialization and learning, and teaching as a profession. Thus, this chapter deals with only one of the themes, school and employment. A 1992 version of this chapter would obviously refer to the many additional works since produced on this issue.

While the democratization of education was undoubtedly one of the main components of the 1960s school reform, the goal of modernizing Quebec by developing a more highly qualified labour force was another. Here, as elsewhere, education was considered one of the most profitable investments on both the individual and collective levels. We have only to recall the slogan of the Liberal Party of Quebec during the 1960s: "education pays." As we know, a lot of water has passed under the bridge since then. The economic crisis, which began in the 1970s and peaked in the early 1980s, resulted in a 1982 unemployment rate of 23 percent among young people aged fifteen to twenty-four. This factor even affected university graduates, thereby challenging certain optimistic perceptions of the school/work link.

---

[1] This text is excerpted from a publication by Pierre Dandurand and Roland Ouellet entitled *Les grandes orientations de la recherche en sociologie de l'éducation au Québec: un bilan biographique*, Les Cahiers du LABRAPS, Laboratoire de recherche en administration et politique scolaires, Faculté des sciences de l'éducation, Université Laval, Série Études et documents, volume 6, chapter II, pp. 23–24. Les Cahiers du LABRAPS have authorized the translation and publication of this work.

In the field of sociology of education and among the major studies already mentioned, two are directly related to this area. One of them, the study conducted by Guy Rocher and Pierre W. Bélanger, *Aspirations scolaires et orientations professionnelles des étudiants* (students' academic aspirations and career choices), the very title of which refers to the choice of a trade or occupation, seeks to explain the career choices of young people and their transition from school to work. It appears that, in general, the analyses based on these data focused primarily on factors determining educational paths, rather than on the actual transition from school to work. However, the study by Lévesque and Sylvain (1982a, 1982b), which specifically analyzes young people's decisions, after completing secondary school, to continue their studies or enter the labour market, and the study by Roberge (1979), which deals more specifically with the transition of young people from the vocational sector to the job market, look closely at this aspect.

Another major study, by Bernard, Demers, Grenier and Renaud (1979), deals directly with the theme of education and employment, thus corresponding more closely to the 1960s slogan on the cause-and-effect link between schooling and income.

A few conclusions should be mentioned here. The first is the confirmation of the positive schooling/income relationship. Although it is true that "education pays" results also show that the profitability of schooling at lower levels has decreased. The secondary school diploma is simply not worth what it was in the 1960s. The inflation of academic degrees has brought about their partial devaluation, resulting in a relative drop in the income that once accompanied them. Allaire, Bernard and Renaud attempt to demonstrate that education must be perceived as a scarce resource and thus likely to create a monopoly, and that schools do more to categorize people than to equip them with skills (Allaire et al., 1979; Renaud et al., 1980).[2]

It should be pointed out that recent studies on the profitability of college and university education reveal that, for the most part, individual and collective investments in college and university education remain profitable (Vaillancourt and Henriques 1986a, 1986b) but that, all things considered, the diploma of college studies (DEC) in the vocational sector is a much better investment than the general DEC. Furthermore, in a critical summary done in the field of economy of education, Lemelin (1988) insists that education is economically profitable but that the individual's experience and branch of education must be considered in light of the glutted labour market (Lemelin, Baril and Robidoux, 1987). In fact, on-the-job training seems, at least from the viewpoint of large companies, to result in positive spinoffs, especially increased productivity and improved labour force adjustment, as indicated in the study conducted by Paquet, Doray and Bouchard in *Les pratiques de formation en entreprises* (1982).

---

[2] A brief, detailed presentation of the main results of this research can be found in an article by Paul Bernard (1982).

The entire issue of on-the-job vocational training is still infrequently studied by education sociologists, which is why the paper by Paquet and Doray is a valuable source of information. Their research shows that a majority of Quebec companies (83%) offer training activities, and that many workers are involved in them. This study, carried out on 1,617 companies with twenty or more employees, shows that training is more accessible to senior level employees, that the employer has complete control over the organization of such activities, and that the training offered is essentially short-term, directly linked to the job in question, and not eligible for purposes of classification. The researchers conclude that this type of training directly fulfils the company's needs in terms of labour force adjustment. However, it essentially disregards workers' needs in terms of increasing their skills, protecting them from layoffs or plant closures, or simply fostering their rise in the workplace hierarchy by providing jobs that give them more stability, higher wages and increased self-esteem (Paquet, 1983).

Other studies have also focused on the issue of vocational education, but this time within the school system. These studies, it should be noted, are remarkable for the diversity of their concerns and approaches. For example, Jean-Pierre Charland (1982) took on the formidable task of summarizing the development of vocational education from the time of the French regime. In his work, the author defends the thesis of the moralization of the working class, which was already present in the monograph by Marcel Fournier (1980) on vocational education at the secondary level. Fournier's work (based on research to which Justo Michelena and Charles Halary originally contributed) includes a questionnaire survey of young students and teachers in this area of study, and is one of the most complete analyses on this issue. It includes a historical overview of the development of vocational education, specifically the institutionalization of this type of education from free apprenticeship contracts to its current form. Fournier then describes the attitudes and behaviour of the students and teachers, which clearly reveal their fairly marginal position with regard to their school. Their proximity to the values conveyed by the work environments they will shortly enter, actually distances them from the culture of the school world. In this study, vocational education programs are defined as a model of the tensions between the logic of school and that of the economy — tensions which shed light on the ever-problematic link between school and the job market.

Institutional analyses were also undertaken by Thérèse Hamel of INRS-Éducation (1982). Several more qualitative studies were conducted on young people in the vocational sector by Marcelle Hardy (1983) and Pierre Côté (1984) on secondary-level vocational education, and by Dandurand and Trudel (1984) on young trainees in the vocational sector. Cournoyer, Drolet and Trottier (1985), also conducted a study which analyzed the long vocational program at the secondary level by comparing the expectations of the school and work environments. Finally, a summary on the status of vocational education was also produced by Pierre Dandurand (1986), who re-oriented it in terms of academic education and the economy.

In this summary, Dandurand refers to the highly structured ranking system of vocational education programs, ranging from the secondary short vocational program to major university faculties, and the fact that these programs are oriented towards positions in the job market that also fall within a strict hierarchy. He points out the various outcomes of these different programs, especially the marginalization of 30 percent of all young people who are still leaving secondary school without having obtained a diploma. He also attempts to show the social importance of skill levels within the context of economic restructuring that results in the disqualification of entire strata of workers, while at the same time calling for increasingly high skill levels from other workers.

This brings us directly to a series of studies that deal with a specific aspect of the links between education and employment, that of youth unemployment. In a special issue on this topic, the *Revue internationale d'action communautaire* (1982) demonstrates to what extent young people are hard hit by unemployment. For example, in 1982 alone, the 15–24 age group accounted for 47 percent of Quebec's total unemployed. The many "Relance"[3] operations undertaken by the ministère de l'Éducation du Québec also provide us with fairly accurate indications of what happens to young people once they leave the school system. We learn that the level of schooling greatly influences young people's access to the job market and that the possibilities of becoming unemployed were, for instance in 1978, 23.5 percent for secondary school graduates, 13.5 percent for college graduates, and 4 percent for university graduates. Although, in comparison to the general sector, students emerging from the vocational sector at the college level and from the long vocational program at the secondary level had better chances of finding employment (9.7% and 16.1% respectively), those completing the short vocational program were the least likely, with an unemployment rate of 32.2 percent (Audet, 1979a and 1979b).

Corbeil demonstrated how dropping out of school or ceasing studies without obtaining a diploma can be a major handicap for young people at the secondary and college level, in the sense that dropping out tends to lead to unemployment, low wages and the least interesting jobs (Corbeil, 1980). It was estimated that in the late 1970s, the percentage of young people who left school before Secondary V, in most cases without diplomas, hovered around 45 percent (Levesque, 1981; Grégoire, 1981).

The dropout situation did, however, improve considerably as the economy rebounded from its 1982 nadir. In the mid- to late 1980s, the unemployment rate for young people has returned to its mid–1970s rate, that is, approximately 15 percent (ministère de la Main-d'oeuvre, de la Sécurité du revenu et de la Formation

---

[3] The following "Relance" studies should be mentioned: Audet, 1982, 1984, 1986; Corbeil, 1979, 1982; Darveau, 1981; Gendron and Jolin, 1979; Lapierre, 1977; Laroche, 1984; Michel, 1987a, 1987b; Vézina and Corbeil, 1984; and others by the ministère de l'Éducation du Québec, 1986a and 1986b. We have not done an exhaustive inventory of all "Relance" studies. For more information, the reader should contact the ministère de l'Éducation du Québec.

professionnelle, 1987, p. 7). The percentage of those who completed secondary school reached a new peak in 1986 of over 72 percent for the same age cohort (ministère de l'Éducation du Québec, 1988, p. 40).[4]

Despite this progress, a considerable number of young people still leave secondary school without a diploma or any type of vocational training and attempt to penetrate a highly competitive job market. In this general context, we must ask ourselves what causes so many young people to drop out of school. Anne La Perrière attempts to answer this in an article entitled: "Quand on le peut: l'école pour éviter le pire" (1982), in which she demonstrates that schools themselves are often to blame for "expelling" students because of their lack of appeal.

The issue of youth unemployment leads us to the more general problem of their social and vocational integration into the job market. This is usually referred to as the inadequacy of school with regard to the job market, or the school-work hiatus. Analyses of this problem often attempt to either emphasize the lack of adjustment between school and the job market, or point out the constraints of the occupational structure or the uncertainties of the economic situation. Hence, in the words of Laflamme (1984), young people's social and vocational integration problems can be explained by a series of socialization (the influence of the education system) and organizational factors (the impact of the labour market).

Many studies have criticized the education system for not only failing to prepare students for "real" life, but for misleading them in their expectations (Cournoyer, 1979, 1984, Bengle and Laflamme, 1979, 1982). The authors argue that the school system pushes students toward a career by forcing them to choose a field of interest early on, resulting in increased frequency of trial and error in the pursuit of their school and vocational courses (Langlois, 1985).

A second theory holds that the education system is not responsible for weaknesses in the economic system, for although teaching programs must take labour market demands into account, the cyclical fluctuations of the economy make any accurate, short-term forecasts almost impossible (Moisset, 1983). From this same line of thought, the CEQ, in an attempt to reformulate the overall problem, attributes the disparities between education and employment more to a deterioration of the labour market than to any chronic inadequacy on the part of the education system (1987). In the same perspective, reference is made to the marginalization of young people by a society which, for reasons of economy specific to the private sector, is no longer capable of integrating them into the work force (Baby, 1985). Thus, it is not a question of blaming schools, but rather of acknowledging the labour market's inability to integrate available workers (Baby, 1986) and of recognizing, as does Laflamme (1984), that integration problems experienced by young people are often the result of social constraints. These in turn are due to the plethora of laws, rules and regulations that overwhelm day-to-day life, govern the working world, and contribute largely to limiting young people's opportunities for social

---

[4] The percentage of school dropouts has risen steadily in Québec since 1986 to reach a rate of 36% for 1991, based on ministère de l'Éducation du Québec data.

integration. As an example of these constraints, Laflamme mentions the certification of knowledge, the institutionalization of the labour market, government regulations, and employment policies.

Other studies have adopted narrower viewpoints by attempting to describe the situation of young people once they have been integrated into the job market. Thus, not only are there few jobs available, but young people must often settle for job insecurity (Hohl, 1982; Lesage, 1986) and the least advantageous working conditions (Girard, Gauthier and Vinet, 1978). They must also deal with powerful protection mechanisms developed by adults to ward off the threat of competition represented by the flood of young people with higher levels of schooling (Fortin, 1986). The few studies done on the perceptions of young people at the university level seem clear in this respect. For them, the work environment is essentially made up of established unionized workers who receive high salaries and whose job security goes hand in hand with professional resistance to change (Hohl, 1982). Despite this, in general, young workers and students have a fairly positive concept of work as a value (Dumas, Rochais and Tremblay, 1982). However, people are far from unanimous with respect to the latter perception. Many claim, on the contrary, that an increasing number of young people are challenging work as the central element of an individual's life (St-Pierre, 1982). What is being disputed is not only work itself, with its organization, productivity, objectives and underlying models for growth, but also work as a way of life (Lesage, 1986).

Further research is needed to clarify these issues and also to find solutions for the school-work hiatus, as suggested by La Perrière (1982). Factors such as the distribution and organization of work, the origins of the insensitivity of school bureaucracy to the life experiences and aspirations of young people, and the culture of youth from various backgrounds (Dandurand, 1986), should all be studied more closely. Within this context, the interesting experiments attempted in alternative schools for dropouts, as reported by Henripin and Proulx (1986), should be noted.

The theme of young people's social and vocational integration is thus gaining widespread popularity, as shown by various publications and presentations made at conferences and symposia attended by education sociologists (Colloque sur les jeunes et le travail, 1981; symposium organized by the Institut québécois de recherche sur la culture: Dumont F., 1986, etc.). However, analyses conducted to date have primarily emphasized the structural and objective aspect of the problem, largely ignoring more subjective approaches such as Baby's (1986), which is based on a "cyclical theory" of integration of young people. The massive onslaught of new computerized technologies and the economic crisis are threatening certain strata of young people with social exclusion and objective marginalization. This longitudinal study, which uses a qualitative approach, should provide us with important information on the way young people deal with the transition from school to the labour market.

The impact of new technologies has also been a focus in links between education and employment insofar as they exercise considerable influence on employment, working conditions and the need for education. In this respect, the research done and the recommendations made by the Centrale de l'enseignement du Québec on each of these themes are an important source of information (CEQ, 1984, 1985 and 1987). This research has enabled us to observe the threat that computerization poses to employment levels, especially to jobs for women and young people's access to the labour market. It has also emphasized the various impacts of computerization on working conditions, such as increased job compartmentalization, tighter control of employer groups over labour, and the fragmentation of the workplace. These issues have also emphasized the importance of adjusting and modifying education content. Finally, they have also pointed out in general, the lack of education and employment information sources in Quebec.

New computer technologies have changed so rapidly that it is no longer possible to assume that education received in school will be applicable in the long term (Baby, 1985). We must therefore think in terms of a continuing education process rather than retraining and upgrading. Initial vocational training should also be looked at. Doray (1986), of the Centre de recherche en évaluation sociale des technologies at the Université du Québec à Montréal, is currently conducting research on the way the education machine (represented here by the educational structures of college instruction) is changing in response to the modifications in work procedures brought about by the introduction of computerized technology.

It is obvious that the interest aroused in vocational education, and more broadly, in the link between school and the labour market, is fostered by the economic situation, which keeps masses of young people out of jobs with the status of unemployed workers and income security recipients. This is a major social problem which the governments, through ad hoc policies, attempt to solve temporarily so as to move on to other things (Provost, 1988). A number of analysts see in job creation policies for young people, and even more in the generalization of employability programs (including on-the-job training sessions and/or retraining programs), the emergence of a new "no-man's-land" between school and the job market, which serves no practical purpose but to maintain in limbo a substantial number of young people whom the labour market can no longer absorb. An important field of research is being defined as a result of the socioeconomic action taken by the governments in the sensitive area of social and vocational integration or reintegration of young people, women, and immigrants — action which relies largely on training and retraining (Dandurand, 1983). An entire series of additional indicators show that the field of vocational education, and indeed education in general, may be subject to sweeping changes in upcoming years. We have only to think of the political willingness to develop on-the-job vocational training, as recommended in the De Granpré report.

These are some of the themes dealing with the school-employment relationship that have sparked the interest of education sociologists over the past decade. Although this summary shows a marked interest in this sector of research, it also shows in many respects that new problems have arisen, creating a field of investigation for education sociologists that is vast but barely explored.

9

Life Trajectories, Action, and Negotiating the Transition from High School

Lesley Andres Bellamy

The link among education, human capital, and human resource development has long been acknowledged. It has been demonstrated repeatedly that participation in post-secondary education makes a difference in terms of future labour market experience, employability, and quality of life. That is, individuals who achieve higher levels of education are more likely to earn higher salaries, hold more prestigious positions in the work force, are less likely to be unemployed, and are more likely to both benefit from and contribute to the robustness of society in general. Post-secondary participation and its consequences have been linked to issues of global competitiveness and economic prosperity. Two recent policy documents released by the Canadian federal government, and initiatives by several provincial governments in relation to human resource development, continue to emphasize the importance of an educated and skilled work force as the "key to prosperity, competitiveness, good jobs, and quality of life" (Learning Well...Living Well, 1991, p.4). According to these documents, the competitiveness of our nation depends on the development of a skilled labour force. Youth, in particular, are targeted in these discussions. In the report entitled *Prosperity through Competitiveness* (1991), it is asserted that "we can ill... ignore the potential of social consequences of a generation of young people ill-equipped to face the challenges of the future" (p.10).

Today, as educational attainment and the demand for credentials surpass a willingness to work as the principal job entry level credential, the "career ladder has been truncated" (Radwanski, 1987) and those with limited education and few skills are likely to be severely limited in their choices of employment and advancement. Coleman and Husén (1985) indicate that the inevitable changes due to the fluctuating nature of the labour market will have grim consequences for poorly prepared youth in developed countries. They refer to those who leave school with the "mandatory minimum" but without the requisite abilities and skills to cope with the demands of the modern work place as a "new underclass." For this group, there is little chance of becoming meaningfully employed.

Yet, Canadian national statistics reveal that nearly 50 percent of Grade 12 graduates do not directly continue on to post-secondary education (Report of the Standing Committee on National Finance, 1987). Given what is known about the benefits of participating in post-secondary education, the demand for a skilled labour force, and the observation that numerous high school graduates do not go on, how individuals make decisions regarding participation in post-secondary education is of increasing interest to policy makers and educational planners.

The purpose of this paper is to report the findings of a study that explored how students, who were in the midst of the transition from high school to various post-high school destinations, perceived these processes. This paper proceeds as follows: first, a brief review of participation studies and related theoretical underpinnings is provided; second, Bourdieu's Theory of Practice is presented, augmented by rational choice theory as posited by Elster, as an alternative theoretical model; and third, the findings of interviews conducted with a sample of high school students in their graduating year are presented.

Approaches to the Study of Post-Secondary Participation

An array of theories, perspectives, and models, including human capital, status attainment, and equality of opportunity have been used to address who attends post-secondary institutions and why. The theoretical bases for these studies correspond, more or less, to one of two broad intellectual streams — the sociological versus the economic — that Coleman (1988) indicates are used to describe and explain social action.

While several important relationships have been revealed in studies that focus on one or the other of these approaches, the adoption of one approach and the neglect of the other is limiting in explaining action. In relation to post-secondary participation, studies that adopt a structural or status attainment approach focus on the first view of action. In these studies it is not unusual to conclude that a measure such as socioeconomic status is related to the probability that an individual will continue on to post-secondary education; however, the usefulness of this type of a measure is incomplete. While an "upper-class" child has a much greater chance of reaching higher education than one from a "working-class" background, not all upper-class students go to university, nor are all working-class students non-participants (Keller and Zavalloni, 1964; Lane, 1972). Härnqvist (1978) asserts that research efforts of this type have likely provided more knowledge about stable and fairly resistant factors behind educational choice than about factors that influence change. As such, these studies provide little insight into how individuals actually make decisions about participation in post-secondary education. Giddens (1984) suggests that factors that influence individuals "always operate via agents' motives and reasons" (p.310). However, without knowledge of these mechanisms, motives or reasons, it continues to remain as difficult to explain why working class kids let themselves get working class jobs (Willis, 1977), as it is to clarify why others escape the social reproductive forces and destinations predicted by their ascribed status (Gambetta, 1987).

On the other hand, the rational actor assumption that is central to many studies of educational participation is also limiting (Elster 1989a, 1989b, Stager 1989). In some of these studies, rational choice theory is rarely explicated in a meaningful way. That is, what researchers mean by "rational action" and the criteria used to assess whether individuals are acting rationally are rarely made clear. Rationality is often treated as a homogeneous concept, when in fact, the rational choice literature is very diverse. For example, practical rationality and its emphasis on the relationship among beliefs, desires, evidence, and action (Elster 1989a, 1989b), provides quite a different analytical framework than a technical account of rationality, or the special case of rate of return on investment, that focuses on maximization of expected utility. Hindess (1989) asserts that, in general, rational choice "accords a very limited role to the significance of social structure or social relations for actors and their actions" (p.36).

In much of the current theoretical debate in the social sciences, a re examination of two disparate views of action have been called for (Coleman, 1986, 1990; Gambetta, 1987; Hindess, 1988; Wharton, 1991). Coleman maintains that the two views of action are not separable. He argues that to adopt either view of action, independent of the other, is misguided, for as defined by the first stream, the actor is treated as though he or she is without an "engine of action" but is completely shaped by the environment, and in the second stream, constraints of the social environment are totally ignored. He suggests that the investigation of action should commence from one conceptually coherent framework, and proceed to introduce elements from the other, without destroying the coherence of the first. Others have suggested that in order to explain the relationship between interaction and structure, both micro and macro levels of analysis are required (Knorr-Cetina, 1981; Lamont and Lareau, 1988).

One approach that integrates the concepts of socialized actor and rational actor can be found in the work of Bourdieu, and Bourdieu and Passeron. In the following section, Bourdieu's Theory of Practice is outlined.

Bourdieu's Theory of Practice

According to Bourdieu (1984), practices (action) can only be accounted for by illuminating the series of effects that underlie them. He proposes that the following formula be used to analyze these effects: *[(habitus) (capital)] + field = practice]* (p.101). As specified in this formula, three concepts, *capital*, *habitus*, and *field* are central to Bourdieu's theoretical formulation. Bourdieu (1984) claims that the primary differences distinguishing the major classes of conditions of existence, derive from the overall volume of capital possessed by an individual. Capital is defined as, "the set of actually usable resources and powers" and exists as many types — as economic, cultural, social, and symbolic capital (p.114). Capital can exist in objectified form, such as material properties, or in incorporated form as in cultural capital, and the kinds of capital "like trumps in a game of cards, are powers which define the chances of profit in a given field" (Bourdieu, 1991, p.230). Of the forms of capital defined by Bourdieu that contribute to the reproduction of the structure of power relationships and symbolic relationships between classes, cultural capital has received the most attention. Of equal importance, however, are his conceptualizations of social capital, habitus, and field.

Bourdieu (1977a, 1986) claims that as groups and organizations within society purport to adopt policies that support equality of opportunity, dominant groups increasingly adopt other indirect mechanisms of reproduction. In the case of equality of opportunity in post-secondary education, the demise of direct mechanisms of reproduction (ascriptive forces such as social position, gender, and race) and the adoption of selection policies based on meritocratic criteria, result in the emergence of other indirect mechanisms of reproduction, in the form of cultural and social capital. These forms of capital originate within the family domain, are transmitted via the educational system, and are converted into educational capital. In this way, social origin, in the guise of cultural and social capital, is able to "exert its influence throughout the whole duration of schooling, particularly at the great turning points of a school career" (Bourdieu and Passeron, 1979, p.13). They assert that "the chances of entering higher education can be seen as the product of a selection process which, throughout the school system, is applied with very unequal severity, depending on the student's social origin. In fact, for the most disadvantaged classes, it is purely and simply a matter of *elimination*" (p.2).

While the influence of social origin, transmitted as cultural and social capital through the habitus or system of dispositions, is relevant to the choice of post-high school destination, action does not take the form of mechanical determinism. Family background provides individuals with social, cultural, and economic capital. This capital, however, must be actively invested. As Jencks et al. (1983) indicate:

> while individuals with high SES parents, high aptitude scores, high grades, and college-bound friends all enjoy appreciable occupational advantages, they only do so if they get more schooling than average (p.6).

When used *rationally,* educational success is facilitated by the possession of various forms of capital. Through shrewd investment of the capital at hand, even individuals from the most disadvantaged classes, those who are most likely to be "crushed by the weight of their social destiny," are able to overcome their excessive handicap, and thus "avoid the common fate of their class" (Bourdieu and Passeron, 1979, p. 25).

As this statement suggests, even Bourdieu and Passeron do not completely abandon the role of rational choice theory in decision making. This paper maintains that the exploration of the relationships among beliefs, desires, and evidence, as espoused by Elster, will provide a key facet in understanding post-secondary participation. However, the rational choice framework, while necessary, is not sufficient. By enveloping this framework in one of parental transmission of social and cultural capital as espoused in Bourdieu's Theory of Practice, a theoretical model that incorporates the first stream within a framework of the second stream, as suggested by Coleman can be advanced, and both the choices that individuals make about post-high school destinations, and the processes underlying these choices, may be further illuminated.

Elsewhere (Bellamy 1992), the interrelationships among these concepts are addressed in their entirety. In this paper, the analysis is delimited to the relationships among dispositions toward and beliefs about post-secondary education, academic capital, and the interrelated concept of cultural capital. The following questions guide the analysis: Does the concept of "disposition" toward post-secondary education, as posited by Bourdieu, contribute to our understanding of choice regarding post-high school destinations? To what extent do individuals act on these beliefs and desires, in light of the available relevant evidence, as posited by rational choice theory? Are these concepts competing, or are individuals' "rational" choices framed by reproductive forces transmitted through social and cultural capital?

Data and Measures

This paper reports the findings of an empirical investigation of educational choice that sought to explore the relationships among the concepts advanced by Bourdieu and Elster. It is based on two sets of interviews conducted with high school students over the course of their graduating year.

In 1989 and 1990, interviews were conducted with British Columbia Grade 12 students. The purpose of the interviews was to 1) determine their post-high school plans, and 2) to explore in depth their perceptions of the processes underlying their decisions regarding post-high school destinations. Below, the selection of schools and students is described, and the interview procedures are explained.

A purposive or judgment sampling strategy was used to select three British Columbia secondary schools in which to conduct the interviews. The aim of the selection strategy was to ensure that one metropolitan, one urban/rural, and one remote school, each typical or modal of the category, was included in the study. Fifteen to twenty students from each school were interviewed twice during the 1989/90 school year. Face-to-face, semi-structured interviews, approximately one hour in length, were conducted in November 1989, and again in May 1990. While the questions guiding the interviews were based on the theoretical framework of this study, student participants were encouraged to discuss decision making, post-high school destinations, and the transition period in their own "voices" and within their own personal contexts (Mishler, 1986).

All interviews were taped, and typed transcripts were prepared from the tapes. Follow-up interviews were completed with all of the original interviewees in May 1990. In preparation for the follow-up interview, each student participant was given a copy of the transcript of her/his initial interview. Discussion of the transcript served as a starting point for the follow-up interview. This process allowed the interviewer and interviewee to work as research collaborators in a joint effort to understand the previous interview and plan for the present stage of the study, and gave interviewees "a voice in the interpretation and use of the findings" (Mishler, 1986, p.127, 132). The purpose of the follow-up interviews was to: 1) verify the data obtained in the initial interviews and explore more fully the themes arising

Table 9-1: Interviewees by Sex and Post-High School Destination, October 1990

	Non-University	University	F/T Work	P/T Work	Other	Unemployed	Back to H.S.	Row Total
Female	9	6	6	4	3	2	0	30
Male	4	4	3	2	0	0	1	14
Total	13	10	9	5	3	2	1	44

from the initial interviews, 2) determine what actions individuals had taken since November 1989 to prepare for the transition from high school, and 3) explore in further depth the processes underlying the decisions students make regarding post-high school destinations, including how students perceived these processes.

Approximately 1,500 typed transcript pages were prepared from the ninety-seven taped interviews. A coding scheme was generated using the technique of constant comparative analysis (Glaser and Strauss, 1967; Goetz and LaCompte, 1984). This scheme was guided by the theoretical framework described earlier. The credibility of the interview data was enhanced by following the tenets of reliability and validity for qualitative data, as outlined by Goetz and LaCompte (1984). In order to preserve the individuality of the student while protecting her/his identity, each interviewee was given a pseudonym. If the student's own name reflected her or his cultural or ethnic background, a comparable pseudonym was chosen.

While a multisite approach was used in the collection of interview data, the primary unit of analysis was the individual. That is, I have focused on how the individual, within a particular context, perceived and made sense of the transition from high school. However, when perceptions varied by geographical region or gender, the context or ascriptive attributes were taken into account.

In October 1990, the 44 interviewees (or their parents) were again contacted by telephone, to ascertain their actual post-high school destinations. Of the 44 individuals contacted in October 1990, 10 were attending university, 13 were attending a community college,[1] 15 were employed (9 full-time, 6 part-time) 2 were unemployed, 3 were participating in travel/exchange programs (other), and 1 had returned to high school to complete graduation requirements. Actual post-high school destinations of the interviewees, by sex, are summarized in Table 9-1.

---

[1] Of these students, 11 were attending the community college nearest to their high school.

Destinations

The first interviews with Grade 12 students took place in late October 1989, approximately six months before high school graduation. While the end of high school was quickly approaching, the transition process — as an overt, conscious exercise — had not formally commenced for most students.

> Carol: May...that's when you'll start thinking about it more...Right now I do think about it but it's not in the planning stages quite yet.

Yet, when asked in the first interview about their plans for the future, most students were able, with varying degrees of specificity and certainty, to articulate their post-high school intentions.

Studies using survey questionnaires to determine post-high school status usually delimit destinations to the concise categories of "university participant" "non-university participant" and "non-participant." As Table 9–1 in the previous section reveals, a complex choice of actual destinations confronted these high school students. An examination of the shifts in students plans over the course of the year is also revealing. While there was considerable movement toward non-university education and work as post-high school destinations between October 1989 and May 1990, there was virtually no movement toward university. Of the 12 students who indicated in October 1989 that they intended to continue to university following high school graduation, 9 followed through with their plans. In contrast, none of the students who were "undecided" in October 1989 went directly to post-secondary schools in the fall of October 1990. Only 1 of the 6 students who planned to work after high school (and in this case work was intended to be a temporary break before commencing university) carried on to a post-secondary institution. Of the 19 students who indicated, in October 1989, that they planned to attend a non-university institution, 7 entered the labour force, 1 was unemployed, and none went to university.

Plans did change during the graduating year of high school. Between May 1990 and October 1990, the most stable group consisted of those students who stated in the first interview that they were university bound. In all but one instance, movement occurred away from intended post-secondary participation toward non-participant status.

What accounts for the durable nature of some students' plans and unstable nature of others? How do they perceive the choices before them? Bourdieu (1990a) states that enlightenment about real causes or real modes of practices must be sought by asking informants the question "why?" Hence, throughout the two interviews, students were invited to discuss "why?" In this way, the relationship among dispositions toward and beliefs about post-secondary education and academic capital are explored.

Dispositions Toward Post-Secondary Education

According to Bourdieu (1984), movement by individuals within a social space does not occur in a random fashion. Rather, this movement is the result of a dynamic relationship where individuals are subjected to the forces that structure the social space in question, *and* where individuals use their own unique properties (e.g. in embodied form as dispositions, or in objectified form as in goods or qualifications) to resist the forces of the field. He asserts that social position and individual trajectory are not independent of one another, for "to a given volume of inherited capital there corresponds a band of more or less equally probable trajectories leading to more or less equivalent positions" which he refers to as "the *field of the possibles* objectively offered to a given agent" (p.110). Hence, all destinations are not equally probable for all origins. He claims that for "given classes of existence" there is a modal trajectory, and that the social positions and the dispositions of the agents who occupy them are strongly correlated.

The common social space for the students in this study was structured by the British Columbia educational system. These students were all in their final year of high school, after having completed their elementary and secondary years in a common school system. Yet, despite thirteen years of participation in an educational system in which the "field of the possibles" was technically the same for all, differences in dispositions toward post-secondary education held by those intending to continue and those with no intention of continuing were remarkable.

The concept of *habitus* is central to Bourdieu's work. Most simply, *habitus* is a system of dispositions that are created and recreated as objective structures and personal history converge. Disposition, for Bourdieu, has a three-fold meaning. First, it is the result of an organizing action, thus similar to the word structure. Second, it implies a way of being, a habitual state. Third, and most important, it expresses the idea of predisposition, tendency, propensity, or inclination (Bourdieu, 1977b). As such, *habitus* is "history turned into nature" (p.78).

Four types of students emerged, according to dispositions. The first group was comprised of those who indicated that they "always" intended to continue to higher education. The second group was characterized by those who "never" planned to continue. The third group consisted of those whose dispositions conflicted with the expectations held for them by others, and the fourth group, while inclined toward post-secondary education, felt that they were on their own in making this decision. Each group is presented separately.

"*I Always Planned to Attend Post-Secondary.*" For one group of students, the prospect of attending a post-secondary institution following high school was described as simply "natural." This natural or habitual state led to a predisposition towards post-secondary education. No other future had been considered. Rather, continuing to post-secondary education was "always assumed" and thus not a decision.

> **Larry:** I haven't spent a lot of time, like what I want is just instinct, like it's just — I've never had to sit down and decide between this or this…It hasn't been a decision [to go to college].

For many of those planning to continue to post-secondary education, the dispositions they held toward post-secondary education — as a natural way of being and as a predisposition or inclination — were directly attributed to parental influence, either as expectations, cultural capital, or both. Parental expectations, according to students, became organizing principles for their subsequent actions.

> **Victor:** Yeah, but I always decided to do that. I always wanted to [go to university]...'Cause I, 'cause my parents kept telling me, like, you know, you have to do this, but I like it too.

Others recognized the association among parents' cultural capital in the form of educational qualifications, the expectations held for them, and their own educational plans. It was naturally assumed that they would continue to higher education because of parents' educational backgrounds — " 'cause my father is highly educated...he's got a masters in education" — or parents' experiences with the post-secondary system.

> **Clive:** They want me to go to [university]. Both of them have gone there before...My Mom and Dad have brainwashed me sort of thing. But I know that's the best way to go.

Parents, based on their own familiarity with and experiences in college or university, were able to breed in their children a level of comfort with the idea of post-secondary participation. This served to demystify the notion of higher education.

Yet, other students ascribed the very lack of parental cultural capital as the driving force behind the expectations held for them. Limited educational opportunities in their own youth and dissatisfaction with their own career paths led parents to encourage their children to use education to improve their futures.

> **Jasmine:** My Mom, since I don't know when, she's been like, "you'll go to school after you graduate" and I guess that's kind of sunk in and it's stayed there...She expects me to do things that she couldn't do like because her family was poor.

For the majority of students intending to continue to higher education, their "natural" dispositions toward post-secondary education were clearly perceived to originate within the family domain. Interviewees acknowledged that long-term inculcation of parental expectations resulted in the *habitus* of these students as a system of congruous dispositions — as the result of an organizing action, a way of being or habitual state and as a predisposition or tendency (Bourdieu, 1977b). In this way, as Janice's comments illustrate (below), parental expectations, often together with parents' cultural capital, served as "structured structures" which in turn became "structuring structures" and dispositions imposed within the family setting were incorporated to the extent that they were "internalized as second nature and forgotten as history" (Bourdieu, 1990b, p.56).

> **Janice:** Well, my mom's in university right now... And, yeah, my step-dad has and my Dad has and my step-mother have [graduated from university]...There's also parental pressure, there's your friends are going and you should go because you get good marks and you're wasting it — I don't know, just a whole bunch of things. But mostly I want to go. Like, there's never been any question, I'm not doing this because my parents or my friends.

Despite acknowledging the role of parental expectations and cultural capital, the individualistic nature of comments such as Janice's lend credence to Bourdieu's claim that as such, incorporated dispositions give practices their relative autonomy.

"It's Not for Me." For the second group of students, post-secondary attendance was described as not within their "field of the possibles." They asserted that intended non-participation was indeed "self-elimination" (Lamont and Lareau, 1988) — for this choice was perceived to be both elective and desired.

Celia: It's not for me, I don't, I just never think about it 'cause like I've known pretty much all my life that I'm not going to go.

The connection between parental expectations and their own dispositions toward post-secondary education was also evident to this group of students. These expectations, however, sharply contrasted with those held by the group who were "naturally" inclined to attend a post-secondary institution following high school.

Mort: It's like, nobody expects me to go on to post-secondary...my Mom doesn't. She's known for years that I'm not going. That's been my plans...[my Mom expects] nothing really.

Unlike the long-term imbuement of parental expectations acknowledged by those "naturally" disposed toward post-secondary education, the *habitus* of students not intending to continue to higher education was portrayed by students as either a long-standing distaste toward school that remained largely untouched by parental expectations, or as torpid attitudes toward schooling structured by a perceived lack of parental direction in their educational lives.

Matt: My Dad doesn't even think I'm going to graduate, so he hasn't really put much into my education...It's my choice what I want to do, they really don't get in the way of what I want to do.

Inevitable post-secondary participation was not embodied as an habitual state, a predisposition or tendency, or as an organizing action. Nor was there a tradition of post-secondary experience by the parents of this group of students. Almost all of the parents of this group of students had attained high school graduation or less.

John: No. From the first day I started school I never wanted to go any farther than high school. That was it. My parents were just happy if I could graduate, 'cause they didn't make it. My Dad was Grade 10, my mother Grade 11.

Thus, parental transmission of cultural resources, in the form of imparting familiarity with the post-secondary system, was absent for these students.

Bourdieu's notion of *hysteresis of habitus* may help to explain the discrepancy between dispositions toward post-secondary attendance and actual opportunity to participate in post-secondary education. *Hysteresis of habitus*, according to Bourdieu, is a structural lag between opportunities and the dispositions to grasp them which causes opportunities to be missed (Bourdieu, 1990b). Thus, while the "opportunity" to attend some post-secondary institution technically exists, the dispositions held by this group of individuals did not coincide with these "opportunities."

"I Know I Should Continue to Post-Secondary, but..." The distinctive nature of those who *"always intended to attend post-secondary"* and those who *"never intended to continue past high school"* was quite easily discernible. However, it would be misleading to generalize these two types of dispositions to all participants and non-participants. Not all students' dispositions matched their parents' expectations or parents' educational backgrounds. Of particular note was a third group of students who, in the autumn of their graduating year, tended to fall either in the "undecided" group or who expressed vague plans to attend a non-university institution following high school.

According to this group of individuals, parents' expectations exceeded students' own dispositions toward post-secondary education.

> **Kevin:** [My parents] want me to go straight to school. Um, I just don't feel like doing that so they making me pay money if I don't go straight to school.

Rather than possessing a congruous system of dispositions, the facets were in conflict. While on one hand dispositions toward post-secondary education bordered on being a natural way of being, on the other hand, students' unique properties, despite high parental expectations, resisted embodiment of dispositions as a predisposition or tendency. Thus, parental expectations, as organizing actions, failed.

"It's Up to Me." For a small number of students, long-term inculcation of dispositions was not expressed as the case; yet they planned to continue to higher education. They claimed that the decision to attend was their own.

> **Joni:** No, it doesn't matter. So it's totally up to me. Like, [my parents] would prefer it 'cause you know there's more job opportunities and stuff to you know go on to some kind of post-secondary education or whatever, but if I don't want to, I don't have to.

Unlike those who were "naturally" inclined to continue to higher education, this fourth group was predisposed to post-secondary participation, but it was not a habitual state. Nor were parental expectations perceived to serve as organizing actions. These students did, however, appear to have one common attribute — they were enroled in academic programs in high school. The relationship between academic capital and dispositions toward post-secondary education is further explored in the next section.

Academic Capital

In analyses of the factors influencing post-secondary participation, one of the strongest is usually that of achievement and curricular differentiation variables or academic capital (Alexander, Pallas, and Holupka, 1987; Bellamy, 1992; Turrittin, Anisef, and MacKinnon, 1983). That is, the higher the level of academic capital (in the form of credentials for university entrance requirements and grade point average), the more likely one is to participate in post-secondary education. A similar relationship between academic capital and post-high school status can also be demonstrated with interview sample data. As Table 9–2 reveals, despite the fact that all of these students were eligible for admission to some post-secondary

Table 9-2: Post-High School Destination by GPA, Curricular Differentiation and Geographic Location

	No Requirements for University				Requirements for University			
Geographic Location	GPA < than 2.50	2.50 to 2.99	3.00 or >	Row Total	GPA < than 2.50	2.50 to 2.99	3.00 or >	Row total
Remote								
Non-participant	4	0	0	4	0	1*	1	2
Non-university	0	0	0	0	1	0	0	1
University	0	0	0	0	0	1	4	5
Urban/ Rural								
Non-participant	1	0	0	1	2	1*	1*	4
Non-university	1	0	0	1	2	5	1	8
University	0	0	0	0	0	1	1	2
Metro								
Non-participant	8	0	0	8	1	0	0	1
Non-university	1	0	0	1	1	0	0	1
University	0	0	0	0	0	0	3	3
Column Total	15	0	0	15	7	9	11	27

Missing Cases 2
* These students were participating in educational exchange programs, and all had definite plans to enrol in a post-secondary program upon their return.

institution, only 2 of the 15 students who did not meet the requirements for university entrance entered some post-secondary institution, compared with 20 out of 27 students with university entrance requirements. Also, the higher one's grade point average, the more likely the individual was to continue to higher education.

Interviewees' participation patterns, by curricular differentiation and grade point average, corroborate the findings of other studies and support Tinto's (1975) conclusion that rather than increasing participation rates among those without the prerequisites for university attendance, community colleges functioned as a redistributive mechanism among those most qualified to participate, by altering the type of post-secondary institution attended. That is, the most academically disadvantaged Grade 12 graduates were not continuing directly to community colleges.

Of students from the remote and metropolitan schools, those with grade point averages of 3.00 or greater were more likely to attend university over a non-university institution. Of those in the urban/rural sample, only 1 out of 6 students with university entrance requirements, but with GPA's in the borderline (2.50 - 2.99) category, continued to university.

According to the group of students who were "naturally" disposed toward post-secondary education, decisions regarding level and type of course work undertaken in high school were made to ensure that the route to an academic future was left open. Were they limited by their choices?

> **Clive:** Limited no. I've opened most of my doors. By taking all the hard courses, it opens me — by just taking marketing or foods or something, it doesn't — most of my doors would be locked and...I'm getting all A's and that...I'm doing 8 [courses]. Not a spare.

Rather than "self-relegation" as defined by Bourdieu and Passeron (1979) and Lamont and Lareau (1988), curricular and course choices for this group of students assured the possibility of future "self-advancement." If limitations did exist for the post-secondary bound, they were expressed as interest-related rather than route-related. Limitations regarding particular courses were perceived as desired, elective "self-elimination."

> **Janice:** I haven't taken physics 12 and stuff like that so I couldn't be an engineer, but I never, ever wanted to be...so I don't think of it as limiting myself.

Curricular choices by those students intending to continue to higher education were oriented to future opportunities in the post-secondary sector. Their choices ensured that exclusion from future desired paths were minimized and their educational investments were maximized. Curricular routes and course selection were portrayed as conscious, door opening strategies that resulted in inclusion in, rather than exclusion from, further education.

However, curricular choices for those who claimed to have no intention of continuing, rather than being future oriented were described as "anything they had to do to get through high school." These individuals described their choices as "self-relegation" into less demanding routes. Were they limited by their choices?

> **Celia:** Oh no, I think I made the right decisions. 'Cause I knew they'd be easy classes...Well, I want to at least graduate...the only reason I'm taking business courses is because it's easy. You know, I'll graduate with that, but, I'm not really into it.

Rather than curricular and course selection as a rite of passage to further education, the goal for these students was high school graduation. Future limitations ensuing from "self-relegation" into less desirable positions were either unrecognized or not acknowledged, or recognized but curiously not perceived as constraining. For example, Leona did recognize the constraining nature of her choices.

> **Leona:** Well, the courses that I'm taking now is not going to help me in my careers I don't think. They're quite mickey mouse I think, the courses I'm taking, but I need it to graduate.

She was aware that she had eliminated the possibility of attending university, "but you know, I just felt that this is the way I wanted it, you know." Despite the "mickey mouse" nature of her courses, she was content with them. Truncated routes were not perceived as problematic.

Others (all of whom became non-participants following high school graduation) lamented their curricular choices. Choices for this group were also perceived to have been "self-relegation," but were now considered to be a personal shortfall in judgment, made at a time when "I just wanted the easy way out, I just wanted to graduate." For these students, choices were also oriented toward graduation, rather than further education.

> **Roy:** Well, I think I [made good choices], but I should have actually tried harder and passed them, this way I wouldn't be where I am now. I'd be a little further ahead…in order to graduate, I had to accept a few of the bad ones I didn't really want — mechanics and cafeteria. I could live without them easily but seeing it will get me to graduate, I'll take it.

Students readily linked the dispositions they held toward post-secondary education to the expectations and cultural capital of their parents, yet discussion surrounding curricular choices was markedly devoid of the parental connection. Rather, curricular choice was described as an individual endeavour. Implicitly, however, the connection was present. Those individuals for whom post-secondary participation was "natural" were all participating in academic programs — programs that were clearly delineated by structured choices and articulated with the next stage of life. In contrast, those who described post-secondary attendance as "impossible" and those whose parents' expectations exceeded their own almost exclusively participated in non-academic programs — programs that by design, led to nebulous destinations. Those who leaned toward post-secondary attendance, but perceived that their future was up to them, were all enroled in academic programs.

Beliefs About Post-Secondary Education

The practical rationality version of rational choice theory posits that in order for an action to be rational, it should represent the best way of fulfilling an agent's desires, given her or his beliefs. Desires and beliefs must be both rational in themselves and internally consistent. In addition, beliefs should be optimally related to the evidence available to the agent (Elster, 1989b). Yet, as Elster concedes, while a given action is defined as a person's desires along with her/his *beliefs* in relation to opportunities, it is not clear how subjective elements — beliefs and desires — and objective elements — evidence — interact to produce an action.

For Bourdieu (1990b) belief is "an inherent part of belonging to the field" (p.67). He asserts:

> Action guided by a "feel for the game" has all the appearances of rational action that an impartial observer, endowed with all the necessary information and capable of

mastering it rationally, would deduce. And yet it is not based on reason (Bourdieu, 1990a, p.11)

Earlier in this paper it was argued that higher levels of education are associated with higher incomes, more prestigious positions in the work force, lower unemployment, and increased general well being. In other words, there appears to be overwhelming evidence to support the claim that it would be *rational* to believe that the route to the "good life" is most likely to be attained through post-secondary education.

What is it that students believe about their future life chances with or without a post-secondary education? Are these beliefs based on prevailing evidence? Do all students hold the same beliefs? What is the relationship between beliefs and dispositions or the *habitus* of the individual?

For the most part, regardless of intended post-high school destination, almost all students expressed the belief that without a post-secondary education their lives — in terms of employment, quality of life, and future career advancement — would be compromised. However, substantial differences are evident in the way these beliefs are incorporated into one's intended practices for participants and non-participants.

"*I Have to Go to Post-Secondary to Get Ahead.*" For those intending to continue to post-secondary education, belief in the notion of "human capital" was firmly entrenched. Schultz (1960) defined human capital as an investment in oneself, for "by investing in themselves, people can enlarge the range of choice available to them. It is one way free men [sic] can enhance their welfare" (p.314). For the majority of those planning to continue to the post-secondary system, the prospect of directly entering the work world — that is, not attending a post-secondary institution at all — was "unthinkable."

> **Marcus:** No. That's not possible. I wouldn't be able to get anywhere in this world. I need post-secondary education to allow me the career, lifestyle, opportunities that I want.

Belief in the concept of human capital was expressed as strongly by the women in this sample as by the men. That is, they believed that self-investment through post-secondary participation would ensure that they too could enhance their welfare and expand their range of choices.

> **Lisa:** I just don't think that the jobs that you'd get right out of high school would be — this may sound arrogant — worthy of myself...I want something better for myself.

Again, the intent to pursue post-secondary education was associated with parents' educational backgrounds.

> **Patti:** No, I've never, that's never been a possibility [not go on to college and university]. 'Cause, just 'cause my parents both work and have gone to university and all that and it's always been to go to school and get an education.

Not all students were as definite about their intentions to continue their studies. While the possibility of not attending a post-secondary institution existed, when weighed against the alternative — a dead end job and low wages — post-secondary participation was deemed to be more likely to lead to a better life.

Linda: Well, in the younger grades I thought so, but I think to succeed you sorta need more education and that now, but I think it would be more beneficial if I did go on to do something.

For the majority planning to attend either community college or university, life without a post-secondary education was anticipated to be unchallenging, repetitive, unstimulating, and unsatisfying.

Nora: Ummm, low paying job, or a job where you don't use much brains in...Not really rewarding.

The possibility of advancement in a career without a post-secondary education was not viewed as necessarily impossible, but risky at best. With the aid of "luck" "winning the lottery" or "connections," a reasonable future might possibly be secured. By "applying yourself" and "really working at it" an individual might be able to transcend limitations imposed by a lack of educational credentials. However, the threat of being "up against people who have gone to post-secondary education" would be omnipresent. The route to a career via post-secondary education was perceived to be easier, involved less risk, and provided more guarantees.

Carla: Oh, well, I'm sure it would if I was, you know, extremely talented or I got a lucky break, or I was a really hard worker...I'd rather just have a degree.

Acquisition of a post-secondary credential was seen, as Collins (1979) asserts, as cultural currency to purchase desired occupations in an era of competitiveness. Moreover, a post-secondary credential was perceived as "a piece of universally recognized and guaranteed symbolic capital, valid on all markets. As an official definition of an official identity, it releases its holder from the symbolic struggle of all against all by imposing the universally approved perspective" (Bourdieu, 1990a, p.136). Again, the perceived value of an academic credential was held as strongly by the young women in the sample as it was by the young men.

The benefits of higher education were also described in relation to learning and education for itself. Post-secondary education was envisioned as the route to a good life, not only in terms of employability and marketable skills, but also in terms of self-actualization. Further education was perceived as an individual "choice" for a better future.

Sally: All the opportunities are there, it's just the individual has to decide that they want that out of life and if they want it then they'll go for it and they will get it...it's the individual's choice to succeed.

Those not intending to participate in post-secondary education indicated that they also had incorporated the "human capital" view that post-secondary education was important for self-advancement.

Karen: If I would be better off [to go to post-secondary]? Oh yeah, I know I would be! Anyone would be!...It would give me more education and give me more I don't know, choices of things.

The contrast between participants' and non-participants' beliefs surfaced when the notion of post-secondary attendance was transferred from an abstract, general discussion of the benefits of post-secondary education to a concrete, personal discussion of "what it would do for me."

"Sure, Post-Secondary Education is Important, It's Just Not for Me." Whereas participants viewed post-secondary attendance as an avenue to "achieve whatever I want in life" "provide a credential to get a job" "help me reach my full potential" and "make me more interesting," non-participants emphasized that without a reason, purpose, or goal, post-secondary participation would be a futile exercise.

Ivan: Um, it matters what you want to do. For — if you want to be a teacher or something, it would be really important that you go, but if you were just going to do little things, um, to the point of general knowledge, I don't think you'd have to go to university or even college or some post-secondary because most of it's covered...[There's no reason to go] unless you really know what you want to do.

Without a definite reason to attend, post-secondary education was as akin to high school attendance — purposeless, unenjoyable, meaningless — another way to drift and not excel at anything. Rather than opening doors, further education was perceived as constraining. Post-secondary participation, in these students' eyes, was seen as postponement of the inevitable — the establishment of a position in the work world. While incumbent participants were convinced that post-secondary education was the minimum requirement for success, non-participants emphasized the importance of high school graduation.

Ivan: You have to have your Grade 12. It's like a requirement just for life in itself nowadays.

The necessity of a high school graduation certificate was not merely recited as the rhetoric of the day. Experience, both lived and vicarious, had already informed them that symbolic capital in the form of a graduation certificate was currently a minimum. This minimum was not only required, but it was sanctioned by these students as a legitimate screening mechanism.

Mort: How can they trust you if you can't finish high school?...Like if you're not smart enough or whatever, you don't have enough commitment to finish high school, well like this is a real job that people are actually depending on you.

These students also recognized that a high school graduation certificate was being rapidly replaced by the need for higher credentials, credentials that were perceived to be associated with skills and knowledge rather than credential inflation.

Whereas a discrepancy (or structural lag) between their dispositions toward post-secondary attendance and opportunity to attend post-secondary education existed for the group who perceived post-secondary participation to be "impossible," strong beliefs about high school graduation, their dispositions toward high school completion and the opportunity to do so were harmonious.

In their study of working class youth, Gaskell and Lazerson (1981) reported that youth who entered the work force directly from high school described their jobs as boring, low status, and with little in the way of opportunities for advancement. For the youth in my study who were headed for the work world, this reality was not something to be discovered — it was expected.

> **Mort:** I think it's going to be a real shock going into the work world. Like I'm not looking forward to that. I can honestly say, I think I hate school now, but I know I'm going to hate work worse. 'Cause monotony, just monotonous.

These students may indeed have "refused what is anyway refused"; however, their remarks did not suggest that they "love the inevitable" (Bourdieu, 1977b, p.77). The future was not described as rosy or bright. Rather, the prospect of chronic employment was perceived and anticipated with dread. Resistance of the inevitable, however, appeared to be minimal. In particular, the one form of resistance that was available to them — that is, post-secondary participation — was not perceived to be a solution.

Despite ubiquitous beliefs about the importance of higher education and insights into what life would be like without it, non-participants had not eliminated work as a legitimate post-high school destination. Whereas the work world was either not within the participants' repertoire of possibilities or was "possible, but I don't want to," non-participants were willing to at least give work a try; only upon failure in the work world would they consider post-secondary education as an option.

> **Matt:** Well, it depends if I get a good job, a steady job, I'll keep that. If it looks like it's going to turn into something. If it's not, I'll go back to school.

These students were aware of the risks of having to compete with those who possessed post-secondary credentials. Yet, despite conceding that the competition would "have the security of a post-secondary education, which is more beneficial to a job," attempting to establish oneself in the work world was worth the risk. If all else failed, they could return to school.

"*I'd Probably Succeed, But I'll Be Better Off with Post-Secondary.*" For a third group of students who intended to postpone entry into the post-secondary system, eventual participation ranged from "probable" to "inevitable." The beliefs held by this group were a hybrid between those "naturally" inclined to attend and the ardent non-participant view.

> **Linda:** If I really wanted to succeed without going on to post-secondary education I believe I could, but I think it would just be easier with some other kind of, or more formal education. I think it would just be more of a guarantee.

The message "If you have it in you to dream, you have it in you to succeed," or variations thereof, was the most common theme expressed in posters that papered high school walls. This message was reflected in these students' remarks; however, the "dream" was deemed more achievable through post-secondary participation.

Perceptions of interrelationships among beliefs about and dispositions toward post-secondary education, and academic capital by Grade 12 students have been explored to help elucidate how the processes of educational choice are created and reproduced. Earlier in this paper, it was pointed out that students' decisions about post-high school destinations are often assumed and expected by researchers, educators, and policy makers to be "rational" decisions. Do students perceive the decisions they have made regarding their planned post-high school destinations to be rational?

Rational Choices and Post-High School Destinations

The students who participated in these interviews were asked simply "Have you made a rational choice regarding your plans for next year?" "Why is (or isn't) it a rational choice?" and "What does the word "rational" mean to you?" Interestingly, almost all students, regardless of their planned post-high school destinations, asserted "yes" — that they had, in fact, made a rational decision regarding their futures. Why was this decision rational?

Rationality, for these high school students, took on a variety of meanings. Some students equated rational with desired or what they wanted to do. For other students, their planned actions were deemed rational according to a perceived normative component. For example, one student asserted that in order to get anywhere he had to go to university, hence his decision was rational. Others described their plans as natural, and hence rational, since an alternative plan had never been entertained. Yet for others, because their plans were *realistic* in terms of their likelihood of attainment, they were also rational. For some, the decision was rational because it was *pragmatic*, *anticipated*, or a *means of exploration*. *Parental influence* also was attributed to the rationality of one's plans. Finally, just having a *future plan* constituted rational action for a few students.

What was regarded as desirable, realistic, pragmatic, normative, or anticipated was not determined simply by acting on desires, given certain beliefs, and based on the evidence. That is not to say that beliefs, desires, and evidence did not play a role in decisions. However, when describing why their decisions were rational, students grounded their responses in relation to the long-term, deeply instilled dispositions that they held toward post-secondary education. As Troy's and Patti's comments illustrate (below), post-high school plans were not just a choice of what one can do. Rather, what one can do, and will do, was the result of long term structuring processes that facilitated a given action.

> **Troy:** Rational is sitting down and thinking about things. Like well I actually shouldn't say that because I didn't really make a conscious decision to go to college I just, like I said, it was just where I was going to go. It was understood, but like if I was sitting here now and didn't know what I was going to do then I'd want to just sit down and go "okay what are my choices?"

Notions of rationality were structured by embodied history in the form of long term dispositions, which were in turn structured by objectified history. In Patti's case, the financial assistance available (and made available), attitudes toward the transition to university from high school, parental expectations, and the presence in the community of a satellite community college, led her to conclude that, of course, her choice was rational.

> **Patti:** Well I think it's more rational than if I went right to university just for all the reasons that it will be cheaper, it's not such a big step yet it's a step and uh, it's sort of building up and I'll be more ready for university. I can pick up my grades a little

more...and financially like it wouldn't be smart of me because where would I get the money to go off to a big university right now? And I don't want my parents paying for it all.

Students were also asked whether a technical account of rationality played a role in their decisions regarding post-high school destinations. When asked whether they calculated the cost of post-secondary attendance and compared it with foregone earnings and whether they anticipated the salary differences between level of education attained and earnings, most students responded "no." Limited knowledge of salaries in relation to careers and their own unclear career directions precluded this type of approach to decision making.

Susan: I'm still not really aware of what careers offer, what rewards, so I'm still trying to find out. So that's partly why I haven't really made any concrete decisions as far as that goes.

For others, the notion of expected rate of return on investment was completely irrelevant.

Janice: No. No I haven't done that. It wouldn't matter what the results were really. I'd still want to be in university. [Why?] 'Cause I don't want to work.

Expected lifestyles, however, were based on what had been experienced up until this point in their lives. Those who described their backgrounds as "middle class" "well off" or "white picket fence sort of thing" intended to maintain or reproduce this lifestyle, and hopefully enhance it.

Clive: I want to be better than my parents. That's what I'm basing myself on. My Dad, he went to university, he makes a good living now, has a nice house, nice cars and I look at that as being if you go to university then you can get those things. You can achieve those things and that's what I base my future on. I want to be like my Dad or better.

It is difficult to disagree with Bourdieu (1990b) that in the case of decisions regarding post-high school destinations, "the *habitus* makes questions of intention superfluous, not only in the production but also in the deciphering of practices and works" (p.58). He maintains that the conditions under which rational calculations could take place very rarely exist in real life decision making situations. Yet, "agents *do* do, much more often than if they were behaving randomly, 'the only thing to do'" (Bourdieu, 1990a, p.11).

Bourdieu suggests that rather than following the prescriptions of rational decision making, individuals instead follow the intuitions of a "logic of practice." This logic of practice is the product of an enduring exposure to conditions not unlike those which individuals are born into. In these conditions, individuals "anticipate the necessary immanent in the way of the world" (Bourdieu, 1990a, p.11). The art of estimating and seizing the "potential opportunities" that are theoretically available to everybody requires the possession of the necessary capital and dispositions related to a given field.

Discussion

The Grade 12 students who participated in the two sets of interviews in October 1989 and May 1990 occupied a unique position in the social space. Although fully incorporated in the practices, routines, and rules of the secondary school system within the educational field, the time had arrived for them to begin to separate from this familiar world. This transition point is one of a very few in life's way that is both predictable and involuntary.

The predictable nature of the transition from high school permits certain strategies to be undertaken, over the long term, to prepare for adult life. As students vividly described, dispositions toward post-secondary attendance were instilled by family and reinforced in school. These dispositions, or habitus, according to Bourdieu (1990a) are the embodiment of the social game in question as a "feel for the game" that occurs in childhood. He asserts that "nothing is simultaneously freer and more constrained than the action of a good player" (p.63). Those planning to continue to post-secondary education, by doing what the game required, were indeed good players. Curricular choices made and grade point averages earned led to the next step in life, a step that had been envisioned for years and one that opened the way to the future.

Those who lacked a "feel" for the post-secondary game were left not knowing how to play it or even that they had a place in the game. Yet, they appeared well aware of the consequences. They held few pretences about the life that awaited them. Limited job opportunities, monotonous work, and bleak futures were anticipated. Escalating credentialism would continue to limit their futures. The group of students who "never" planned to continue to post-secondary education recognized the importance of further education; however, without positive dispositions toward post-secondary participation, they were unable to translate their beliefs into action. As such, their dispositions obfuscated the ability to recognize the chances offered to them through the non-university system. Curricular decisions, by the most disadvantaged because of limited cultural, and academic capital, were still described as the "right" choices. Minimal anger was expressed, nor was a sense of injustice perceived.

Did students make rational decisions about their futures? According to the tenets of practical rationality as espoused by Elster, it could be argued that some students did make rational decisions based on what they desired, the beliefs they held, and the evidence that was available. For others, inconsistency among desires, beliefs, evidence, and action could lead to the conclusion that decisions regarding post-high school destinations did not meet the requirements of rational action. But what does this tell us? It is far more enlightening, through the use of concepts of habitus, cultural, and academic capital, to uncover why certain beliefs are held, how desires (or dispositions are formed), and how evidence is amassed, and hence what action is taken.

10

First Nations Empowerment in Community Based Research

Schuyler Webster and Herbert Nabigon

> I looked again and saw the Indian Nations of this sacred Turtle Island,
> The ones you put here first and showed them their sacred way.
> They too were despised and desecrated by those so blind and greedy.
> But the sands of time run through the glass
> And this time of times is nearly over.
> The longest and the darkest and the coldest hour of the night
> Is the one just before the new day returns.
> Now is the time of hope.
> Now is the time to rise up.
> Now we must take into our hands the power of self-determination.
> We must stand up in our places in the sun.
> I give thanks for this new day. Kitchi meegwetch!
>
> Arthur Solomon, *Songs for the People*

The emerging movement to affirm Aboriginal Rights for the establishment of First Nations self-government has far reaching implications for private and public research endeavours, including the study of the schooling and employment of native youth. The principles that govern the conduct of community based research are assuming growing importance both for the native community and researchers. The process of communicating informed consent must be guided by codes that reflect a community partnership in creating the framework for participatory research. Native empowerment over research conducted in native communities has to be guided by criteria that ensure that outcomes more clearly focus on the strengths of the host culture — not only in identifying barriers, but also in fostering ownership of the solutions. A respect for and awareness of indigenous community belief systems must reflect the cultural and inter-cultural diversity of the population group.

A community-specific consultation process can contribute to creating an environment wherein native and non-native participants can share and examine value orientations and perceptions. In the early stages of the consultation process, indigenous involvement can assist in two important ways; first, in ensuring that a community-specific perception of the problem being investigated is communicated; second, in determining how the findings are utilized. This process requires no small effort on the part of both community participants and researchers.

Conducting transcultural research at the community level requires that the typical relationship between expert and non-expert be re-examined. Native commentary and assessment throughout all stages of the research process may help in creating continuity and in maintaining informed consent before embarking upon subsequent activities. Traditional native leadership throughout the consultation process is a vital component in ensuring guidance and input from recognized local expertise. There exists a need to expand the boundaries of research to include rights of the community. In discussing and articulating these rights we must first assume that native communities exist as "living systems." Additionally, a fundamental understanding of the historical profile of the community can lend a retrospective dimension to those policies that have had profound impacts upon the cultural, social, economic, and political systems of First Nations communities.

The following section provides an example of dilemmas encountered in one community based reserve project and raises several questions concerning control as a protection for First Nations against inaccurate or misleading research results. The paper then discusses approaches that might be followed in ensuring that research is conducted in ways which respect the cultural traditions and integrity of native communities.

Issues for Transcultural Research

It has not always been understood, nor accepted, in behavioral sciences that cultural values, attitudes, and beliefs can influence research results and can lead to unanticipated conflicts if research design and methodology fail to reflect the strengths of community culture. A primary concern of First Nation communities, spiritual leaders, political, professional, and other indigenous advocacy groups is that problems being researched should not add to the litany of "culture bound syndrome" stereotypes. Issues of alcohol addiction, violence, and other social pathologies plaguing indigenous populations are often interpreted as a failure of native culture to adapt to stressful socio-economic conditions. As Beauvais (1989) points out, "...we know that socio-economic stress can lead to increased substance abuse, and is undoubtedly a better prediction in a population than any exotic cultural explanation" (p. 28).

Historically, community based models of assessment or research have treated the dynamics of culture as peripheral to the goal of constructing methodologies that produce "sound" and "reliable" data. Perceptions of community assessment suffer from a "poverty of vision" wherein the "locus of control," so central in creating a sense of community ownership, is often diminished in favour of the jurisdiction of scientific inquiry. Research strategies are required to increase understanding of both the native world view and the meaning attached to the expressions of this world view.

The inability to translate social research concepts designed for mainstream community profiles into social policy frameworks more germane to the socio-cultural context of minority populations has far reaching implications. For example, a native community alcohol study conducted at North Slope Barrow, Alaska in 1979 concluded that the rapid increase of financial benefits derived from oil development and the native community's inability to adapt were in a large part responsible for the existing alcohol problems and other pathologies plaguing the community. An implicit assumption of this conclusion was that retention of cultural values created "a society of alcoholics" (Foulks, 1989: 13).

The North Slope study revealed several failures in the research strategies utilized in organizing a community index of the quality of life of a specific native community:

- Failure to obtain informed consent
- Failure to ensure a proactive structure for community input and assessment throughout all phases of the research
- Failure to separate ethnographic issues from the social pathologies being investigated
- Failure to expand the boundary of causal factors
- Failure to establish a collaborative relationship
- Failure to develop reporting procedures that protect against premature and misleading study results. (Adapted from contributions to *American Indian and Alaska Native Mental Health Research*, 1989.)

The structure for organizing community information must clearly articulate the goal of "community partnership" at each phase of the project, as well as establishing a sustaining supportive structure beyond the survey phase. Furthermore, the organizing elements must reflect a continuum that "unites those themes for fostering self-reliance within a context of transactions that are mutually beneficial to both the individual and the community, enhancing the potential for community aspirations and ensuring that community empowerment help identify solutions through organizing a supportive and responsive set of institutional arrangements that reaffirm the integrity of traditions and cultures" (Red Horse, 1982).

Successful First Nations community based research models in Canada that have facilitated the process of empowerment include: the Nitchee Institute for native based traditions and teachings for alcohol addiction services and research; the Alkali Lake Bands cultural network model for revitalization of native traditions and practices as a response to alcohol dependency; and the Native Human Services program at Laurentian University. The latter utilized a developmental cultural network model in order to formulate a community directed structure for establishing an Honours Bachelor of Social Work program. The Laurentian model retains a guiding philosophy through active community representation that serves to enhance and reinforce the "community partnership."

The following principles are recommended as a means of empowering subjects in the development and implementation of First Nations research (*American Indian and Alaska Native Mental Health Research*, 1989).

- That cultural values and belief systems of the host community be understood and respected

- That clear articulation of informed consent as a community right be recognized
- That development of a community consultation process which ensures First Nations participation and validation of the research design and methodology criteria be established
- That traditional leaders be recognized as sources of local expertise
- That a training component for First Nations communities be made available
- That confidentiality rights be extended to participating First Nations communities
- That publication and presentation of community research be under First Nations control
- That decisions about the public disclosure of premature study results be under the control of the community
- That employment practices related to the research project reflect native preference and be under local control
- That ongoing community consultation be maintained in the development of policy, organizational action steps, research design, and fiscal support
- That the primary document for presentation and dissemination of research results be made available in the aboriginal language of the community

Other Methodological Considerations

Recognizing aboriginal people as representative of a highly heterogeneous population is often made problematic because existing literature reinforces stereotypical homogeneous universal trait characteristics. Ethno-behavioural patterns of communication necessitate expanding the contextual continuum which may account for variation among and between aboriginal populations. Hence, popular notions of impassiveness, limited eye contact, noncompetitiveness and other misleading universal trait generalizations must be viewed from perceptions both within and outside of the cultural context. Additionally, the unique linguistic, socio-economic, religious, educational and political impact associated with assimilationist policies must be considered as alternative explanations.

Upon closer examination we find that, in fact, many variations exist among and within native cultures. The Navajo of Southwestern United States, for example, prefer eye contact. The Sechelt Band of British Columbia has prospered economically through land development, yet, the value which they place on their native identity remains an important unifying element of community. Many native cultures recognize individual autonomy as an important component of community success. "Consequently, portrayals of the collective Indian personality, although useful in establishing dialogues that can lead to enhanced understanding, must also

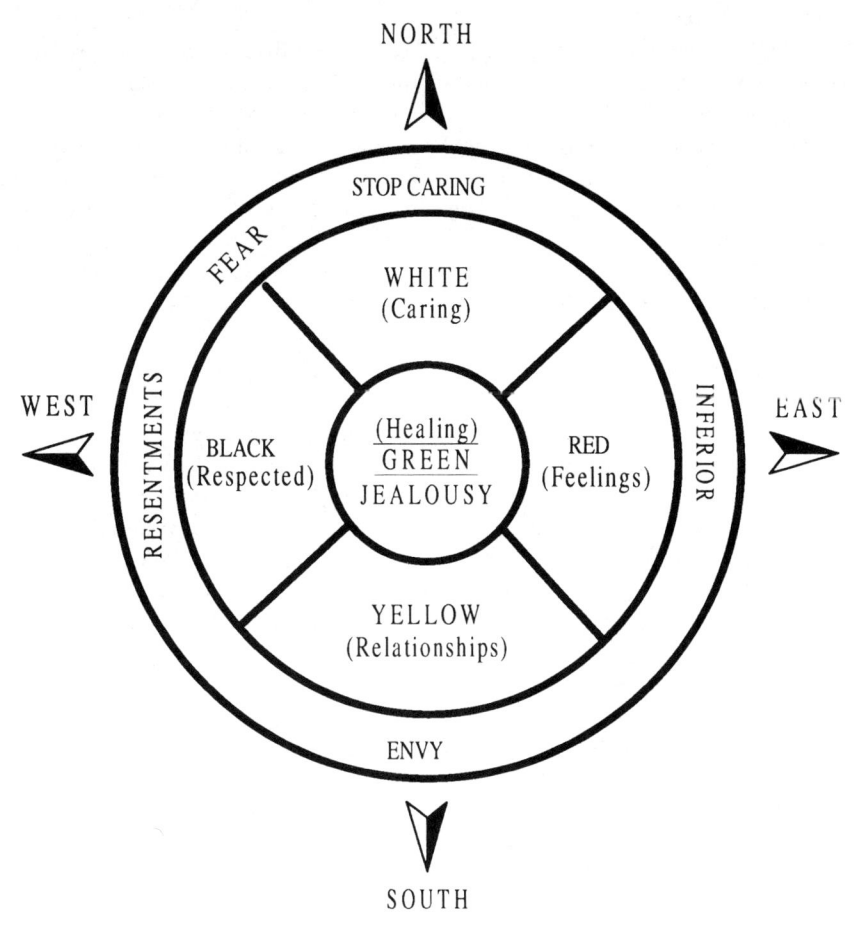

```
                          NORTH
                            ▲

                       STOP CARING
                    ╱ FEAR ╲
                   ╱   WHITE   ╲
                  ╱   (Caring)   ╲
         R                              I
         E                              N
  WEST   S   BLACK  (Healing)  RED     F   EAST
   ◀     E  (Respected)  GREEN  (Feelings)  E   ▶
         N              JEALOUSY        R
         T                              I
         M      YELLOW                  O
         E   (Relationships)            R
         N                              
         T      ENVY
                    ▼
                  SOUTH
```

Source: Cree Oral Tradition

Figure 10-1: Medicine Wheel

be viewed as preliminary to more important awareness of contemporary Indian lifestyles" (Dinges, Trimble, Manson and Pasquale, 1981: 244).

Investigations of cultural orientation through native family systems have focused narrowly upon the individual interaction between the non-native and native. Value orientation must expand the interpretation of native behaviourial patterns. "Cultural investigations have identified numerous family types including traditional, transitional, bicultural, and pan-traditional. These however, do not appear to measure 'Indianness,' but instead capture differential transactional styles among Indian families. Many cultural features remain constant: family structure, incorporation and relational bonding, and Indian preferences in social behaviour" (Red Horse, 1980: 466).

Attempts have been made to explain the limited utilization by urban-dwelling natives of medical, mental health and social services. However, a study of native medical service utilization patterns in the city of Saskatoon, Saskatchewan, found that the persistence of a traditional native medical system did not preclude the use of access to Western medical services. "In most cases where a healer was contacted for a health problem, this was after consultation with a physician. Individuals who reported simultaneous utilization of Western and traditional medical services invariably consulted a physician first, then a healer. The utilization of traditional services does not detract from the utilization of Western services" (Waldram, 1990: 16).

Other investigations that seem to contradict popular assumptions concerning the characteristics of native population groups have raised new questions about the utility of relying upon traditional techniques for measuring self-concept. Lower self-concept and personality formation within native populations has previously assumed significant negative self-concept. Lefley, however, reported that several studies of American Indian youth "found positive self-concept, competence, and optimism for the future" (Fuchs and Havighurst, cited in Lefley, 1982: 66). Trimble noted that "self-perception of 791 American Indians from 114 different tribes on a six-scale self-perception measure showed a moderately positive self image" (Trimble cited in Lefley, 1982: 66).

Lefley (1982) indicated that with the exception of Trimble's study, "construct and criterion validates, particularly those exemplifying appropriate conceptual and behaviourial correlates of positive self-concept in a given culture, have been rarely considered" (p. 66). Trimble's study "utilized native input to translate meanings and definitions of attitudes toward self." Native scales of self-perception are not yet generally used in standard training for social science research. Integrating native commentary and meaningful participation into research strategies could improve dialogue between First Nations communities and non-native investigators, and lead to meaningful research results.

The Cultural Paradigm

The aboriginal population is estimated to be 1.5 million with 11 different language groups and 53 dialects across Canada. The cultural, social, economic, political, and geographic landbase of aboriginal people has been adversely affected by intrusive, prescriptive, and burdensome governmental policies. The result is that aboriginal communities have suffered under often hostile policies designed to eradicate their cultural and language systems. As a response to these conditions, aboriginal people can be found to practice unique lifestyles that may be viewed as existing along a continuum. Within this continuum, native communities may be found to be traditional, transitional, or contemporary-adaptive. Within those several native belief systems, cultural practices and traditions may exist relatively intact in the traditional setting; however, in the contemporary adaptive community a process of cultural revitalization may be occurring.

As a cultural paradigm, aboriginal belief systems can contribute a unique perspective to understanding the values, attitudes, and perceptions of a native world view. The guiding philosophy of our approach acknowledges and reflects the world view of one of the prevailing native community belief systems. This world view interprets community relations in ways that are consistent with native realities rather than with non-native interpretations of these realities. The following description articulates a native world view on community. The spiritual interpretation of this native world view is divided into four sacred directions (see Figure 10–1). These directions are used to search for harmony and peace from within. Researchers should be aware of both the symbols and the beliefs systems which the "Colours" reflect. Interpreting native experience through the Colours may be an effective way of both facilitating communication and maintaining the integrity of the research project.

Historically, aboriginal cultures have transmitted their knowledge generationally through oral tradition. The medicine wheel is a sacred and complex symbol which represents abstractions difficult to capture in written form. Elders assume an important role in imparting the inherent vitality and meanings associated with the medicine wheel. It is for this reason that Elders continue to play such a meaningful role in this process.

East

It is believed that the creator began life in the east, where the colour red is symbolized. Aboriginal people are represented in the east. The creator bestowed the gifts of food, feelings, and vision for the people.

All life begins with the colour red. Red is a symbol of renewal. In the spring, the east wind breathes new life into our mother, the earth; the animals have their young and we use those animals for food. The spring teaches us to be grateful for life.

There is a strong relationship between food and feelings. Good food brings us good feelings. When we feel good about ourselves, we enjoy vision. In contrast to good feelings, feelings of inferiority also come from this direction. Feelings of inferiority can make us feel that we are not as good as other people. Today, many people experience inferior feelings and strong anger that comes from the east. Anger from the east can be translated into many of our domestic problems. Traditional teachings from this direction bring a message of peace and harmony into our communities.

South

The colour yellow is a symbol of summer, time, relationship, and the sun. At midday, the sun is facing south. The heat of summertime teaches us patience. We are helped to understand self through our relationships with family, extended family, friends, and community. It takes time to understand our identity as human beings. We learn and understand "self" by interacting with peers and acquiring values that are transmitted through our parents.

Puberty is a time of change for all young people. Adolescence is often a time of crisis. For the young native, it is a time to define their nativeness. The process of defining cultural heritage takes precedence over all activities, including education. It is during this period of self-exploration that a young person's academic grades may begin to decline. Educators and some parents forget to take this factor into consideration when there is a crisis at school. Elders and traditional teachers help to understand and defuse the crisis.

The opposite of a good relationship is envy. Envy can be defined as wanting what someone else has, but not willing to work for it. Envy needs to be diffused in sacred healing circles. Oriental people are represented in the south.

West

The colour black is a symbol of fall, respect, reason and water. Our bodies are largely made of water and this connects us to the lakes. Water helps us to see more clearly.

Respect means to look twice at everything we do. The quality of our inner life is enhanced when we understand and implement the word "respect." Many adolescents have a difficult time reviewing their inner life because of change and crisis. Native spiritual leaders have an intimate understanding of adolescence and healing ceremonies are made available to help the young people. There are times when older children have to share in the responsibilities of taking care of younger siblings. This practice can foster inner hostilities and resentments in adolescents because of the great changes they are undergoing. Elders and traditional teachers can conduct sacred ceremonies to defuse resentments. Feelings of resentment destroy any self-respect we may have. Black people are represented in the west.

North

The colour white is a symbol of winter, caring, movement and air. It is a peaceful colour that symbolizes peace. In the winter, the earth rests and the animals sleep.

Caring can be defined by our level of interaction, within family, school, community and nation. Isolation usually indicates that problems exist and that they need to be dealt with accordingly. An action plan is usually devised outlining caring behaviour that is intended to defuse isolation and not caring about responsibilities and self. Native Elders and traditional teachers understand the sacred nature of caring and its implications. How we interact and behave towards each other is observed and when requested, appropriate levels of interventions are mobilized. Caucasians are represented in the north.

Green is a healing colour and it is the symbol of Mother Earth. Green is also a symbol of *balance* and *listening*. The Earth nurtures all the colours and all living things. The dark side can be defined by five little rascals. They are inferiority, envy, resentment, not caring and jealousy. It means we stop listening. Spiritual leaders emphasize we should listen and pay attention to the dark side of life. The first step towards healing is relearning how to listen to our dark side. Listening helps us to make the appropriate changes from negative to positive behaviour.

Finally, the spiritual teachings of honesty and kindness permeate all of the five colours. Sage and sweetgrass remind us of self-honesty and self-kindness.

These elements of the prevailing belief system are presented as a first step in the consultation process and require that traditional elders play a vital role in the process of understanding the context of the community.

Conclusion

Tradition can both bridge gaps in cultural support experienced by native adolescents and provide cultural validation for their experiences. These belief systems are considered healthy and must be explored further as a method to prevent confusion at a critical time in the development of the native adolescent's cultural identity.

For example, the medicine wheel can assist community, school officials and students in exploring perceptions of problems that contribute to high drop-out rates. More importantly, a deeper sense of principle is conveyed which acknowledges important community and culture-specific perspectives not only in identifying problems, but also in crating a sense of ownership for the solutions. Furthermore persons participating in this process may feel empowered to make changes according to the relationship between the colours and the change required from an individual as well as a community standpoint. The Medicine Wheel is not limited as an expression of traditionality. Its application within indigenous support systems is well-documented as a source of interpretive balance, interpersonal renewal and community aspiration, all of which can and do change over time.

Native tradition can be an effective source of cultural renewal and can strengthen community aspirations for defining native success in the broader society, yet it is not itself a panacea for change. A multi-frontal effort must include expanding the human, technical, and financial resources available to First Nations communities in order to facilitate economic and educational stability. The retention of their culture values should not prevent natives from participating successfully in education or the labour market.

By engaging native communities at every level of the research endeavour — from the definition of the research problem, the conceptualization of the model, the conduct of field work, to the integration and application of the results, scholars (native and non-native alike), can contribute to a deeper understanding of the native experience.

11
Panel Studies of the Transition from School to Work: Some Methodological Considerations [1]

Harvey Krahn, Clay Mosher and Laura C. Johnson

For most young people, the process of leaving the education system and entering the work world involves significant role changes. The replacement of unpaid studying by paid labour is typically accompanied by a movement from dependence on parents to independent living and, some time later, by marriage or entry into a long-term relationship. Thus, the transition from school to work also signals the transition from youth to adulthood (Hogan and Astone, 1986).

Social scientists have not ignored this process, as demonstrated by the scores of studies in the past few decades of educational aspirations and attainment, career decision-making, occupational outcomes, and family formation. However, substantial economic, demographic, and social changes in the 1980s appear to have made the transition process more complex and difficult for North American youth. Consequently, academics, educators, and policy-makers have renewed their interest in the changing transition from school to work.

Given the dynamic nature of the subject matter, panel studies that survey the same individuals at several time-points have often been recommended (e.g., Mason, 1985: 23; Anisef et al., 1986: 67). Compared to cross-sectional studies which collect data at a single time-point, panel studies are much more useful for documenting the process of transition and for determining cause-and-effect relationships (Menard, 1991: 5). But because of their cost (both money and time), few panel studies have been completed. There appear to have been no nationally representative panel studies of the school to work transition in Canada.[2] However,

---

[1] Financial support for the multi-year study described in this paper was provided by the Social Sciences and Humanities Research Council of Canada, the Alberta and Ontario governments, the Canadian Solicitor General, the cities of Edmonton and Toronto, the University of Alberta and Laurentian University, and the Royal Bank of Canada. Along with the authors of this paper, the research team included Graham S. Lowe and Timothy F. Hartnagel (University of Alberta), Julian Tanner (University of Toronto), and John Lewko, Geoff Tesson and Carol Hein (Laurentian University).

[2] Statistics Canada's follow-up surveys of college and university graduates (e.g., Clark et al., 1986)

two large province-wide follow-up studies of youth leaving school were completed in Ontario in the 1970s. Porter et al. (1982) surveyed twelfth-graders in 1971 and 1972, and eighth-graders in 1971 and 1976. Six years after first surveying a sample of Grade 12 students, Anisef et al. (1980) recontacted them in 1979 to ask about their educational and occupational attainments. More recently, Sharpe and Spain (1991) have completed the first of several planned follow-up surveys of large samples of high school graduates and dropouts in Newfoundland.

The Canadian research literature also contains several useful single-community panel studies of the transition process. In her Hamilton study, Looker (1985) compared the 1981 occupational attainments of several hundred young women and men to the aspirations they had expressed six years earlier. Gaskell and Lazerson (1980) interviewed a small sample of Vancouver high school graduates before they left school in the spring of 1977 and then again after they had entered the labour force a year later. Hagan (1991) recontacted almost 500 Toronto youth, thirteen years after first interviewing them when they were in high school in 1976.

The four-year (1985–89) study of high school and university graduates described in this paper is another addition to this short list of Canadian panel studies. Our discussion of the design and implementation of this three-city study (Edmonton, Toronto and Sudbury) is organized around a series of critical methodological issues which researchers should consider when planning future panel studies of the transition from school to work. At the same time, the examples we draw from our research findings highlight several important features of the changing transition process in Canada.

We begin by arguing that the reference period, the social and economic context within which young people leave school and enter the labour force, must be taken into account when trying to explain the transition process. In other words, the results of transition studies completed a decade or more ago may not be completely generalizable to the current cohort of Canadian youth, even though these earlier studies can provide valuable over-time comparisons. We then use the description of our four-year panel study to suggest that researchers should:

1. Employ sampling designs, that allow a wide range of sub-sample comparisons over an extended period of time;

2. Implement data collection strategies that limit sample attrition, a significant problem in panel studies;

3. Develop measures that take advantage of the panel design but which are also sensitive to the "process" of transition as experienced by youth;

---

are national in scope but have typically used retrospective questions in a single survey to construct a data set that covers a several-year time period. Although published sources are unclear, the 1987 survey appears to have a panel design component. In contrast, the National Longitudinal Surveys of Youth Labor Market Experience (Borus, 1984) have used repeated surveys to obtain large-sample, nationally representative panel data on the transition experiences of teenagers and young adults in the USA. The Canadian graduate surveys are examples of "retrospective panel designs," as compared to the "prospective panel design" (Menard, 1991: 4) used in the US study.

4. Build data file structures that facilitate analysis of the panel data;
5. Employ analysis techniques appropriate to the subject matter and the research design.

Reference Period Effects

Compared to the 1960s and 1970s, the transition from school to work, and from youth to adulthood, has become a more prolonged and complex process. Young people are remaining in the education system longer, and are mixing school and work in a variety of different ways. The linkage between educational attainment and occupational outcomes appears to have weakened. Canadian youth are waiting longer to leave their parents' home and set up their own residence (Boyd and Pryor, 1989; Johnson, 1988), and are postponing parenthood (Schlesinger and Schlesinger, 1989). These changing patterns are related to several significant demographic, social, and economic trends that have been transforming Canadian society.

A very large baby boom cohort has meant that, until a few years ago, larger numbers of youth were moving through the education system and into the labour force (Foot and Li, 1986). The proportion of young people continuing on to higher education has also increased. By 1986, one in four 18 to 24 year old Canadians were engaged in some form of post-secondary education (Statistics Canada, 1988). There has been a simultaneous trend towards more young people working part-time while attending school (Cohen, 1989). As young people remain longer in the education system, and begin working sooner, the distinction between "student" and "worker" roles has been blurred (Krahn and Lowe, 1991).

The recession of the early 1980s saw Canadian youth unemployment rates rise rapidly to 19.9 percent by 1983. Joblessness among the young might have climbed even further, but for the larger proportion of young people staying on in school. Youth unemployment rates subsequently dropped, because of an economic recovery and also because of the dramatic decline in the size of the youth cohort. By 1987, there were half a million fewer youth (age 15 to 24) in Canada than there had been when this age group was at its largest in 1980 (Gower, 1988). Consequently, competition declined for the types of jobs typically held by youth.

These demographic, educational, and labour market trends have been occurring alongside a longer-term pattern of structural change in the Canadian labour market. Since mid-century, Canada has become a service-based economy. Today, more than 70 percent of employed Canadians work in the service sector (Lindsay, 1989). Service sector expansion has involved the creation of both good jobs and bad jobs (Economic Council, 1990). The former are much more common in the upper tier services (distributive and business services, public administration and the education, health and welfare sectors), while the latter are more often found in the lower tier retail trade sector and the other consumer services. This segmentation of employment opportunities is reflected in substantial differences in pay, job security, benefits, and skill demands (Krahn, 1992).

Young labour force participants have been much more likely to find themselves in lower-paying, low skill jobs (Myles et al., 1988), and young student workers have been heavily over-represented among these lower tier service sector workers. But there is evidence that a significant number of university graduates may also be having difficulty moving out of this "student labour market" (Krahn and Lowe, 1990; Krahn, 1991a). A recent study of 1976, 1982 and 1986 college and university graduates demonstrates that employment outcomes for both groups have declined (Davies et al., 1991). As indicated by the risk of unemployment, the incidence of part-time work, and other job quality measures, it is evident that the "good jobs" that previous cohorts of post-secondary graduates could reasonably expect were harder to find by the end of the 1980s. These changes cannot be simply attributed to the economic cycle, since the post-recession (1986) graduates did not fare better than those who left school at the height of the recession.

Thus, while we may not have observed the "radical restructuring" of the youth labour market that researchers have documented in Britain (Ashton et al., 1990: 2), we have witnessed some significant changes in the process of transition from school to work in Canada. Hence, while studies of previous cohorts can highlight important questions and provide useful comparisons, they will not reflect the experiences of contemporary youth. In many ways, the graduates of the 1980s are unique. The social, demographic, and economic forces that structured their transition out of school must be taken into account when describing and explaining this process.

We should also not generalize to the graduates of the 1990s. Youth unemployment has risen again in the past year (Thompson, 1991), but a smaller youth cohort offers hope that it will not reach the levels observed in the early 80s. However, structural changes in the Canadian economy continue. Given the on-going cutbacks in employment by large corporations and government departments, it is very likely that the lower tier services will provide a larger share of new jobs. Part-time and other forms of non-standard work will probably become more common (Krahn, 1991b). Consequently, we might expect to see more underemployment among young, well-educated Canadians. Alternatively, the smaller number of labour force entrants, and predicted skill shortages, may counter these trends. Thus, while it is evident that labour market changes continue, it is difficult to predict the type and extent of transition problems that future youth cohorts might face.

The panel study (1985–89) of high school and university graduates described below was initially designed to address problems of unemployment among youth. As unemployment declined while other structural changes continued, and as we began to see that unemployment was only one of many possible experiences in a longer process of transition from school to work, additional research questions were addressed in subsequent waves of data collection. The following discussion of methodological concerns will be of interest to researchers planning similar panel studies, but it also highlights some of the substantive findings that emerged from analyses of data collected in the study.

Research/Sampling Design

The ideal panel study of the transition from school to work would involve a large, national sample including high school dropouts along with high school, college/technical school, and university graduates. The study would extend over half a decade or more, and would include a minimum of two follow-up surveys after the baseline data collection. Large-sample, multiple-wave, nationally representative panel studies are extremely expensive, which explains why they have not been done in Canada. Province-wide panel studies with a similar design would be somewhat less expensive, but still very costly.[3] While our study was not representative of a complete province, it did cover three cities (in two provinces), included both high school and university graduates, and involved four waves of data collection. Hence, it did have a broader scope than several other single-community Canadian panel studies.[4] Cost considerations meant that college and technical school graduates were omitted, along with high school dropouts.[5]

Baseline (Year 1) data were collected in the spring of 1985 from high school and university seniors in Edmonton, Toronto and Sudbury. We chose these cities for pragmatic reasons (members of the research team lived in them), but recognize that they also reflected some of the diversity in the Canadian economy. Toronto is the largest urban centre in the country and typically, has had a very strong local economy. Edmonton is a moderate-size city with a reasonably diversified economy, while Sudbury is a good example of the single-industry communities scattered across the country. When the study began, the unemployment rate was about 6 percent in Toronto compared to 12 percent in the other two cities.[6]

---

[3] Despite these costs, several province-wide panel studies of the school-to-work transition have been completed in Canada. Porter et al. (1982) initially surveyed 9,000 Ontario students (in grades eight, ten and twelve) in 1971. The twelfth-graders were resurveyed a year later while the younger respondents were surveyed a second time in 1976. In 1979, Anisef et al. (1980) resurveyed 1,522 of their original 1973 sample of 2,555 twelfth-graders. This study also included two earlier follow-up surveys in 1973 and 1974. More recently, Sharpe and Spain (1991) have completed one follow-up survey of over 2,100 Newfoundland high school dropouts and two follow-ups of a sample of over 9,000 high school graduates, and are planning several additional waves of data collection.

[4] Gaskell and Lazerson (1980) interviewed a non-random sample of 80 Vancouver youth before leaving high school and again a year later. Looker (1985) resurveyed 76 percent of the 400 randomly-selected young people in her Hamilton study six years after her initial survey (see, also Looker and Pineo, 1983). In 1989, Hagan (1991) recontacted 490 of the 693 Toronto youth (grades 8 to 12 from four different schools) he had first interviewed in 1976.

[5] A parallel cross-sectional study of high school dropouts was completed in Edmonton in 1985. It employed semi-structured interviews to collect information from a sample of 162 early school-leavers (Tanner, 1990; Hartnagel and Krahn, 1989).

[6] Today (mid–1992), these inter-city differences have almost disappeared, with all three cities registering unemployment rates in excess of 10 percent in April, 1992. While previous trends would suggest that the Toronto rates would decline first, these temporal changes merely reinforce our earlier conclusion that the reference period and other contextual factors must be taken into account when commenting on the transition process.

While highlighting these important community differences, we still recognize that a three-city sample cannot possibly reflect the whole of Canada. Smaller urban centres and rural regions were omitted, as were the east and west coast provinces, Quebec, and the northern Territories. Graduates of community colleges and technical schools and early school-leavers did not participate in the study. Thus, our observations about the transition process are generalizable only to larger urban centres in English Canada. Nevertheless, this population still includes a large proportion of Canadian youth. In addition, the study can provide valuable comparisons to similar studies conducted elsewhere in Canada.

Although our study was restricted to three cities, we tried to build as much diversity as possible into the sampling design. The three cities represented three distinct local labour markets. We tried to survey large numbers of both academic and non-academic stream high school students, while five major faculties were included in the university sample. These sampling decisions have proved to be very useful, allowing us to examine, for example, employment opportunities for university and high school graduates in different cities (Krahn and Lowe, 1990), varying levels of underemployment among graduates from different faculties (Redpath, 1991), and differences in drug and alcohol use among high school seniors in different communities (Tanner and Krahn, 1991). Given that funding for large-scale panel studies will be equally difficult to obtain in the future, researchers studying the transition process would be advised to build critical comparisons such as these into their smaller-scale research designs.

Our initial (1985) university sample covered the five largest faculties (Arts, Business, Education, Engineering, Science) at the University of Alberta, the University of Toronto, and Laurentian University. A systematic sample was generated by choosing every third name (every second name in Sudbury) on lists of undergraduate students scheduled to receive their degree that spring. Professional faculties such as Law or Medicine were excluded because of small enrolments and specialized labour markets. Inclusion of these students in the sample would have added to the study but compromises were necessary.

This (university) sampling design netted a small number (less than 10%) of mature students (anyone 30 years of age or older). We processed the Year 1 data collected from these individuals, but did not include this information in our working data-sets and did not re-survey these graduates in subsequent years. Looking back, we would not make the same decision again. Universities are beginning to attract more mature students and, as we have learned, the school-to-work transition has become a prolonged process which, for many, involves movement in and out of educational institutions. The interrupted transition process is clearly of interest to researchers examining the relative contributions of age, experience, training and formal education to successful employment outcomes.

Turning to the high school sample, we would also reconsider our decision to begin the study with high school seniors. Given the large numbers of students working while attending school, it is evident that the process of transition from school to work begins long before the end of the senior year. Consequently, baseline data collected from tenth-graders, for example, could be very useful. This earlier start would also provide valuable information about the formation of career and higher education aspirations, and about the impact of early course and program choices on subsequent educational options.[7]

We were unable to randomly select high school students in our baseline survey.[8] Instead, we attempted to build as much variation as possible into the sample by contacting schools in middle-class and working-class neighbourhoods, seeking permission to survey academic and vocational classes, and making every effort to convince all students present to participate in the study. The final sample contained students from six Edmonton high schools, twelve schools in Toronto, and seven in Sudbury.

We did not put extra emphasis on race or ethnicity when constructing our initial sample. If we were to begin again today, we would add racial mix to our criteria for choosing schools, particularly in Toronto where the population is becoming much more ethnically and racially diverse. The interacting effects of race, gender and class on the transition from school to work cannot be ignored (see James, 1990, as well as the papers by James, Mandell and Looker in this book).

The Year 1 survey in May of 1985 was followed by a complete second wave of data collection in May of 1986 (Year 2) and a third survey in May of 1987 (Year 3). Our inability to immediately raise money for the fourth wave of data collection postponed this survey till June of 1989 (Year 5). We also completed a small "mini-survey" in the fall of 1985, six months after the baseline survey. This questionnaire contained a short set of questions about education and employment status, and about problems of unemployment for those who had not found work.

If we could start over again, we would not use the same time schedule. We have become very conscious of the extent to which the transition from school to work has become a prolonged process (Krahn and Lowe, 1991). In the spring of 1989, four years after graduating, over half (58%) of the high school sample were still planning to return to school in the fall, either full-time or part-time, compared to 36 percent of the university sample (who had received their undergraduate degrees four years earlier). Thus, given limited resources, a research design that resurveyed respondents every two years, over a longer period of time, would be much more useful than a series of back-to-back annual surveys.

---

[7] Porter et al. (1982: 40) recognized this fact when they included eighth, tenth and twelfth grade students in their initial sample. Hagan's (1991) Toronto panel study also included students from grades 8 through 12.

[8] Gaining access to high schools was more difficult than we had expected. In Edmonton, for example, school board officials would not give us access to school records, a problem also encountered by Porter et al. (1981: 41) in their earlier Ontario study. Edmonton school board officials allowed us to approach a range of high schools, but the principals of these schools could refuse to participate, as could individual teachers. With permission from a teacher, we would meet with the class, describe the study, and send home letters explaining the study to parents. If a parent provided written approval (students 18 and older were allowed to make their own decision), their child could then complete the questionnaire on our second visit to the school.

The disadvantages of an extended time-frame are the basic disadvantages of a panel study. Longer gaps between data-collection points increase the probability of losing contact with sample members. Even with a one-year break between surveys, retrospective questions will be needed to enquire about education and work experiences during the previous twelve months. The longer the time period covered by such questions, the greater the problems of measurement reliability. One can, of course, ask questions only about current status (e.g., what kind of job do you have now?), and compare the answers to those provided for similar questions asked two or more years earlier. However, if it is the "process" of transition that is of interest, questions about specific experiences in the time between surveys are very important. Recognizing these problems, we would still recommend a minimum of two years between data collection points.

Data Collection Strategies

Baseline data from high school graduates were collected in classrooms in May and June of 1985. Members of the research team described the study to students in a first meeting, and then returned a week later to administer the questionnaire. Precise information on the number of students not present was unavailable, but we estimate that our first wave of data collection had a response rate close to 90 percent.

University graduates were surveyed by mail in April 1985, before the end of term. A cover letter describing the study and a return-addressed stamped envelope accompanied the questionnaire. In Edmonton and Sudbury, the initial mailing was followed over the next three weeks by a reminder letter (to everyone in the sample), a second questionnaire and cover letter to those who had not responded by this point, and a second reminder letter. After this, phone calls were made to several hundred students who had not responded to our earlier appeals, asking them to complete the questionnaire.

In Toronto, university officials would not provide us with a list of graduates, although they were willing to send out the first questionnaire package and one reminder letter. This difference in procedure had a significant effect on baseline response rates, which reached 64 percent in Edmonton, 50 percent in Sudbury, but only 34 percent in Toronto. Our experience in this first data collection effort, and in subsequent years when both the high school and university samples were contacted by mail, highlights the need for a great deal of persistence (multiple mailings and follow-up telephone calls) in pursuing respondents and convincing them to participate. The importance of aggressive follow-up procedures to reduce sample attrition cannot be over-emphasized.

Panel studies require respondents to give up their anonymity, so it is very important that they be guaranteed confidentiality. Respondents in the baseline (1985) survey were asked to provide their name, home address and telephone number on the last page of the questionnaire. High school sample members were asked to tear off this page and hand it in separately, and were promised that this information would be stored in a safe location away from the questionnaires. Year

Table 11-1: Sample Sizes and Response Rates, by City and Sample, 1985-89

	Year 1 May, 1985		Year 2 May, 1986		Year 3 May, 1987		Year 5 June, 1989	
	H.S.	Univ.	H.S.	Univ.	H.S.	Univ.	H.S.	Univ.
Edmonton	983 [894]*	589 [533]	665 (68%)#	458 (78%)	547 (56%)	421 (71%)	504 (51%) (56%)+	392 (67%) (74%)
Toronto	754 [674]	519 [433]	412 (55%)	358 (69%)	296 (39%)	326 (63%)	207 (27%) (31%)	287 (55%) (66%)
Sudbury	492 [338]	227 [221]	240 (49%)	156 (69%)	187 (38%)	128 (56%)	125 (25%) (37%)	90 (40%) (41%)
Total	2,229 [1,906]	1,335 [1,187]	1,317 (59%)	973 (73%)	1030 (46%)	875 (66%)	836 (38%) (44%)	769 (58%) (65%)
Total	3,564 [3,093]		2,289 (64%)		1,905 (53%)		1,605 (45%) (52%)	

* Number of Year 1 respondents who provided their name and address for follow-up purposes.
\# Percent of total Year 1 sample who completed follow-up survey.
\+ Percent of Year 1 respondents who provided follow-up information.

1 university sample members who were contacted by mail were given the same promise.

Nevertheless, some Year 1 sample members were unwilling to provide follow-up information. In the high school sample, this meant we had no way of returning to them. While we could identify the university sample members who did not provide follow-up information (since we had mailed the questionnaire to them), we took their unwillingness to fill in the last page as an indication that they did not wish to be contacted again. Thus, while a total of 2,229 high school seniors completed the first survey, only 1,906 (86%) provided the information needed for follow-up. In the university sample, 1,187 (89%) of the 1,335 Year 1 respondents gave us their name, address and phone number (Table 11–1).

All of the follow-up surveys for both samples were completed by mail, using a modified version of the Year 1 university procedures. The last reminder letter was omitted since our experience in 1985 showed it to have little additional effect on response rates. Instead, we found it more effective to move immediately to telephone calls after mailing the second questionnaire package. Since funding for this panel study was patched together from various sources, with the Edmonton component of the study being better funded, more resources were devoted to follow-up efforts in this city, resulting in substantially higher response rates.

Our final 1989 response rate was only 38 percent of all those who completed the Year 1 questionnaire for the high school sample compared to 58 percent for the university sample. The difference is simply explained — university students who were not interested in the study ignored our first questionnaire and never became part of the study. However, most high school students participated in the initial in-class survey. The disinterested then dropped out of the study in the next year or two (Table 11-1). If we use only those who provided follow-up information in Year 1 as our base, our final response rates are obviously higher (44% for high school graduates and 65% for university graduates). Nevertheless, the fact remains that large numbers of those who began the study failed to stay with it over four years.[9]

When preparing for the second follow-up survey (Year 3, 1987), we made the decision not to contact those who had failed to return the Year 2 questionnaire. Our reasoning was that the final data sets would contain large blocks of "missing data" if some of these individuals re-entered the study. Thus, in each successive survey only those who had remained participants throughout were contacted. No doubt, if we had returned to the other original participants, some would have re-joined the study, raising the long-term response rates. Recognizing now that not all of our panel data analyses will include information from all time-points covered in the study, we are less convinced of the correctness of the original decision. However, we are very aware that the construction of multi-year data sets would have been complicated considerably if we had attempted to re-contact these individuals.

Several months before each follow-up survey we sent sample members a Newsletter that included general findings, information about how the data were being used (e.g., government reports, academic publications), and details about the next wave of data collection. The Newsletters also included a request for respondents to phone (collect) if they had moved to a new address. Newsletters returned to us by the Post Office indicated which sample members needed to be located before starting the follow-up. We believe these Newsletters also helped maintain the interest of respondents. Our limited research budget had no room for payments

---

[9] Compared to other Canadian panel studies, our over-time response rates are somewhat low. Looker (1985) was able to resurvey 76 percent of her original Hamilton sample six years after her baseline study. Anisef et al. (1980: 43) reported a response rate of 60 percent of their six-year follow-up of Ontario twelfth-graders, while Hagan (1991) managed to reinterview 72 percent of his original Toronto sample thirteen years later.

Table 11-2: Currently Living with Parents by City, Sample and Sex, 1985-89

Percent*

Living with Parents(s)	1986 Female	1986 Male	1987 Female	1987 Male	1989 Female	1989 Male
High School						
Edmonton	87.6	88.2	79.8	86.1	54.4	64.1
Toronto	94.2	95.1	87.5	83.5	72.1	81.4
Sudbury	92.8	91.1	79.7	83.9	55.1	61.8
Total	90.0	90.4	81.6	85.1	58.8	68.3
University						
Edmonton	31.5	34.4	23.6	28.6	14.3	13.2
Toronto	56.9	59.4	45.3	51.9	25.6	36.8
Sudbury	28.8	25.0	16.5	25.0	6.2	8.3
Total	41.3	42.0	31.3	36.1	17.6	20.7

*Percentages for each year calculated with the final Year 4 sample (see Table 11-1) as the base.

to respondents, but we felt that a Newsletter could be an effective way of showing that we appreciated continued participation in the study.

When forced to trace respondents who had moved, we relied most on the home address and phone number provided in Year 1. In subsequent surveys, we added to our data base by asking respondents for the name and telephone number of a friend who might be phoned if we lost contact. A few respondents were traced through provincial government Drivers License agencies, but we quickly learned that young people are very slow to update their address after they move. Each year, a handful of respondents would phone and report their change of address.

Ultimately, the reluctance of respondents to complete another questionnaire had the largest effect on our response rates, since there were very few sample members who we were unable to locate. Tracing the university graduates was more difficult

Table 11-3: Percent Still Living in the City Where They Completed High School/University by City, Sample, and Sex, 1987 and 1989

Percent*

	High School Sample				University Sample			
	1987		1989		1987		1989	
Still Living in:[#]	Female	Male	Female	Male	Female	Male	Female	Male
Edmonton	94.0	94.6	86.9	91.1	61.1	58.7	53.2	47.1
Toronto	98.1	96.1	95.2	88.3	76.8	74.5	66.9	68.9
Sudbury	76.8	76.8	69.6	66.1	15.2	37.5	16.7	16.7

* Percentages for each year calculated with the final Year 4 sample (see Table 11-1) as the base.
[#] Percentage of individual city sample.

than locating the high school sample members. In 1985, when first surveyed, 48 percent of the complete university sample (57% in Toronto, 47% in Edmonton, and 29% in Sudbury) were living with their parents, compared to 96 percent of the high school sample (Krahn, 1988). By 1989, few of these university graduates were living at home (Table 11-2). While members of the high school sample were beginning to leave home, the majority had not yet done so. However, Toronto respondents in both samples were still most likely to be living with their parents, no doubt because of the higher cost of housing in that city.

University graduates were also much more likely than high school sample members to have moved to another city (Table 11-3). This table also reveals large city differences in mobility patterns, with Sudbury respondents being considerably more likely to have moved. By 1989, one-third of the Sudbury high school sample had left the city, compared to roughly one in ten Edmonton and Toronto high school graduates. As for the university sample, only 17 percent of the Sudbury respondents were still living in the city where they had obtained their degree, compared to 69 percent of University of Toronto graduates and almost half (47%) of University of Alberta graduates. Differential employment opportunities in the three local labour markets obviously account for much of these city differences.

Sample Attrition

As already noted, sample attrition was more problematic in Sudbury and Toronto (Table 11-1). The higher response rates in Edmonton result from the additional resources that local members of the research team could devote to data collection, and probably have little to do with the characteristics of Edmonton sample members. However, it is quite likely that other respondent characteristics are systematically related to the probability of remaining in the study. Attrition bias was assessed by separating all 3,564 Year 1 respondents into two groups, those who remained in the study through Year 5 and those who dropped out. Chi-square tests of the relationship between this binary variable and a range of Year 1 measures were used to determine the existence of any attrition bias. Specifically, we examined the effects of gender, educational orientation, labour force experience, and socio-economic background on attrition, separately for the high school and university samples and, within them, for each of the three cities (see Krahn and Mosher, 1992, for more details).

Beginning with the high school sample, in all three cities females were significantly more likely than males to remain in the study through to Year 5. For the three cities combined, 45 percent of the female high school graduates in the baseline survey completed all of our questionnaires, compared to 32 percent of males.

In each city, high school graduates in an academic program were significantly more likely to stay in the study (53% compared to 28% of those in non-academic programs). Similarly, students who reported higher grades in their senior year (1985) were more likely to still be participating in the study in 1989. The "survival rate" for those with self-reported grades of 80 percent or higher was 50 percent. Somewhat fewer (41%) of those with grades between 70% and 79% responded at all four time-points, compared to 35 percent of those in the 60% to 69% range, and 29 percent of those with grades under 60%. In each city, those who planned to continue their education in the fall of 1985 were somewhat more likely to remain in the study, but the difference was statistically significant only in Edmonton. Thus, in general, we observe that less academically-oriented members of the original high school sample were more likely to drop out of the study by Year 5.[10]

Compared to educational orientation, labour market experience while attending high school has only a marginal impact on attrition. In Edmonton, but not in the other two cities, sample members who had held a paying job while in high school were significantly less likely to remain in the study. In Toronto, respondents reporting a period of unemployment prior to graduation were less likely to complete all of the follow-up questionnaires (25% compared to 34% of those reporting no previous unemployment).

---

[10] Anisef et al. (1980: 43) observed a similar pattern of attrition in their province-wide Ontario survey in the 1970s. Hagan (1991: 572) reports that young people with a lower self-assessment of their school performance were more likely to drop out of his study between 1976 and 1989.

High school graduates from a higher socio-economic background were more likely to participate in this panel study through to Year 5, although significant relationships were not found for each indicator of SES and in each of the three cities. In the total high school sample, 32 percent of those who identified their parents' financial situation as "below average" remained in the study, along with 36 percent of those who answered "average," and 43 percent of respondents who reported their parents' financial situation as "above average." As for their own financial status, respondents stating that it was "above average" were more likely to have responded at all four time-points (43%), compared to 32 percent of those who answered "below average."

A higher proportion of those with a professional/managerial father remained in the study through to Year 5 (46% compared to 34% of those whose father had a lower status occupation). Similarly, respondents with a better-educated father had a higher survival rate. A larger proportion of those born in Canada (41% as opposed to 28% of those born elsewhere) remained in the study in Year 5, although the relationship was not statistically significant in the Sudbury sub-sample. For the total high school sample, a significantly higher proportion of those from an English-speaking family were still in the study in 1989.

As in the high school sample, significantly more female university graduates (62% compared to 53% of males) remained in the study in Year 5 (although this relationship was not significant in the Sudbury sample). While age and marital status varied little in the high school sample in 1985 (the majority of respondents were between the ages of 17 and 19 and almost all were single), there was some variation in the university sample. However, neither age nor marital status affected the probability of dropping out of this panel study.

For the university sample as a whole, there was no attrition bias by faculty. Nevertheless, a significant relationship was found in the Edmonton sub-sample where the lowest survival rate (56%) was found among the Science graduates, compared to 67 percent for Arts, 68 percent for Business, 73 percent for Education, and 74 percent for Engineering. Self-reported grades were not significantly related to attrition, and neither were plans to continue education in the fall of 1985. Only one of the six sub-sample tests involving labour force experience measures revealed a significant relationship.

While SES measures were systematically related to attrition in the high school sample, the pattern was not as strong or as consistent in the university sample. In fact, for several SES indicators, university sample members from higher status families were somewhat more likely to drop out of the study (Krahn and Mosher, 1992). The much weaker link between socio-economic status and attrition in the university sample may result from the limited SES variation among university students who tend to come from middle-class backgrounds. However, native-born university sample members, and those from English-speaking homes, were significantly more likely to remain in the study (although these relationships were not significant in the Toronto and Sudbury sub-samples).

Summing up, the university sample reveals fewer systematic attrition biases than the high school sample. In both samples, females were significantly more likely to stay with the study. While less school-oriented high school graduates were more likely to drop out of the study, a similar pattern was not found among the university graduates. Both the high school and university samples suffered from greater loss of non-Canadian born and non-English speaking members, a pattern that was particularly apparent in Edmonton. But while lower SES was associated with a lower survival rate in the high school sample, there was no clear and systematic SES bias in the university sample.

These attrition biases must be taken into account when analyzing data from this study, which already over-represents middle-class, more school-oriented youth in its basic design (since high school dropouts and young people choosing technical or vocational post-secondary training were not surveyed). As previous research has shown, SES is a significant factor in determining whether or not young people go on to higher education which, in turn, strongly influences career outcomes (Anisef et al., 1980; Porter et al., 1982). Hence, total-sample findings from this study should not be casually generalized to all youth. Nevertheless, there is still sufficient SES variation within the samples to allow comparisons of the transition experiences of young people from different socio-economic backgrounds. If such analyses reveal SES differences, class-specific conclusions must be drawn. If no differences are found, broader generalizations may be appropriate.

Measurement Issues

The topic of measurement in survey research is a large one, and measurement issues in panel research designs can be particularly complex. The following observations only begin to address such issues, but may still be of value to other researchers planning panel studies of the transition from school to work.

Measurement problems arose very early in our study when School Board officials (in Edmonton) objected to a number of questions we had hoped to include in the Year 1 questionnaire because of their concerns about possible negative reactions from parents. For example, we had hoped to test the frequently hypothesized relationship between youth unemployment and crime with before and after graduation measures of delinquency. However, we were forced to compromise with very general questions rather than the specific measures we had planned to use, because we were also asking respondents for their name and address. We did include the preferred measures in subsequent follow-up surveys which no longer required School Board approval, but our analyses have been handicapped because of our crude baseline measures (Hartnagel and Krahn, 1988).

We included most of the questions from the baseline survey in each of our follow-up surveys, since we wanted to monitor changes over time in both statuses and attitudes. However, the development of each follow-up questionnaire was a struggle, because we could not include as many questions on new issues as we would have liked. In retrospect, we would probably stagger the inclusion of many of the questions, since only some over-time analyses require frequently repeated measures. For example, we would still include questions about specific employment and educational experiences in each questionnaire, but might ask about political attitudes, leisure activities, and family plans in every second wave of data collection.

A majority of the items in our questionnaires were of the forced-choice variety but we also included a significant number of open-ended questions. Such measures were sometimes chosen because we wanted to ask about general reactions to subjects on which young people might not have well-formed opinions, without prompting them. For example, in Year 2 of the study we included an open-ended question asking for reactions to a hunger strike on behalf of Canadian youth by a Canadian senator (Krahn and Lowe, 1987).

In the baseline survey, we used forced-choice (agree-disagree) measures to assess young people's explanations of unemployment (Lowe et al., 1988). Sensing that we might be helping create some opinions with a long list of possible "explanations," we shifted to an open-ended format when asking about the same issue in Year 3. Similar concerns about planting ideas in respondents' minds discouraged us from using check-lists for questions about job search plans, or forced-choice measures when enquiring about motivations for working part-time while in high school (Lowe and Krahn, 1992), or for living at home with parents (Johnson, 1988).

In some cases, we might have used a forced-choice measure if we had known something in advance about the range of possible answers. However, before asking sample members, we really had no idea of how they used computers in their jobs (Lowe and Krahn, 1989), of the types of advice they might offer to some other young person looking for a job, or what they might have seen as a positive feature of personal unemployment.

In short, clearly-stated forced-choice questions are essential for documenting many aspects of the transition from school to work. Alternatively, open-ended questions may provide a better picture of the process from the perspective of the young person going through it. Unfortunately, responses to open-ended questions are costly to process. They are also difficult to analyze, given their categorical level of measurement, higher amounts of non-response, and the tendency of many respondents to provide multiple answers. But while open-ended questions may not lend themselves easily to sophisticated quantitative analysis, they do incorporate a valuable qualitative element into survey research designs.

Data File Structure

A few comments about data file structures might also be useful. In our baseline (1985) survey, we used different questionnaires for the high school and university samples because not all our questions were relevant to both groups. For example, we wanted to ask high school graduates more questions about relationships with their parents, while questions about student loans and choice of faculty did not apply to them. If we had put all of the common questions at the beginning of each questionnaire and the sample-specific questions at the end, as we did in the follow-up surveys, we would not have spent as much time reorganizing the variables in the two Year 1 data sets before merging them.

In each of our follow-up surveys we included the same set of identifying variables (sex, day, month and year of birth) so that we could confidently merge the follow-up data with the correct cases in the baseline data. Even with access to these variables we were uncertain about a few cases. Some respondents married and changed their names and a few invariably made mistakes in their answers. We encountered several "sex changes" when matching data from one year to the next, but were able to reverse them after checking birth dates and additional information on educational activity and previous employment. We cannot emphasize enough the importance of planning ahead for such data-merging problems.

Panel studies as large as ours can create cumbersome data sets. We have found it most convenient to construct a series of data files of varying size and shape. Our largest-sample file contains only Year 1 information for all 3,564 participants in the baseline study. A second data set with twice as many variables contains Year 1 and 2 data, but only for the 2,289 individuals who stayed with the study till 1986. Our third and fourth data sets contain more variables and fewer respondents, respectively. When beginning an analysis project, we choose from among these data sets, depending on the time-frame we wish to cover.

Analysis Techniques

While panel data can address questions that could not be answered with cross-sectional surveys, more sophisticated analysis techniques are often required. We have not employed such techniques in all of our analyses.[11] Frequently, like most other previous users of panel data in Canada, we have incorporated data from multiple time-points, but without using repeated measures of the same concept. For example, when examining on-the-job use of computer skills, Year 1 variables were among the indicators used to account for employment outcomes measured in Year 3 (Lowe and Krahn, 1989). An equivalent analysis could have been done with data from a cross-sectional survey that incorporated retrospective questions. The advantage of using panel data for such analyses lies in the greater reliability of the baseline measures, as compared to retrospective questions that might be prone to memory problems.

We have begun to operationalize the transition process by constructing typologies of transition groups on the basis of educational activity in each of the years covered by our study. In an analysis of young workers in the service economy based on the 1985–87 data, we identified four distinct groups: "students" who had remained in school full-time for twenty-four months; "workers" who had not completed any full-time education during this time; and two intermediate groups who had mixed school and work in different ways (Krahn and Lowe, 1990).

---

[11] In some cases, we have simply used cross-sectional data from a single wave of data collection (e.g., Lowe et al., 1988; Tanner and Krahn, 1991).

However, the analysis strategies described above still do not take full advantage of our panel data, which can provide insights into cause and effect processes denied to users of cross-sectional data. A recent paper (Empson-Warner and Krahn, 1992) that examines the effects of unemployment experiences on occupational aspirations of high school graduates begins to move in this direction. In this analysis of 1985–86 Edmonton data, occupational aspirations in Year 2 were modelled as a function of aspirations in Year 1, experiences of unemployment in the intervening twelve months, and other important control variables. Thus, differences in baseline aspirations are taken into account in this regression analysis, as are their potential effect on unemployment, the theoretically important variable in this model.

This structural equation approach is probably the most common method of analyzing panel data (Kessler and Greenberg, 1981). We expect to use it in a number of analyses currently planned, particularly those examining changes over time in attitudes and goals. Event history analysis (Allison, 1984), which focuses on the probability of a given event occurring to an individual within a specific time period, and on the effects of other factors on this probability (or hazard rate), also seems particularly well-suited to studies of the transition from school to work. We plan to use this technique to examine movement between jobs, in an out of educational programs, and into different family statuses.

Summary

The transitions from school to work, and from youth to adult roles, are intertwined. Researchers risk missing an important part of the picture if they study only one, and not the other. They should also remain conscious of the diversity of transition experiences. Gender, race, region, and socio-economic background can have significant effects on the educational and career opportunities available to youth. In addition, the transition from school to work has become a more complex, prolonged, and often interrupted affair. Many Canadian youth are active labour force participants long before they leave the educational system. Many also continue to move in and out of the education system after beginning full-time jobs. Thus, it is imperative that researchers conceptualize and study "transition" as a process, not as an event.

Panel studies are excellent research vehicles for studying this process of transition, but they are also very costly. Hence, researchers should consider a number of important methodological issues when designing and implementing such studies. Since few will have access to the funds needed to complete province-wide (or larger) panel studies, every effort should be made to incorporate as much variation as possible into the baseline sample of a smaller-scale panel study. With more sub-sample comparisons built into a research design, the likelihood increases that the study will portray the wide diversity of young people's transition experiences. In addition, panel studies should be extended over at least five or six years, in order to satisfactorily cover the extended process of transition from school to work.

Assessments of attrition in previous panel studies have revealed that less school-oriented youth are more likely to drop out of such studies, as are young people from lower SES backgrounds. Since significant levels of sample attrition could seriously damage a study's generalizability, researchers should employ the full range of data collection techniques required to maintain high response rates in each follow-up survey.

Forced-choice questions lend themselves best to the types of quantitative analysis one would want to undertake with panel data. However, open-ended questions can be a valuable addition to a study of the transition from school to work, even if their answers are difficult to process and analyze. Open-ended questions are more likely to provide information about the transition process from the perspective of the subject.

Researchers undertaking panel studies of the school-to-work transition (or any other subject) could simplify their analyses considerably by planning, in advance, how they will organize and structure their data files. They will also get more value from their study if they attempt to use some of the more sophisticated data analysis techniques that have been developed for panel data.

Finally, over the past decade we have observed substantial industrial shifts and a decline in labour market opportunities, particularly for youth. While the size of the youth cohort has declined, the proportion of young people entering post-secondary institutions has increased. At the same time, many young people appear to be postponing exit from their parent(s)' home and entry into marriage or a long-term relationship. These trends suggest that the school-to-work transition experiences of Canadian youth in the 1980s may have been very different from those of earlier cohorts, and will no doubt differ from those of the next cohort. In short, researchers studying the transition process must take the reference period into account.

Bibliography

CAUT Bulletin (1990). "Research and Development in the Mulroney Era" December.

Abella, Rosalie (1984). "Equality in Employment." *The Commission on Equality in Employment.* Ottawa: Ministry of Supply and Services.

Abrahamsson, K. (1986). *Adult Participation in Higher Education.* Stockholm: Almquist and Wiksell International.

Alexander, K.L., and A.M. Pallas (1984). "Curriculum reform and school performance: an evaluation of the 'new basics'." *American Journal of Education,* 92(4), 391–420.

Allaire, André, Paul Bernard and Jean Renaud (1979). "Qui s'instruits'enrichit?" *Possibles,* 3(3-4), Spring, 13–33.

Allaire, André, Paul Bernard and Jean Renaud (1981). "Scolarité et revenu en début de carrière: une relation inflationniste." *Cahiers de recherche sociale,* 22(3), 361–378.

Allison, P.D. (1984). *Event History Analysis: Regression for Longitudinal Event Data.* Beverley Hills: Sage.

Ambert, A. (1976). *Sex Structure,* (2 ed.) Toronto: Longman Canada.

American Council for Education (1976). *Guide to the Evaluation of Education in the Armed Services.* Washington: Office of Educational Credit and Certification, American Council for Education.

American Council for Education (1976). *National Guide to Educational Credit for Training Programs.* Washington: Office of Educational Credit and Certification, American Council for Education.

American Indian and Alaska Native Mental Health Research (1989). *The Journal of the National Centre,* 2(3), Special Issue.

Anderson, D.S., and C. Blakers (eds.) (1983). *Youth, Transition, and Social Research.* Canberra: Australian National University Press, 130-152.

Anisef, Paul, J.G. Paasche and A.H. Turrittin (1980). *Is the die cast? Educational achievements and work destinations of Ontario Youth: A six-year follow-up of the critical juncture high school students.* Toronto: Ministry of Colleges and Universities.

Anisef, Paul, Norman Okihiro and Carl E. James (1982). *Losers and Winners: The Pursuit of Equality and Social Justice in Higher Education.* Toronto: Butterworth & Co.

Anisef, Paul, M-A. Bertrand, U. Hortian and Carl E. James (1985). *Accessibility to Post-Secondary Education in Canada: A Review of the Literature.* Ottawa: Secretary of State.

Anisef, Paul, E. Baichman, D. Northrop and J. Tibert (1986). *Models and methodologies appropriate to the study of outcomes of schooling in Ontario's multicultural society.* Toronto: Ontario Department of Education.

Anisef, Paul, and Etta Baichman-Anisef (1991). *Evaluating Canadian University Education Through the Use of Graduate and Employer Surveys.* Ottawa: Association of Universities and Colleges of Canada. Commission on the Inquiry on Canadian University Education.

BIBLIOGRAPHY

Armstrong, H., and P. Armstrong (1975). "The segregated participation of women in the Canadian labour force, 1941-71." *Canadian Review of Sociology and Anthropology*, 12, 370-384.

Armstrong, P., and H. Armstrong (1978). *The Double Ghetto*. Toronto: McClelland and Stewart.

Armstrong, P., and H. Armstrong (1983). *A working majority: What women must do for pay.* Ottawa: Prepared for the Canadian Advisory Council on the Status of Women.

Armstrong, P., and H. Armstrong (1990). *Theorizing Women's Work*. Garamond: Toronto.

Ashton, D., and D. Field (1976). *Young Workers*. London: Hutchinson and Co. Ltd.

Ashton, D., M. Maguire and M. Spilsbury (1990). *Restructuring the Labour Market: The Implications for Youth*. London: MacMillan.

Ashton, D., and G. Lowe (eds.) (1991). *Making Their way: Education, Training, and the Labour Market in Canada and Great Britain*. Toronto: University of Toronto Press.

Audet, Marc (1979a). *Relance 1978. Étude de l'efficacité de la formation au secteur professionnel et au secteur général du niveau collégial et au niveau secondaire auprès des sortants de juin 1977*. Québec, Gouvernement du Québec, ministère de l' Éducation, Direction des politiques et plans.

Audet, Marc (1979b). *Relance à l'université*, Québec, Gouvernement du Québec, ministère de l'Éducation, Direction des politiques et plans.

Audet, Marc (1982). *Relance à l'université 1980*. Vue d'ensemble, Québec, Gouvernement du Québec, ministère de l'Éducation.

Audet, Marc (1984). *Relance à l'université 1983. Les disciplines*. Québec, Gouvernement du Québec, ministère de l'Éducation.

Audet, Marc (1986). *Relance à l'université 1984*. Québec, Gouvernement du Québec, ministère de l'Éducation.

Audet, Marc (1989). *Qu'advient-il des diplômes et diplomées universitaires?* Québec: ministère de l'Enseignment Supérieure et de la science.

Axelrod, Paul (1982). *Scholars and Dollars: Politics, Economics and the Universities of Ontario, 1945-1980*. Toronto: University of Toronto Press.

Axelrod, Paul (1986). "Service or Captivity? Business-University Relations in the Twentieth Century." In W.A. Neilson and C. Gaffield (eds.), *Universities in Crisis: A Medieval Institution in the Twenty-first Century*. Montreal: Institute for Research on Public Policy.

Axelrod, Paul (1990). *Making a Middle Class Student Life in English Canada During the Thirties*. Montreal: McGill-Queen's University Press.

Aylward, A. (1991). *A study of factors influencing female nontraditional career choice in Newfoundland and Labrador*. Unpublished master's thesis, Memorial University of Newfoundland, St. John's.

Baby, Antoine (1985). "Insertion des jeunes et pratiques de l'orientation professionnelle." *L'orientation professionnelle*, 21(2), 69-82.

Baby, Antoine (1986). "Dans les années d'aujourd'hui, c'est plutôt décourageant... plus on avance dans le temps, plus c'est difficile." Jalons d'une problématique conjoncturelle de l'insertion sociale et professionnelle des jeunes. Québec, Université Laval, Faculté des sciences de l'éducation, May 1986, 41 (mimeo).

Baker, D. (1987). "The influence of role-specific self-concept and sex-role identity on career choices in science." *Journal of Research in Science Teaching*, 24(8), 739-756.

Baker, M. (1985). *What will tomorrow bring? A study of the aspirations of adolescent women*. Ottawa: Canadian Advisory Council on the Status of Women.

Beauvais, F. (1989). "Limited notions of culture ensure research failure." *American Indian and Alaska Mental Health Research: Journal of the National Centre* 2(3), 25-28.

Becker, Howard, Blanche Geer, Everett Hughes and Anselm Strauss (1968). *Making the Grade*. University of Chicago Press: Chicago.

Belanger P. and G. Rocher (1976). *Aspirations et Orientations de Étudiants (ASOPE)*. Montreal: Université de Montréal.

Bell, Stephen (1990). "Using Matching Grants to Facilitate Corporate-University Research Linkages: A Preliminary Examination of Outcomes from One Initiative," *The Canadian Journal of Higher Education*, 20(1), 57–73.

Bellamy, L.A. (1991). "Transitions from high school: determinants, decisions, and destinations." Paper presented at the Canadian Sociology and Anthropology Association Conference. Queen's University, Kingston, Ontario.

Bellamy, L.A. (1992). "Paths on life's way: destinations, determinants, and decisions in the transition from high school." (Unpublished doctoral dissertation.) University of British Columbia.

Benbow, C.P., and J.C. Stanley (1982). "Intellectually talented boys and girls: Educational profiles." *Gifted Child Quarterly*, 26(2), 82–87.

Bengle, Normand and Claude Laflamme (1979). "L'information scolaire et professionnelle et l'inévitable rupture entre l'école et le marché du travail." *Revue des sciences de l'éducation*, V(3), 401–422.

Bengle, Normand, and Claude Laflamme (1982). "Le secteur professionnel dans l'enseignement secondaire et dans la société," *Revue des sciences de l'éducation*, VIII(2), 271–292.

Bercuson, David et al., (1984). *The Great Brain Robbery*. Toronto: McClelland and Stewart.

Bernard, Jessie (1981). *The Female World*. The Free Press: New York.

Bernard, Paul, André Demers, Diane Grenier and Jean Renaud (1979). *L'évolution de la situation socio-économique des francophones et des non-francophones au Québec (1971–1978)*. Montréal, Office de la langue française, Gouvernement du Québec.

Bernard, Paul (1982). "L'insignifiance des données," Bref essai contre la stigmatisation positiviste. *Sociologie et sociétés*, XIV (1), 65–82.

Bibby, Reginald, and Donald Posterski (1985). *The Emerging Generation: An Inside Look at Canadian Teenagers*. Toronto: Irwin Publishers.

Billingsley, Brenda, and Leon Muszynski (1985). *No Discrimination Here? Toronto Employers and the MultiRacial Workforce*. Toronto: Social Planning Council of Metropolitan Toronto.

Blackburn, R.M., and M. Mann (1979). *The Working Class in the Labour Market*. London: Macmillan.

Blau, P.M., and O.D. Duncan (1967). *The American Occupational Structure*. New York: John Wiley and Sons.

Blishen, B.R., W.K. Carroll and C. Moore (1987). "The 1981 socioeconomic index for occupations in Canada." *Canadian Review of Sociology and Anthropology*, 24(4), 465–488.

Bloom, T.K. (1985). "Expectations of entry level-work attitudes: the employer's view." *Journal of Industrial Teacher Education*, 22(3), 25–36.

Boak, T., and C.J. Boak (1990). *Career Interest and Knowledge: Influencing Factors*. St. John's: Memorial University of Newfoundland, Faculty of Education.

Borus, M.E. (ed.) (1983). *Tomorrow's Workers*. Lexington: D. C. Heath and Company.

Borus, M.E. (ed.) (1984). *Youth and the Labor Market: Analyses of the National Longitudinal Survey*. Kalamazoo, Mich.: W.E. Upjohn Institute for Employment Research.

Boulet, J., and L. Lavallee (1984). *The Changing Economic Status of Women*. Ottawa: Economic Council of Canada.

Bourdieu, P. (1977a). "Cultural reproduction and social reproduction." In J. Karabel and A.H. Halsey (eds.) *Power and Ideology in Education*. New York: Oxford University Press, 487-511.

Bourdieu, P. (1977b). *Outline of a Theory of Practice*. Cambridge: Cambridge University Press.

Bourdieu, P., and J. Passeron (1979). *The Inheritors*. Chicago: University of Chicago Press.

Bourdieu, P. (1984). *Distinction*. Cambridge: Harvard University Press.

Bourdieu, P. (1986). "The Forms of Capital." In J.C. Richardson (ed.) *Handbook of Theory and Research for the Sociology of Education*. New York: Greenwood Press, 241-258.

Bourdieu, P. (1990a). *In other words: Essays Toward a Reflexive Sociology* (M. Adamson, Trans.) Stanford: Stanford University Press. (Original work published in 1982, 1987).

Bourdieu, P. (1990b). *The Logic of Practice* (R. Nice, Trans.) Stanford: Stanford University Press. (Original work published in 1980).

Bourdieu, P. (1991). *Language and Symbolic Power* (G. Raymond & M. Adamson, Trans.). Cambridge: Harvard University Press. (Original work published in 1977, 1984, 1983, 1984).

Boyd, M. (1982). *Sex Differences in the Canadian Occupational Attainment Process*. Toronto: Oxford.

Boyd, M., J. Goyder, F. Jones, H. McRoberts, P. Pineo and J. Porter (1985). *Ascription and Achievement*. Toronto: Oxford.

Boyd, M. and E.T. Pryor (1989). "The cluttered nest: the living arrangements of young Canadian adults." *Canadian Journal of Sociology* 14: 461–77.

Breakwell, G.M., C. Fife-Schaw and J. Devereux (1988). "Parental Influence and teenagers' motivation to train for technological jobs." *Journal of Occupational Psychology*, 61, 79–88.

Breton, R. (1972). *Social and academic factors in the career decisions of Canadian youth*. Ottawa: Department of Manpower and Immigration.

Brown, Phillip (1991)."Schooling and Employment in the United Kingdom." In David Ashton and Graham Lowe (eds.) *Making Their Way: Education Training and the Labour Market in Canada and Britain*. University of Toronto Press: Toronto, 85-108.

Burstein, M., N. Tienhaara, P. Hewson and B. Warrander (1975). *Canadian Work Values: Finding of a Work Ethic Survey and a Job Satisfaction Survey*. Ottawa: Manpower and Immigration.

Burris, V. (1983, August). "The social and political consequences of overeducation." *American Sociological Review*, 48, 454–67.

Byrne, E.M. (1978). *Women and Education*. London: Tavistock Publications.

Campbell, P.B., and J.A. Gardner and Winterstein (1984). *Transition patterns between education and work*. Columbus, OH: The National Center for Research in Vocational Education, Ohio State University. (Eric Document Reproduction Service No. ED 240 272)

Campbell, R.T. (1983). "Status attainment research: End of the beginning or the beginning of the end?" *Sociology of Education*, 56: 47–92.

Canada. Department of Manpower and Immigration (1989). *Canadian Classification Dictionary of Occupations*.

Canadian Association for Adult Education (1982). *From the adult's point of view*. Toronto: CAAE/ICEA.

Canadian Research Committee on Practical Education (1951). *Two Years After School*. Toronto: Canadian Education Association.

Carnoy, Martin, and Henry Levin (1985). *Schooling and Work in the Democratic State*. Stanford University Press: Stanford, California.

Centrale de L'Enseignement du Québec (1984). *Nouvelles technologies, emploi et aménagement du temps de travail.* XXIXe Congrès, C.E.Q.

Centrale de L'Enseignement du Québec (1985). *Actes du colloque sur les nouvelles technologies, la division du travail, la formation et l'emploi, apprivoiser le changement.* C.E.Q., Sainte-Foy.

Centrale de L'Enseignement du Québec (1987). *L'école et l'emploi: pour une problématique formation-emploi renouvelée.* C.E.Q., Sainte-Foy.

Charland, Jean-Pierre, and Nicole Thivierge (1982). *Bibliographie de l'enseignement professionnel au Québec,* (1850–1980). Québec, Institut québécois de la recherche sur la culture, 482.

Clark, W., and Z. Zsigmond (1981). *Job Market Reality for Postsecondary Graduates: Employment Outcome by 1978, Two Years After Graduation.* Ottawa: Ministry of Supply and Services.

Clark, Warren, M. Laing and D. Rechnitzer (1986). *The Class of 82: Summary Report on the Findings of the 1984 National Survey of Graduates of 1982.* Ottawa: Secretary of State.

Clark, H., and H. Sloan (1958). *Classrooms in Factories.* Rutherford, N.J.: Institute for Research, Dickenson University.

Clarke, John, and Paul Willis (1988). "Youth and the Transition into Adulthood." In Roger Dale, Ross Ferguson and Alison Robinson (eds.), *Frameworks for Teaching.* Hodder and Stoughton: London, 370-395.

Clausen, J. (1986). *The Life Course: A Sociological Perspective.* New York: Prentice Hall.

Cockburn, C. (1987). *Two Track Training.* Hampshire: MacMilliam Education Ltd.

Cogle, Francis L., and Grace E. Tasker (1982). "Children and Housework." *Family Relations,* 395–399.

Cohen, J. (1991)."Is an education, for the sake of it, passé?" *Toronto Star* (11 Sept.,1991) A25.

Cohen, G.L. (1989). "Youth for hire." *Perspectives on Labour and Income* (Summer), 7–14.

Coleman, J.S. and T. Husén (1985). *Becoming adult in a changing society.* Paris: OECD.

Coleman, J.S. (1986). "Social theory, social research, and a theory of action." *American Journal of Sociology,* 91(6), 1309–1335.

Coleman, J.S. (1988). "Social capital in the creation of human capital." *American Journal of Sociology,* 94(Supplement), S95-S120.

Coleman, J.S. (1990). *Foundations of Social Theory.* Cambridge: The Belknap Press of Harvard University Press.

Collins, R. (1979). *The Credential Society.* New York: Academic Press.

Colloque les Jeunes et le Travail. Secrétariat permanent des conférences socio-économiques du Québec. Quebec, June 1981, 179.

Corbeil, Paul (1979). *Relance 1978, Abandon ou poursuite des études chez les étudiants sortants des niveaux secondaire et collégial pour l'année 1976–1977* (Summer). Québec, Gouvernement du Québec, ministère de l'Éducation.

Corbeil, Paul (1980). "L'abandon scolaire et le marché du travail." *Critère,* 29, (Fall) 43–61.

Corbeil, Paul (1982). *Relance, Les finissants du secondaire. Enquête sur les finissants de 1978–1979* et *Enquête sur les finissants de 1979–1980.* Québec, Gouvernement du Québec.

Cote, M. (1990). The labour force: into the 90's. *Perspectives,* Spring, 8–16.

Côté, Pierre (1984). *Les décrocheurs de l'enseignement professionnel court: leur abandon scolaire et leur insertion sociale et professionnelle.* Québec, INRS - Éducation.

Council for Adult and Experiential Learning (1977). *Experiential Learning: An Annotated Selection Guide*. Columbus: Maryland CAEL.

Cournoyer, Monique (1979). *L'École, c'est pas la vraie vie ou c'est mieux d'en savoir plus que pas assez: une étude des attentes des étudiants face à l'école secondaire*. Montreal, C.E.C.M., (Dec.).

Cournoyer, Monique (1984). *Le cheminement scolaire des décrocheurs du secondaire professionnel court*. First draft, INRS Éducation.

Cournoyer, Monique, Jean-Yves Drolet and Claude Trottier (1985). *La formation professionnelle "longue" au secondaire: attentes du milieu scolaire et du milieu du travail*. Les Cahiers du Labraps, Série Études et recherche, 2(1).

Cuneo, C., and J. Curtis (1975). "Social ascription in the educational and occupational status attainment of urban Canadians." *Canadian Review of Sociology and Anthropology*, 12(1), 2–24.

Curtis, B., D.W. Livingstone and I.H. Smaller (1992). *Stacking the Deck*. Toronto: Our Schools/Our Selves.

Dandurand, Pierre (1983). "Crise, État et politiques de main-d'oeuvre," *Revue internationale d'action communautaire*. 10(50), 101–117.

Dandurand, Pierre (1984). "La recherche en sociologie de l'éducation au Québec." *Prospectives*, 20(1-2), (Feb./Apr.) 69–75.

Dandurand, Pierre, and F. Trudel (1984). *C'est rien qu'un stage. Recherche exploratoire sur les stages en milieu de travail des jeunes du secondaire professionnel*. Rapport de recherche, Montreal, Department of Sociology, University of Montreal, May/June.

Dandurand, Pierre (1985). "L'érosion d'une innovation. L'école polyvalente." *Relations*, (513), Sept. 226–228.

Dandurand, Pierre (1986). "Situation de la formation professionnelle au Québec." In Fernand Dumont, (ed.) *Une société des jeunes?* Québec: Institut québécois de la recherche sur la culture, 210-236.

Dantan, N., A. Greene and H. Reese (1986) (eds.). *Life-span Developmental Psychology*. Hillsdale, N. J.: Lawrence Erlbaum.

Darveau, Micheline (1981). *Cheminement scolaire des femmes et quelques aspects de leur intégration au marché du travail*. Québec, Gouvernement of Québec, ministere de l'Éducation, Direction des politiques et plans.

Davies, S., B. O'Grady and C. Mosher (1991). "Exploring trends in the transition from education to employment of Canadian post-secondary graduates." Paper presented at the Annual Meetings of the Canadian Sociology and Anthropology Association, Kingston, Ontario.

Day, D. (1990). *Young women in Nova Scotia: A study of attitudes, behavior, and aspirations*. Nova Scotia Advisory Council on the Status of Women.

Dean, John, P. White and William Foote (1970). "How do you know if the informant is telling the truth?" In L.A. Dexter, *Elite and Specialized Interviewing*. Evanston: Northwestern University Press, 119–131.

Deboer, G. (1984). "A study of gender effects in the science and mathematics course-taking behaviour of a group of students who graduated from college in the late 1970s." *Journal of Research in Science Teaching*, 21 (1), 95–103.

Deem, Rosemary (1980). *Schooling for Women's Work*. Routledge and Kegan Paul: London.

Denton, F.T., A.L. Robb and B.G. Spencer (1980). *Unemployment and Labour Force Behavior of Young People: Evidence from Canada and Ontario*. Toronto: University of Toronto Press.

Denton, M. et al. (1987). *Unemployment Survey of 1985 Graduates of Ontario Universities*. Toronto: Ontario Ministry of Education.

Department of the Secretary of State (1990 Draft Report). *The Flow of Graduates from Higher Education and Their Entry into Working Life.* Country Report: Canada.

Derber, C. (1978). "Unemployment and the entitled worker: job entitlement and radical political attitudes among the youthful unemployed." *Social Problems*, 26, 26–37.

Devereaux, M. (1985). *One in Every Five.* Ottawa: Statistics Canada and Education Support Section, Secretary of State.

Deverell, John (1991). "Report Slams Performance of Universities," *The Toronto Star*, (15 Aug.) A11.

Dexter, Lewis Anthony (1970). *Elite and Specialized Interviewing."* Evanston: Northwestern University Press.

Dinges, N., J. Trimble, S. Manson and F. Pasquale (1981). "Counselling and Psychotherapy with American Indians and Alaskan Natives." In A. Marsella and P. Pederson (eds.). *Cross-Cultural Counselling and Psychotherapy.* New York: Pergamon Press, 243–276.

Doray, Pierre (1986). "Nouvelles technologies et formation: transformations des pratiques éducatives dans les techniques physiques des CÉGEPS "(Oct.). Centre de recherche en évaluation sociale des technologies. Montreal, University of Quebec, Montreal, (mimeo).

Dragastin, S.E., and G. Elder Jr. (eds.) (1975). *Adolescence in the Life Cycle: Psychological Change and Social Context.* Washington, D.C.: Hemisphere.

Duffy, Ann, Nancy Mandell and Norene Pupo (1989). *Few Choices: Women, Work, and Family.* Garamond: Toronto.

Dumas, Suzanne, Gérard Rochais and Henri Tremblay (1982). *Une génération silencieusement lucide?: vers un profil socio-culturel des jeunes de 15 à 20 ans.* Québec, Gouvernement of Québec, ministere of l'Éducation, Direction de la recherche.

Dumont, Fernand (ed.) (1986). *Une société des jeunes?* Québec, Institut québécois de la recherche sur la culture, 397.

Economic Council of Canada (1965). *Towards Sustained and Balanced Economic Growth.* Second Annual Review Ottawa: Queen's Printer.

Economic Council of Canada. (1990). *Good Jobs, Bad Jobs: Employment in the Service Economy.* Ottawa: Minister of Supply and Services Canada.

Economic Council of Canada (1992). *A Lot to Learn: Education and Training in Canada.* Ottawa: Minister of Supply and Services.

Elder, G. Jr. (ed.) (1985). *Life Course Dynamics: Trajectories and Transitions.* Ithaca, New York: Cornell University Press.

Ellis, R. (1987). *Post-Secondary Cooperative Education in Canada.* Ottawa: Science Council of Canada.

Elster, J. (1989a). *Nuts and Bolts for the Social Sciences.* Cambridge: Cambridge University Press.

Elster, J. (1989b). *Solomonic Judgements: Studies in the Limits of Rationality.* Cambridge: Cambridge University Press.

Employment and Immigration Canada (1981). *Labour Market Development in the 1980s.* Ottawa: Minister of Supply and Services

Employment and Immigration Canada (1989). *Success in the Works: A Profile of Canada's Emerging Workforce.* Ottawa: Minister of Supply and Services Canada.

Employment and Immigration Canada (1990). *Canadian Occupational Projection System.* Ottawa: Minister of Supply and Services Canada.

Empson-Warner, Susan, and Harvey Krahn (1992). "Unemployment and occupational aspirations: a panel study of high school graduates." *Canadian Review of Sociology and Anthropology*, 29(1): 38-54.

Erikson, G.L., and L.J. Erikson (1984). "Females and science achievement: evidence, explanations, and implications." *Science Education*, 68(2), 63–89.

Eurich, N. (1985). *Corporate Classrooms*. Lawrenceville, N.J.: Carnegie Foundation for the Advancement of Teaching, Princeton University Press.

Evans, N. (1984). *Exploiting Experience*. London: Further Education Unit.

Fitzpatrick, J.L., and T. Silverman (1989). "Women's selection of careers in engineering: Do traditional-nontraditional differences still exist?" *Journal of Vocational Behaviour*, 34, 266–278.

Fleras, A., and J.L. Elliott (1992). *Multiculturalism In Canada*. Scarborough: Nelson Canada.

Foot, D.K. and J.C. Li (1986). "Youth employment in Canada: a misplaced priority?" *Canadian Public Policy*, 12: 499–506.

Fordham, Signithia (1988). "Racelessness as a Factor in Black Students' School Success: Pragmatic Strategy or Pyrrhic Victory?" *Harvard Educational Review*, 58(1).

Fortin, Pierre (1986). "Conjoncture, démographie et politique: Où va le chômage des jeunes au Québec?" In Fernand Dumont (ed.) *Une société des jeunes?* Québec, Institut québécois de la recherche sur la culture, 191-209.

Foulks, E.F. (1989). "Misalliances in the Barrow alcohol study." American Indian and Alaska Mental Health Research. *Journal of the National Centre*, 2(3), 7–17.

Fournier, Marcel. (1980). *Entre l'école et l'usine*. Montréal, Éditions coopératives Albert Saint-Martin et C.E.Q.

Friendly, Martha, Saul V. Levine and Linda Hagarty (1979). "Adolescents in the Urban Social Context." In W. Michelson, S. Levine, A-R. Spina et al., *The Child in the City: Change and Challenges*. Toronto: University of Toronto Press.

Fuller, Mary (1983). "Qualified Criticism, Critical Qualifications." In Len Barton and Stephen Walker (eds.), *Race, Class and Education*. London: Croom and Helm Publishing.

Gallup Canada (1990). "1 in 4 Adults Set for Classes." *Toronto Star*. (15 Nov.) A14.

Gambetta, D. (1987). *Were they pushed or did they jump? Individual decision mechanisms in education*. Cambridge: Cambridge University Press.

Gaskell, Jane and Marvin Lazerson (1980–81). "Between School and Work: Perspectives of Working Class Youth." *Interchange*, 11(3), 80–96.

Gaskell, Jane and Arlene McLaren (1987). *Women and Education: A Canadian Perspective*. Detselig: Calgary, Alberta.

Gaskell, Jane (1992). *Gender Matters from School to Work*. Buckingham, U.K.: Open University Press.

Gecas, V., and M.L. Schwalbe (1986). "Parental behaviour and adolescent self-esteem." *Journal of Marriage and the Family*, 48 (1), 37–46.

Gelpi, E. (1985). "Lifelong education and international relations." Wain, K. (ed.), *Lifelong Education and Participation*. B'Kara: University of Malta Press.

Gendron, Diane and Jean-Pierre Jolin (1979). *Enquête auprès des finissants de juin 1977 de l'enseignement professionnel du niveau secondaire*. Québec, Gouvernement du Québec, Ministère du travail et de la main-d'oeuvre.

Giddens, A. (1984). *The Constitution of Society*. Berkeley: University of California Press.

Ginzburg, C. (1976). *The Cheese and the Worms*. Toronto: Penguin Books.

Girard, Michel, Hervé Gauthier and Alain Vinet (1978). *Les jeunes Québécois et le travail*. Québec, Office de planification et de développement du Québec.

Glaser, B.G., and A.L. Strauss (1967). *The Discovery of Grounded Theory. Strategies for Qualitative Research*. Chicago: Aldine.

Goetz, J.P., and M.D. LaCompte (1984). *Ethnography and Qualitative Design in Educational Research.* San Diego: Academic Press, Inc.

Gottfredson, L.S. (1981). "Circumscription and compromise: a developmental theory of occupational aspirations." *Journal of Counselling Psychology,* 28, 545–579.

Government of Canada (1983). *Learning a Living in Canada.* Report of the Skill Development Leave Task Force. Ottawa: Ministry of Supply and Services.

Government of Canada (1991). *Prosperity Through Competitiveness.* Ottawa: Minister of Supply and Services Canada.

Government of Canada (1991). *The Prosperity Initiative: A Summary.* Ottawa: Ministry of Supply and Services Canada.

Government of Ontario (1986). *Educational Statistics, Ontario.* Toronto, Ministry of Education.

Government of Ontario (1990). *People and Skills in the New Global Economy.* A Premier's Council Report. Toronto: Queen's Printer for Ontario.

Gower, D. (1988). "The 1987 labour market revisited." *The Labour Force.* Statistics Canada (January): 84–111.

Grandy, J. (1987). "Trends in the selection of science, mathematics, or engineering as major fields of study among top-scoring SAT takers." *Research Report.* (Report No. ETS- RR–39). Educational Testing Service, Princeton, N.J. (ERIC Document Reproduction Service No. ED 289 740).

Grant, C.A. and C.E. Sleeter (1988). "Race class and gender and abandoned dreams." *Teachers College Record,* 90(1), 19–40.

Grégoire, Réginald (1981). *La formation et l'insertion sociale des jeunes de 15 à 18 ans dans la société: un défi pour toutes les institutions.* Québec, Gouvernement du Québec, ministère de l'Éducation, Section de la planification.

Griffith, Alison, and Dorothy Smith (1987). "Constructing Cultural Knowledge: Mothering as Discourse."In Jane Gaskell and Arlene McLaren (eds.), *Women and Education: A Canadian Perspective.* Detselig: Calgary, Alberta, 87-104.

Grude, J., L. Osberg, F. Wien, M. MacDonald and M. Kilfoil (1991). "Disadvantaged workers in a competitive, technology driven economy: Firm case studies from rural Nova Scotia." Paper presented to the Canadian Sociological and Anthropology Association, Kingston, Ontario.

Haas, Jack, and William Shaffir (1977). "The Professionalization of Medical Students: Developing Competence and a Cloak of Competence." *Symbolic Interaction,* 1, 71–88.

Hackett, G., N.E. Betzer, and M.S. Doty (1985). "The development of a taxonomy of career competencies for professional women." *Sex Roles,* 12 (1), 393–409.

Hagan, John (1991). "Destiny and drift: subcultural preferences, status attainments, and the risks and rewards of youth." *American Sociological Review* 56 (5), 567–82.

Hall, Roberta, and Bernice Sandler (1982). *The Classroom Climate: A Chilly One for Women?* Association of American Colleges.

Hall, Oswald, and Bruce McFarlane (1962). *Transition from School to Work.* Report #19 of the Interdepartmental Skilled Manpower Training Research Community. Department of Labour, Ottawa: Queen's Printer.

Haller, A., O.L. Otto, R. Meier and G. Ohlendorf (1974). "Level of occupations aspiration: An empirical analysis." *American Sociological Review,* 39, 113–121.

Hamel, Thérèse (1982). *L'enseignement professionnel au Québec: vers une soumission plus étroite de l'école à l'entreprise?* Québec, INRS-Éducation.

Hamilton, S.F., and J.L. Powers (1990). "Failed expectations: Working class girls' transitions from school to work." *Youth and Society,* 22 (2), 241–262.

Hardy, Marcelle (1983). *Les élèves de l'enseignement professionnel court: leur origine sociale et leurs rapports à l'école d'après une analyse d'entrevues.* Québec, Gouvernement du Québec, ministère de l'Éducation.

Härnqvist, K. (1978). *Individual demand for education.* Paris: OECD.

Hartnagel, Timothy F., and Harvey Krahn (1988). "Methodological issues with self-reported crime and delinquency: an analysis from a Canadian study of the transition from school to work." In M.W. Klein (ed.), *Cross-National Research in Self-Reported Crime and Delinquency,* Dordrecht: Kluwer Academic Publishers.

Hartnagel, Timothy F., and Harvey Krahn (1989). "High school dropouts, labour market success and criminal behaviour." *Youth and Society,* 20(4), 416–44.

Head, Wilson (1975). *The Black Presence in the Canadian Mosaic.* Toronto: Ontario Human Rights Commission.

Henripin, Marthe, and Lucie Proulx (1986). *Les écoles de chance: retourner aux études pour apprendre à réussir.* Québec, Gouvernement du Québec, ministère de l'Éducation, Direction générale des politiques et des plans, Direction de l'éducation permanente, 4 vols.

Henry, Frances, and Effie Ginzberg (1985). *Who Gets The Work: A Test of Racial Discrimination in Employment.* Toronto: The Social Planning Council, January.

Henry, Frances, and Effie Ginzberg (1988). "Racial Discrimination in Employment." In James Curtis et al., *Social Inequality in Canada: Patterns, Patters, Policies.* Scarborough: Prentice-Hall Canada Inc.

Hindess, B. (1988). *Choice, Rationality, and Social Theory.* London: Unwin Hyman.

Hogan, D. (1981). *Transitions and Social Change: The Early Lives of American men.* New York: Academic Press.

Hogan, D.P., and A.M. Astone (1986). "The transition to adulthood." *Annual Review of Sociology* 12, 109–30.

Hohl, Janine (1982). "Apprendre l'insécurité d'emploi." *Revue internationale d'action communautaire,* 8(48), 83–90.

Holland, J. (1985). *Making Vocational Choices* (2 ed.). New Jersey: Prentice-Hall Inc.

Houser, B.B., and C. Garvey (1985). "Factors that affect nontraditional vocational enrolment among women." *Psychology of Women's Quarterly,* 9, 105–117.

Hubner-Funk, S. (1983). "Transition into occupational life: Environmental and sex differences regarding the status passage from school to work." *Adolescence,* 18(71), 709–723.

Hunter, A.A. (1981). *Class Tells: On Social Inequality in Canada.* Toronto: Butterworth & Co.

Hunter, A. (1988, Oct.). "Formal education and initial employment: Unravelling the relationships between schooling and skills over time." *American Sociological Review.* 53, 753-65.

Illich, I. (1971). *Deschooling Society.* New York: Harper and Row.

Isabelle, R. (1984). *La reconnaissance des acquis de formation.* Montreal: Federation of CEGEPS.

James, Carl E. (1990). *Making It: Black Youth, Racism and Career Aspirations in a Big City.* Oakville: Mosaic Press.

Jencks, C., J. Crouse and P. Mueser (1983). "The Wisconsin model of status attainment: a national replication with improved measures of ability and aspiration." *Sociology of Education,* 56(1), 3–18.

Johnson, Laura (1988). "The new extended family: patterns of youth employment and family configuration in three Canadian cities." Paper presented at the Special Interest Meeting on Research at the 15th European Symposium of the International Council on Social Welfare, Noordwijkerhout, The Netherlands.

Kairamo, K. (ed.) (1989). *Education for Life: A European strategy*. London: Butterworths Scientific Limited.

Keller, S., and M. Zavalloni (1964). "Ambition and social class: a respecification." *Social Forces*, 43, 58–70.

Kelly, A. (1988). "Option choice for girls and boys." *Research in Science and Technological Education*, 6(1), 5–23.

Kerckhoff, A. (1990). *Getting Started: Transition to Adulthood in Great Britain*. Boulder: Westview Press.

Kessler, R.C., and D.F. Greenberg (1981). *Linear Panel Analysis: Models of Quantitative Change*. New York: Academic Press.

Kirby, Sandra, and Kate McKenna (1989). *Experience, Research, Social Change: Methods From The Margins*. Toronto: Garamond Press.

Knorr-Cetina, K. (1981). "The micro-sociological challenge of macro-sociology: towards a reconstruction of social theory and methodology." In K. Knorr-Cetina and A. Cicourel (eds.), *Advances in Social Theory and Methodology*. London: Routledge and Kegan Paul, 1-48.

Krahn, Harvey and G.S. Lowe (1987). "Youth action." *Policy Options* 8(5), 13–14.

Krahn, Harvey (1988). "A Study of the Transition from School to Work in Three Canadian Cities: Research Design, Response Rates and Descriptive Results." Edmonton: University of Alberta, Department of Sociology.

Krahn, H., and G.S. Lowe (1990a). *Young workers in the service economy*. Working Paper no. 14. Ottawa: Economic Council of Canada.

Krahn, H., and G.S. Lowe (1990b). "The school to work transition in Edmonton, 1985–1989." Final Research Report. Edmonton: University of Alberta, Department of Sociology.

Krahn, H., and G.S. Lowe (1991). "Transitions to work: findings from a longitudinal study of high school and university graduates in three Canadian cities." In D. Ashton and G.S. Lowe (eds.), *Making Their Way, Education, Training, and the Labour Market in Canada and Britain*. Toronto: University of Toronto Press.

Krahn, Harvey (1991a). "Youth employment." In R. Barnhorst and L. Johnson (eds.), *The State of the Child in Ontario*. Toronto: Oxford University Press.

Krahn, Harvey (1991b). "Non-standard work arrangements." *Perspectives on Labour and Income*, Winter, 35–45.

Krahn, Harvey (1992). "Quality of Work in the Service Economy". *General Social Survey Analysis Series*, no. 6. Ottawa: Minister of Supply and Services.

Krahn, Harvey and Clay Mosher (1992). *The Transition from School to Work in Three Canadian Cities: Research Design and Methodological Issues*. Edmonton: Population Research Laboratory, Department of Sociology, University of Alberta.

La Perrière, Anne (1982). "Quand on le peut: l'école pour éviter le pire." *Revue internationale d'action communautaire*, 8(48), 69–82.

Laflamme, Claude (1984). "Une contribution à un cadre théorique sur l'insertion professionnelle des jeunes." *Revue des sciences de l'éducation*, X(2),199–216.

Lamont, M. and A. Lareau(1988). "Cultural capital: allusions, gaps, and glissandos in recent theoretical developments." *Sociological Theory*, 6, 153–168.

Lane, M. (1972). "Explaining educational choice." *Sociology*, 6, 255–266.

Langlois, Simon (1985). "Les rigidités sociales et l'insertion des jeunes dans la société québécoise." *L'orientation professionnelle*, 21(2) 48–68.

Lapierre, Roger (1977). *Relance 1976. Étude de l'efficacité de la formation reçue dans les spécialités professionnelles au collégial et au secondaire*, Québec, Gouvernement du Québec, ministère de l'Éducation.

Laroche, Gabriel (1984). *Les finissants du secondaire professionnel sur le marché du travail. Enquête auprès de la promotion de juin 1981*. Résultats pour le Québec et par région au 31 mars 1982, Québec. Gouvernement du Québec, Ministère de la Main-d'oeuvre et de la sécurité du revenu.

Lee, V.E. (1987). Identifying potential scientists and engineers: An analysis of the high school – college transition. Report 2: multivariate analysis of the high school class of 1982. Congress of the U.S., Washington, D.C. Office of Technology Assessment. (ERIC Document Reproduction Service No. ED 308 063)

Lefley, H.P. (1982). "Self-perception and primary prevention for American Indians." In Spero Manson (ed.), *New Directions in Prevention Among Indian and Alaskan Native Communities*. Oregon Health Sciences University: Portland, 65–90.

Lemelin, Clément, Benoit Robidoux, and Robert Baril (1987). "La demande d'éducation des jeunes québécois." In *L'actualité économique, revue d'analyse économique*, 63(1), 5–25.

Lemelin, Clément (1988). "Bilan critique des recherches en économie de l'éducation." *Revue des sciences de l'éducation*, XIV(2), 115–182.

Lesage, Marc (1986). *Les vagabonds du rêve, vers une société de marginaux*. Montreal: Boréal Express.

Levesque, Mireille (1981). "L'école ne mériterait-elle ni les honneurs ni l'indignité?" *Prospectives*, 17(2), 61–66.

Levesque, Mireille, and Louise Sylvain (1982a). *Poursuivre ou non ses études après l'école secondaire. Analyse d'un processus de décision. Synthèse de recherche*. Québec, Conseil supérieur de l'éducation, Éditeur officiel.

Levesque, Mireille, and Louise Sylvain (1982b). *Après l'école secondaire: étudier ou travailler, choisit-on vraiment?* Québec, Conseil supérieur de l'éducation, Éditeur officiel.

Levine, Arthur, and Eric Riedel (1987). "The College Student: A Changing Constituency." In Philip G. Altbach and Robert O. Berdahl (eds.), *Higher Education in American Society*. Buffalo, N.Y.: Prometheus Books.

Lindsay, C. (1989). "The service sector in the 1980s." *Canadian Social Trends*, Spring, 20–23.

Lindsey, Linda (1990). *Gender Roles*. Prentice-Hall: Englewood Cliffs, New Jersey.

Livingstone, D.W. (1983). *Class, Ideologies and Educational Futures*. London: Falmer Press.

Livingstone, D.W. (1985). *Social Crisis and Schooling*. Toronto: Garamond Press, 1985.

Livingstone, D.W. (1987). "Job skills and schooling." *Canadian Journal of Education*, 12(1), 1–30.

Livingstone, D.W., and R.E. Bowd, (1990, June 3). "Deciphering 'underemployment': The relations between occupational class, education-job mismatch and political attitudes in Ontario, 1982–90." Paper presented at Annual Meeting of Canadian Association of Foundations of Education, Victoria, BC.

Livingstone, D.W., D. Hart and L. Davie (1991). *Public Attitudes Toward Education in Ontario*. Toronto: OISE.

Lojkine, J. (1986). "From the industrial to the computer revolution: First signs of a new combination of material and human productive forms." *Capital and Class* 29, (Summer) 111–29.

Looker, E.D. (1977). "The role of value elements in the intergenerational transmission of social status." Ph.D. Dissertation, McMaster University.

Looker, E.D., and P.C. Pineo (1983). "Social psychological variables and their relevance to the status attainment of teenagers." *American Journal of Sociology* 88(6), 1195–1219.

Looker, E.D. (1985). "Fuelling a gender-segregated labour market: gender and the transition from school to work." In G. Mason (ed.), *Transitions to Work*. Winnipeg: Institute for Social and Economic Research, 150-68.

Looker, E.D., and K. McNutt (1989). "The effects of occupational expectations on the educational attainment of males and females." *Canadian Journal of Education*, 14, 352–366.

Looker, E.D., M. Denton, and C. Davis (1989). "Bridging the gap: Incorporating qualitative data into quantitative analyses." *Social Science Research*, 18(4), 313–331.

Looker, E.D. (1991). "Interconnected transitions and their costs: gender and rural urban differences in the transition to work." Paper presented at the Transition to Work Conference, Toronto.

Lowe, G.S., H. Krahn and J. Tanner (1988). "Young people's explanations of unemployment." *Youth and Society* 19(3), 227–49.

Lowe, G.S., and Harvey Krahn (1989). "Computer skills and use among high school and university graduates." *Canadian Public Policy* 15(2), 175–88.

Lowe, G. S., and Harvey Krahn (1992). "Do part-time jobs improve the labour market chances of high school graduates?" In B.D. Warme, K.L.P. Lundy, and L.A. Lundy (eds.). *Working Part-time : Risks and Opportunities*. New York: Praeger.

Lucas, R. (1971). *Minetown, Milltown, and Railtown*. Toronto: University of Toronto Press.

MacKinnon, N., and P. Anisef (1979). "Self assessment in the early educational attainment process." *Canadian Review of Sociology and Anthropology*, 16, 305–319.

Maizels, J. (1970). *Adolescent Needs and the Transition from School to Work*. London: Athlone Press.

Martin, W., and A.J. Macdonell (1982) (eds., 2nd edition) *Canadian Education: A Sociological Analysis*. Scarborough: Prentice Hall.

Mason, G. (ed.) (1985). *Transitions to Work*. Winnipeg: Institute for Social and Economic Research.

Mathews, J. et al. (1988). "Towards flexible skill formation and technological literacy: challenges facing the education system." *Economic and Industrial Democracy*, 9, 497–522.

Maywood, A.G. (1982). "Vocational education and the work ethic." *Canadian Vocational Journal*, 18(3), 7–12.

McColl, A.G. (1950). "Progress of the Canadian Research Committee on Practical Education." *Canadian Education*, 5(2), 30–32.

Menard, Scott (1991). *Longitudinal Research*. Beverly Hills: Sage.

Michel, Pierre (1987a). *Relance au secondaire. Promotion 1984–1985. Situation au 31 mars 1986*. Québec, Gouvernement du Québec, ministère de l'Éducation, Direction des études sur l'emploi et les carrières.

Ministère de l'Éducation du Québec (1986a). *Relance au secondaire. Promotion 1983–1984. Situation au 29 mars 1985*. Québec, Gouvernement du Québec.

Ministère de l'Éducation du Québec (1986b). *Relance au collégial. Promotion 1983–1984. Situation au 29 mars 1985*. Québec, Gouvernement du Québec.

Ministère de l'Éducation du Québec (1988). *Indicateurs sur la situation de l'enseignement primaire et secondaire*. Québec, Gouvernement du Québec, Éditeur officiel.

Ministère de la Main-d'oeuvre et de la Sécurité du Revenu (1987). *La main-d'oeuvre et l'emploi au Québec et dans ses régions*, Québec, Gouvernement du Québec, Éditeur officiel.

Mishler, E.G. (1986). *Research Interviewing*. Massachusetts: Harvard University Press.

Moisset, Jean J. (1983). "Système d'éducation et système économique." In R. Cloutier, J.J. Moisset, and R. Ouellet (eds.), *Analyse sociale de l'éducation,* Montreal: Boréal Express, pp. 225–251.

Moss, Penny, and Donald Rutledge (1991). "Issues in Education." In Laura Johnson and Dick Barnhorst (eds.), *Children, Families, and Public Policy in the 90s*. Toronto: Thompson Educational Publishing, 135-152.

Myles, J., G. Picot and T. Wannell (1988). "The changing wage distribution of jobs, 1981–1986." *The Labour Force, Statistics Canada* (October): 85–138. (cat. no. 71–001)

Myles, J. (1990, 20 Feb.). "Economic restructuring and Canadian labour." Paper presented at Atkinson College — Ontario Federation of Labour Seminar Series on Ontario and the Global Economy, Toronto.

Natural Sciences and Engineering Research Council of Canada (1989). *Ten years to 2000: A strategy document*. Canada: Minister of Supply and Services Canada.

Neilson, W.A., and C. Gaffield, (eds.) (1986). *Universities in Crisis: A Medieval Institution in the Twenty-first Century*. Montreal: Institute for Research on Public Policy.

Nevitte, N., R. Gibbins, and P.W. Codding (1990). "The career goals of female science students in Canada." In Marianne Gosztonyi Ainley (ed.), *Despite the Odds: Essays on Canadian Women and Science*. Montreal: Vehicule Press (reprinted from the *Canadian Journal of Higher Education* 1988).

Newson, J., and H. Buchbinder (1988). *The University Means Business*. Toronto: Garamond Press.

Nobert, L. (1990). *Profile of higher education in Canada*. Ottawa: Secretary of State.

Noeth, R.J., H.B. Engen and P.E. Noeth (1984)." Making career decisions: A self-report of factors that help high school students." *The Vocational Guidance Quarterly*, 240–248.

Novek, Joel (1985). "University Graduates, Jobs and University-Industry Linkages." *Canadian Public Policy*, XI(2), 180–195.

O'Connor, J. (1984). *Accumulation Crisis*. New York: Basil Blackwell, 1984.

Ogbu, John U. (1988). "Class Stratification, Racial Stratification and Schooling." In Lois Weis (ed.), *Class, Race, and Gender in American Education*. State University of New York Press: New York, 163-182.

Ontario Council on University Affairs (1990). *If the Future Were the Past: the Likely Consequences of Maintaining Current Policies of Base Funding for Ontario Universities*.

Orr, Patrick (1985). "Sex Bias in Schools: National Perspectives." In Judith Whyte et al., (eds.), *Girl Friendly Schooling*. Methuen: London, 7-23.

Otto, L.B. (1987). "Parents: Key Advisors." *VocEd*, 62(6), 37–39.

Paquet, P., P. Doray, P. Bouchard, avec la collaboration de Diane Grenier (1982). "Sondage sur les pratiques de formation en entreprises," in *Commission Jean*, Commission d' étude sur la formation des adultes, Annexe 3, Montréal, Gouvernement du Québec.

Paquet, P. (1983). "Les pratiques de formation en entreprise au Québec." *Revue internationale d'action communautaire*, 9(49), 102–113.

Pilkington, Gwendoline (1983). *Speaking with One Voice: Universities in Dialogue with Government*. Montreal: McGill University.

Pineo, P., J. Porter and H. McRoberts (1971). "The 1971 census and the socioeconomic classification of occupations." *Canadian Review of Sociology and Anthropology*, 14(1), 91–102.

Pineo, P.C., and E.D. Looker (1983). "Class and conformity in the Canadian setting." *Canadian Journal of Sociology*, 8(3), 293–317.

Pollard, K., and W.P. O'Hare (1990). "Beyond high school: The experience of rural and urban youth in the 1980's." Staff Working paper. Washington, D.C.: Population Reference Bureau Inc.

Porter J. (1965). *The Vertical Mosaic*. Toronto: University of Toronto Press.

Porter, Marion R., J. Porter and B.R. Blishen (1979). *Does Money Matter? Prospects for Higher Education in Ontario*. Toronto: Macmillan of Canada.

Porter J., Marion R. Porter and B.R. Blishen (1982). *Stations and Callings: Making It Through the School System*. Agincourt: Methuen.

Pratt, John (1985). "The Attitudes of Teachers." In Judith Whyte (ed.), *Girl Friendly Schooling*. Metheun: London, 24-35.

Premier's Council (1990). *People and skills in the new global economy*. Toronto: Queen's printer for Ontario

Prosperity Secretariat (1991). *Learning Well...Living Well: A Discussion Paper*. Ottawa: Ministry of Supply and Services.

Provost, Monique (1988). *Les nouveaux phénomènes sociaux: la catégorie sociale jeunesse*. Annexe à la commission d'enquête sur la santé et les services sociaux. Québec, Gouvernement du Québec.

Radwanski, G. (1987). *Ontario study of the relevance of education, and the issue of dropouts*. Toronto: Ministry of Education.

Rea, Kenneth (1987). "The Political-Economic Record." In Higher Education Group (ed.), *Governments and Higher Education: The Legitimacy of Intervention*. Toronto: OISE, 145–169.

Red Horse, J.B. (1980). "Family structure and value: orientation in American Indians." *Social Casework*, 61(8), (Oct.) 451–526.

Red Horse, J.B. (1982). "American Indian community mental health: A primary prevention strategy." In Spero Manson (ed.), *New Directions in Prevention Among Indian and Alaskan Native Communities*. Oregon Health Sciences University: Portland, 217–32.

Redpath, Lindsay (1991). "The Causes and Consequences of Education-Job Mismatch: A Study of Underemployment Among Canadian University Graduates," 1985–87. Unpublished PH.D. dissertation, University of Alberta.

Reed, D. (1981). *Education for Building a People's Movement*. Boston: South End Press.

Renaud, Jean, Paul Bernard and Monique Berthiaume (1980). "Éducation, qualification professionnelle et carrière au Québec," *Sociologie et sociétés*, XII(1), (Apr.) 23–52.

Report of the Provincial Access Committee (1988). *Access to advanced education and job training in British Columbia*. British Columbia: Ministry of Advanced Education and Job Training.

Revue Internationale d'Action Communautaire (1982). Les jeunes et le chômage, (numéro thématique) automne, 8/48.

Richmond-Abbott, Marie (1992). *Masculine and Feminine: Gender Roles Over the Life Cycle*. McGraw-Hill: Toronto.

Roberge, Pierre (1979). *Le nombril vert et les oreilles molles: l'entrée des jeunes Québécois dans la vie active dans le second tiers des années 1970*. Quebec, Faculté des sciences de l'éducation. University of Laval, and Montreal, Department of Sociology, University of Montreal. Les Cahiers d'A.S.O.P.E., IV, 110.

Roe, A. (1953). "A psychological study of eminent psychologists and anthropologists, and a comparison with biological and physical scientists." *Psychological Monographs: General and Applied*, 67(2).

Rosenthral, N.H., and M. Pilot (1988). "Information needs for initial and ongoing work transition." *Journal of Career Development*, 15(1), 20–41.

Rossi, A. (1985). *Gender and the Life Course*. New York: Aldine.

Royal Commission on Employment and Unemployment (1986). *Building on our strengths*. (Final Report). St. John's: Queen's Printer.

Royal Commission on the Status of Women (1970). *The Status of Women in Canada*. Ottawa: Information Canada.

Rubensen, K. (1989). "Swedish adult education policy in the 1970s and 1980s." In S.J. Ball and S. Larsson (eds.), *The Struggle for Democratic Education: Equality and Participation in Sweden*. London: Falmer Press, 117–36.

Rumberger, R.W. (1981). *Overeducation in the U.S. Labor Market*. New York: Praeger.

Sadker, Myra, David Sadker and Susan S.Klein (1986). "Abolishing Misconceptions About Sex Equity in Education." *Theory Into Practice*, 25 (Fall): 219–26.

Sanayal, Bikas C. (1991). "Higher Education and the Labour Market." In Philip G. Altbach (ed.), *International Higher Education: An Encyclopedia*. New York: Garland Publishing Inc. Vol. 1, 142–167.

Sandberg, D.E., A.A. Ehrhardt, C.A. Mellins, S.E. Ince and H.F. Meyer-Bahlburg (1987). "The influence of individual and family characteristics upon career aspirations of girls during childhood and adolescence." *Sex Roles*, 16(11/12), 649–667.

Schlesinger, B., and R. Schlesinger (1989). "Postponed parenthood: trends and issues." *Journal of Comparative Family Studies* 20(3), 355–363.

Schulenberg, J.E., F.W. Vondracek and A.C. Crouter (1984). "The influence of the family on vocational development." *Journal of Marriage and the Family*, (Feb.), 129–143.

Schultz, T.W. (1961). "Investment in human capital." *American Economic Review*, 51(1), 1–17.

Secretary of State (1991). *Profile of higher education in Canada*. Ottawa: Minister of Supply and Services Canada.

Selltiz, C., M. Johoda, M. Deutsch and S.W. Cook (1965). *Research Methods in Social Relations*. New York: Holt, Rinehart and Winston.

Selman, G., and P. Dampier (1991). *The Foundations of Adult Education in Canada*. Toronto: Thompson Educational Publishing.

Serbin, L.A., and C. Sprafkin (1986). "The salience of gender and the process of sex-typing in three-to-seven-year-old children." *Child Development*, 57, 1188–1199.

Sewell, W.H., A.O. Haller and A. Portes (1969). "The educational and early occupational attainment process." *American Sociological Review*, 34, 82–92.

Sharpe, Dennis B., and William H. Spain (1991). "The Class of '89: Initial Survey of Level III (Grade 12) High School Students." St John's: Centre for Educational Research and Development, Memorial University of Newfoundland.

Shemesh, M. (1990)."Gender-related differences in reasoning skills and learning interests of junior high school students." *Journal of Research in Science Teaching*, 27(1), 27–34.

Silverman, Eliane, and Janelle Holmes (1992). *We're Here, Listen to Us!: A Survey of Young Women in Canada*. Canadian Advisory Council on the Status of Women. Ottawa.

Skolnik, Michael (1991). "Higher Education in Canada." In Phillip G. Altbach (ed.), *International Higher Education: An Encyclopedia*. New York: Garland Publishing Inc. Vol. 2, 1067–1080.

Smart, Carole (1990). "The Legal and Moral Ordering of Child Custody." Unpublished paper, Department of Sociology, University of Warwick, England.

Social Sciences and Humanities Research Council (1990). "Strategic Grants Guide for Applicants," Ottawa:S.S.H.R.C.

Solomon, A. (1990). *Songs for the People: Teachings on the Natural Way*. Toronto: New Canada Publications.

Spain, W.H., and D.B. Sharpe (1990). *The early school leavers: initial survey*. St. John's: Memorial University of Newfoundland, Centre for Educational Research and Development.

Spain, W.H., D.B. Sharpe, T. Wiseman and A.S. Wiseman (1987). *Youth transition into the labour market: a longitudinal study design.* St. John's: Memorial University of Newfoundland, Institute for Educational Research and Development.

Spenner, K.I., and R.A. Rosenfeld (1990). "Women, and work and identities." *Social Science Research*, 19, 266–299.

St-Pierre, Céline (1982). "Les jeunes et le travail: remise en question ou fuite en avant." *Revue internationale d'action communautaire*, 8(48), 158–164.

Statistics Canada (1984). *Women and the World of Work.* Ottawa: Minister of Supply and Services.

Statistics Canada (1988). *Education in Canada: A Statistical Review for 1986–87.* Ottawa: Minister of Supply and Services Canada, Cat. no. 81–229.

Statistics Canada (1988). *Enrolment in Universities in Canada.* Ottawa: Minister of Supply and Services Canada.

Statistics Canada (1991). *Labour Force Annual Averages.* 1990. Ottawa: Minister of Supply and Services Canada.

Streeck, W. (1989). "Skills and the limits of neo-liberalism: The enterprise of the future as a place of learning." *Work, Employment and Society*, 3(1), 89-104.

Sunter, D. (1992). "Juggling school and work." *Perspectives*, 4(1), 15–21.

Super, D. (1980). "A life-span, life-space approach to career development." *Journal of Vocational Development*, 16, 282–298.

Tamir, P., and P. Gardner (1989). "The structure of interest in high school biology." *Research in Science and Technological Education*, 7(2), 113–140.

Tanner, Julian (1991). "Reluctant Rebels: A Case-Study of Edmonton High-School Dropouts." In David Ashton and Graham Lowe (eds.), *Making Their Way: Education Training and the Labour Market in Canada and Britain.* University of Toronto Press: Toronto, 109-129.

Tanner, Julian, and Harvey Krahn (1991). "Part-time work and deviance among high school seniors." *Canadian Journal of Sociology* 16(3), 281–302.

Task Force on Mathematics and Science Education (1989). *Towards an achieving society* (final report). St. John's: Queen's Printer.

Teichler, Ulrich (1989). "Research on Higher Education and Work in Europe." *European Journal of Education*, 24(3).

Terman, L.M. (1954). "Scientists and non-scientists in a group of 800 gifted men." *Psychological Monographs: General and Applied*, 68(7).

Thomas, A. (1989a). *The Utilization of Prior Learning Assessment as a Basis for Admission and the Establishment of Advanced Standing in Education in Canada.* Toronto: OISE.

Thomas, A. (1989b). "An Evaluation of the Ontario 'Equivalent Standing for Mature Students' Policy'." Toronto: OISE.

Thomas, A. (1991). "Social Education in Japan: A Canadian Perspective." Kingston: Proceedings of the Annual Meeting of the Canadian Association for the Study of Education, Queens University.

Thomas, A. (1993). "Transitions from school to work—and back: A new paradigm." (In this volume).

Thompson, T. (1991). "The labour market: mid-year review." *Perspectives on Labour and Income*, Supplement, (Fall), 1–10.

Tinto, V. (1975b). "The distributive effects of public junior college availability." *Research in Higher Education*, 3(3), 261–274.

Tough, A. (1978). "Major learning efforts: Recent research and future directions." *Adult Education*, 28, 250 - 63.

Tough, A. (1979). *The adult's learning projects: A fresh approach to theory and practice in adult education* (2 ed.). Toronto: OISE.

Turrittin, A., P. Anisef and N. MacKinnon (1983). "Gender differences in educational achievement: a study of social inequality." *Canadian Journal of Sociology*, 8(4), 395–420.

Vaillancourt, François, and Irène Henriques (1986a). "La rentabilité des études collégiales." *Recherches sociographiques*, 27(3) 481–493.

Vaillancourt, François, and Irène Henriques (1986b). "The returns to University Schooling in Canada." *Analyse de politiques*, 12(3), 449–458.

Vézina, Lucie, and Paul Corbeil (1984). *Relance au collégial. Les sortants de 1976 à 1981.* Québec, Gouvernement du Québec, ministère de l'Éducation, Direction des politiques et plans.

Wakil, S. P. (ed.) (1975). *Marriage Family and Society.* Toronto: Butterworth & Co.

Waldram, J.B. (1990). "The persistence of traditional medicine in urban areas: The case of Canada's Indians." *American Indian and Alaska Native Mental Health Research* 4(1), 9–31.

Walker, Stephen, and Len Barton (ed.) (1982). *Gender, Class and Education.* The Falmer Press: London.

Walkerdine, Valerie (1989). *Democracy in the Kitchen: Regulating Mothering and Socializing Daughters.* Virago: London.

Walkerdine, Valerie (1990). *Schoolgirl Fictions.* Verso: London.

Walsh, J. (1989). "Managing the transition from school to work." *Canadian Vocational Journal*, 25(2), 23–25.

Waniewiez, I. (1976). *Demand for Part-Time Learning in Ontario.* Toronto: OISE/OELA.

Weinfeld, M. (1990). "Trends in Ethnic and Racial Inequality." In James Curtis and Lorne Tepperman, *Images of Canada*, Scarborough: Prentice-Hall Canada Inc.

Weis, Lois (1990). *Working Class Without Work.* Routledge and Kegan Paul: London.

Welton, M. (ed.) (1987). *Knowledge for the people: The struggle for adult learning in english-speaking Canada, 1828–1973.* Toronto: OISE/OELA.

Wharton, A.S. (1991). "Structure and agency in socialist-feminist theory." *Gender and Society*, 5(3), 373–389.

Whyte, Judith, Rosemary Deem, Lesley Kant and Maureen Cruickshank (1985). *Girl Friendly Schooling.* Metheun: London.

Williams, T. (1988). *Studying education-work transitions among Australian youth.* Victoria: Australian Council for Educational Research.

Willis, P. (1977). *Learning to Labour.* Farnborough, Hants: Saxon House.

Wilson, K., and J. Boldizer (1990). "Gender segregation in higher education: effects of aspirations, mathematics achievement, and income." *Sociology of Education*, 63, (Jan.) 62–74.

Young, R.A. (1983). "Career development of adolescents: an ecological perspective." *Journal of Youth and Adolescence*, 12(5), 125–134.

Youniss, J., and J. Smollar (1985). *Adolescent Relations With Mothers, Fathers, and Friends.* Chicago: The University of Chicago Press.

Zureik, E., and R. Hiscott (1982). *The Experience of Visible Minorities in the Work World: The Case of MBA Graduates.* Toronto: Ontario Human Rights Commission, August.

Index

A

aboriginal peoples, 162
  belief system, 165-167
  communities, 164
  cultural paradigm, 164-165
  language, 162
  lifestyle, 164
  population characteristics, 164
  self government and, 159
academic capital, 147, 154, 157
adult education, 91-92, 94, 100, 123
  popular demand for, 91
  underemployment and, 98-99
advanced capitalism
  educational contradictions of, 97, 100, 113
aspirations
  academic, 48, 83, 130, 141, 143, 147, 150, 152, 154, 157, 181
  career, 3-5, 8, 20, 23, 39, 41, 49, 66, 72, 74-76, 78, 81, 83-85, 97-98, 134, 170, 175, 186
  of parents for children, 24, 26, 28, 33
  vocational, 66, 68, 70, 109

B

baccalaureate graduates
  satisfaction of, 111-112
Blacks
  employment experiences of, 3, 6-20
Blacks'
  self image, factors contributing to, 6-20

Bourdieu's theory of
  practice, 138-141, 143-144, 146, 149, 156-157

C

career choice
  educational decisions and, 68
  families and, 23, 66-67, 82
  framework for understanding, 66-71
  gender and, 67, 83-85
  personal orientation and, 68
  understanding of, 130
  See also family influence of
career pathways, 65-66, 71, 75-76, 86
  prediction of, 78

D

dropouts, 3, 32, 45, 57, 132-134, 170, 173, 183
  studies of, 37

E

education
  beliefs about post-secondary, 150
  formal, informal, and non-formal, 91
  gender differences and, 28, 37, 40, 47, 49, 51, 53, 55, 67, 69, 83-84, 86
  goal-achievement and, 5
  limits of, 118-121
  parental support for, 26-28, 66-68, 70, 72, 74-75, 78, 82, 85, 140, 144-147, 150, 155

participation in
post-secondary, 138-139
egalitarianism, 23-24, 26, 28-30, 32-33, 35, 40
employee satisfaction, monitoring of, 110
employers, concerns of, 61, 96-98, 108-110, 113, 119, 121

F

family, influence of, 21, 23-24, 31, 40, 51, 53-55, 59, 61-64, 66-67, 72-75, 78, 80-82, 84, 86-87, 140, 145, 157, 163, 165
family, influence on educational attainment and career
marriage plans and, 44, 46, 51-55, 63-64, 169, 187
First Nations
empowerment in community-based research, 159-167

G

gender, 69
gender tracking and the transition to work, 21-22, 24, 32-34, 37-38
transition to work and, 6, 21-24, 26, 28-29, 32-35, 37-40, 43, 46-48, 51-55, 61-62, 69, 75, 78, 81, 83-86, 175, 181, 186
urban/rural differences and, 43, 61-63
gender equity scale, 24, 28, 33

H

high school graduates
destinations of, 142-143, 155

L

labour market, education and, 4, 21-22, 28, 33, 35, 56, 91, 103, 187
lifelong learning, 89, 91, 101, 118, 123
chronic underemployment and, 89

P

parental educational background, 75
See also education
part-time work
employment rates, 107-108
women and, 6, 32, 51, 53, 55, 73
youth and, 118, 120, 171-172, 184
prior learning assessment, 120-123

Q

Quebec
education and employment, 129-135

R

race
social construction of, 6
work experience and, 9
racial prejudice
as a factor in educational and occupational
attainment, 4-9, 19, 40, 175, 186
reference period, effects of, 68, 170-171, 187
rural-urban differences in the transition to work, 141, 149, 174

S

science education, 65, 85-86
career pathways to, 65-76, 83-84
gender bias and, 21, 35, 41, 67, 70-71, 75, 82, 84-87
interest and motivation for, 75-76, 78, 80-82, 84

self-concept, 3, 8, 66-67, 86, 164
social class, as a factor in educational attainment, 4, 18, 20, 27-28, 31, 40, 66, 94, 97, 124, 153, 175
social science education, 21, 67-69, 71, 106-107, 109
stop outs, 3

T

transcultural research, issues for, 160
transition to work
   from high school, 137
   from school to work and back, 117-127, 129
   future research, 85
   panel studies of, 169

U

underemployment
   adult education participation and, 98
   chronic, 96
   lifelong learning and, 89, 96, 98-100, 104, 172, 174
unemployment, youth and, 57, 62-63, 106-108, 129, 132-133, 151, 171-173, 175, 181, 183-184, 186
universities, graduates, and the marketplace, 103-115
university degrees and fields of study, 106-108
university graduate surveys findings and issues, 106
urban-rural differences in the transition to work, 55-57, 59-63

W

work
   challenges on the job, 11
   preparing for world of, 7
   values and attitudes towards, 131

Printed in Canada